About The Author

Ian Wishart is an award-winning journalist and author, with a 25 year career in radio, television and magazines, a #1 talk radio show and three #1 bestselling books to his credit. Together with his wife Heidi, they edit and publish the news magazine *Investigate*

For Neville, Dianna, Yvonne, Mal, Warren, Diana, but most of all for Heidi, the love of my life, for everything you have done and everything you have carried. This one's for you. To God be the glory.

The
DIVINITY
CODE

Ian Wishart

HOWLING AT THE MOON PUBLISHING LTD

First edition published 2007
Howling At The Moon Publishing Ltd
PO Box 302-188
North Harbour
North Shore 0751
NEW ZEALAND

www.thedivinitycode.tv
email: editorial@investigatemagazine.com

ISBN 978-0-9582401-2-3

Typeset in Adobe Garamond Pro
Cover concept: Ian Wishart, Heidi Wishart, Bozidar Jokanovic
Book Design: Bozidar Jokanovic

*To get another copy of this book airmailed to you anywhere in the world, or
to purchase a fully text-searchable digital edition,
visit our website:*

WWW.THEDIVINITYCODE.TV

CONTENTS

PROLOGUE

AND SO IT BEGINS...

Dawkins' Challenge

"I shall suggest that the existence of God is a scientific hypothesis like any other...even if God's existence is never proved with certainty one way or the other, available evidence and reasoning may yield an estimate of probability far from 50%"

Richard Dawkins, *The God Delusion*

WHEN I WROTE MY PREVIOUS book *Eve's Bite* earlier this year, there were some things I left unsaid. Not because I was afraid of saying them but because *Eve's Bite* – which deals with social engineering in the West – was not really the forum to explore those issues in.

You see, over the past 24 months there has been an explosion of anti-God books on to the market – Richard Dawkins' *The God Delusion* merely being one of the most recent examples. That's fine, it's a free world. But informed debate cannot exist if you are not getting all sides of the story.

The truth is, far from Dawkins' and others' claims, there's a growing, gnawing, accelerating suspicion within the scientific community that God may indeed exist and – horrors – be engaging with the natural world.

Yet the other reality is that our modern world is segmented into a range of different religions. If this "God" that science grudgingly concedes exists, then whose "God" is he/she/it?

In *The Divinity Code*, I am not attempting to blindly convert anyone to Christianity - I figure you are all smart enough to make your own choices in life. But laying my cards on the table, yes, I myself am a Christian. As an investigative journalist I had been trained to be skeptical about all things, and 26 years ago when I began my career I was at the time an atheist, and someone who believed only naturalism and science could explain the world and provide progress.

My journey to skepticism had been helped by books like the 1982 bestseller, *The Holy Blood & The Holy Grail*, which suggested Christ had never died on the cross but survived, married Mary Magdalene, moved to the south of France, had a couple of kids etc. Those of you who've read Dan Brown's *The Da Vinci Code* may recognise this plotline and its variations.

I used my position as a journalist to run anti-God stories wherever I could, interviewing skeptical luminaries like Professor Lloyd Geering about the Gospel of Thomas supposedly driving nails into traditional Christian beliefs. I even, in my personal life, briefly teamed up with other atheists to try and "deprogramme" Christians in staged "interventions".

This, then, is my background.

Despite all that, I eventually became a Christian – initially on pure faith alone because it went against what I perceived to be the credible evidence against it. Later, much later, I discovered that the atheist and skeptical literature I'd read had left out a lot of crucial information – a discovery that shocked me when I came across it. It was the "Inconvenient Truth" for atheism: data and information that didn't fit the argument and so was deliberately put to one side or dealt with out of context.

As a journalist, this jolted me to a realisation. Any argument that cannot withstand robust debate is not a good argument. A reporter should follow the evidence where it leads, not merely where he or she wants it to lead. As an investigative journalist, I knew professionally that the omission of major, inconvenient facts was a sign that I needed to worry about the credibility of the books I was reading, regardless of what I had wanted to believe in them.

Fast-forward to the latest crop of "God" books from Dawkins, Hitchens, Harris, Dennett and the like. They may be bestsellers, but are their arguments simply the triumph of flashy rhetoric over meaningful substance?

I guess the real question is this: are you sufficiently secure in your own belief or lack of belief to read further? How do your current views about life, the universe and everything stack up against evidence, rather than just rhetoric?

The Divinity Code is not a book full of airy-fairy moralising. Instead, I'm applying Richard Dawkins' dictum that much of religion is testable:

"I shall suggest that the existence of God is a scientific hypothesis like any other...even if God's existence is never proved with certainty one way or the other, available evidence and reasoning may yield an estimate of probability far from 50%."

On this much, Dawkins and I agree. Belief one way or the other is not built on 100% proof but on the balance of probabilities.

In taking up Dawkins' gauntlet, this does not mean that science can 100% prove God's existence or non-existence. Like all religious believers, I argue that the supernatural is, by definition, outside the reach or control of a branch of human study that restricts itself only to investigating the natural.

Like Dawkins, however, and like advocates of Intelligent Design, I argue that the fingerprints of God – if they exist – can in principle be found embedded in the natural world. Dawkins, of course, believes the evidence to be so non-existent as to almost be zero. This book, on the other hand, presents evidence that I believe makes the existence of God almost certain.

Unlike Dawkins, who has been known to avoid confronting evidence that doesn't fit his arguments, I have taken the opportunity in *The Divinity Code* to examine the best evidence I can find from skeptics and deal with it head-on.

While there are a multitude of arguments raging about religion, and it would certainly take about eight books this size to deal with them all, I have chosen what I believe are the strongest challenges mounted by most critics.

By the very nature of the subject, however, we are dealing with issues of religious belief and proof one way or the other. And if Dawkins and Christopher Hitchens can make a spirited attack on religion, I can equally make a spirited attack on unbelief. It is my contention that belief in a higher power is not only rational – it is far more rational than skepticism.

Do I succeed? You be the judge.

CHAPTER I

THE QUEST FOR FIRE

"The God Hypothesis comes in many versions. Historians of religion recognize a progression from primitive tribal animisms, through polytheisms such as those of the Greeks, Romans and Norsemen, to monotheisms such as Judaism and its derivatives, Christianity and Islam"

Richard Dawkins, *The God Delusion*

N O ONE ALIVE TODAY KNOWS for sure when the first human emerged, nor do we know when the first person looked at the stars and wondered about the meaning of life. We do know that religious rituals of some kind existed – even among Neanderthal cultures, where graves have been found featuring the deceased in the company of prized possessions, generally indicating a possible belief in the afterlife.[1]

It is true that we don't actually know very much at all about human history. As Professor Robert Winston points out in the BBC series *Walking With Cavemen*, all the bones and fossils found in the world relating to human evolution could fit in a cardboard box in the boot of a small car.

The task of investigating human history is made even harder by, ironically, ancient global warming. As a paleontologist adviser to New Zealand's national Te Papa Museum once explained to me, humans traditionally build settlements close to the sea – a major source of food. During the Ice Ages, sea levels dropped by around 150 metres and beaches receded, meaning people living in warmer climes had to move their villages to match the new tidelines, sometimes – like on America's west coast – up to 160 kilometres further out.

People often have this impression of the Ice Ages as a time when the

---

[1] http://en.wikipedia.org/wiki/Neanderthal

entire planet was cold. Not so. The ice simply pushed the temperate and tropical zones closer to the equator. It rained heavily on jungles and lakes in what is now the Sahara desert, for example.[2]

As the ice melted somewhere between 10,000 and 6,000 years ago (and by many scientific accounts it happened fast), the sea rose again quite rapidly, quickly drowning the villages and cities lining the shores in those ancient times. To get a feel for what happened, imagine the city where you live. If the sea level were to rise by 150 metres, how far inland would you have to go to remain on the mainland? In my case, Auckland, the city's highest piece of land is the Mt Eden volcanic crater. At 196m high, the sea would wash against the hill three quarters of the way up. With that kind of deluge, it is obvious that virtually an entire city of 1.1 million people would vanish beneath the waves. In the case of Sydney, Australia, only 50 metres above sea level, the new shoreline would be the base of the Blue Mountains, 100 km west of the city; Los Angeles would no longer be the City of Angels but the City of Islands.

Give it 6,000 years underwater, pointed out my paleontologist, and any hope of finding these cities under 20 or 30 metres of sand and sediment, 150 metres underwater and up to 100 km out to sea, would be akin to finding the proverbial needle in a haystack.

As a result, he told me, it's a pretty safe bet that the vast majority of human history is submerged and lost to us. Apart from one or two brief fluctuations several million years ago, the sea levels on earth have never been higher than they are now.[3]

Several things emerge from this revelation. Firstly, that when our scientists are digging for fossils – particularly human or hominid – they are digging in areas that would have been considered outback hill-country 10,000 years ago – far from the larger settlements on the [now submerged] coast. It's hardly surprising, then, that the image we get of our ancestors is one of, well, fossilized hillbillies. It's the difference between finding New York, and finding Walton's Mountain.

Secondly, the same thing applies to animal fossils – we're digging up a large number of cave bears, woolly mammoths, dire wolves and other such creatures particular to these locations, and we have no way of digging up the vast herds of creatures who roamed the plains closer to the coastline. Therefore when we talk of "evolution" at all, we should acknowledge that much of what science currently does is guesswork.

Thirdly, all of this has a major bearing on the arguments of atheist writers

2   http://www.usask.ca/geology/classes/geol206/iceoceans.html
3   ibid

like Richard Dawkins, Christopher Hitchens and Sam Harris. Their collective efforts to debunk religion in general and Christianity in particular rely heavily on a presumption that they know most of what there is to know about human history. As I've just established in the space of less than one page: that's a pretty flawed and dangerous presumption to make.

Let's return to the concept of submerged cities to illustrate the point. In 2000, a Canadian expedition searching for sunken Spanish galleons located what appears to be an underwater city off the western coast of Cuba, 650 metres (2,132 feet) below the surface of the Caribbean Sea, on an earthquake faultline.[4] Using an expensive remote controlled submersible with robot cameras, they videoed massive granite blocks, between two and five metres in length each, forming various structures. According to news reports in the Canadian and American press, the granite is not native to the area and the nearest possible source today is central Mexico. The underwater "city" is estimated to be around 7,000 years old. If correct, it was built by a civilization that predated the invention of the wheel in Sumeria in the Middle East. Unless, of course, the Sumerians were only re-discovering older technology lost in the disappearance of older civilizations.

The submerged architecture in Cuba is not the only example of its kind. There is speculation that underwater blocks discovered in the Bahamas 40 years ago are also the remains of a submerged town or city, and *National Geographic* has reported on one submerged city found off the coast of India.[5] Now another, even more spectacular, has been added to the list:

"The remains of a huge underwater city off the western coast of India may force historians and archaeologists to radically reconsider their view of ancient human history. It's believed that the area was submerged when ice caps melted at the end of the last ice age, 9-10,000 years ago.

"Marine scientists say archaeological remains discovered 120 feet underwater in the Gulf of Cambay off the western coast of India could be over 9,000 years old. The vast city – which is five miles long and two miles wide – is believed to predate the oldest known remains in the subcontinent by more than 5,000 years.

"The site was discovered by chance last year by oceanographers from India's National Institute of Ocean Technology who were conducting a survey of pollution. Using sidescan sonar – which sends a beam of sound waves down to the bottom of the ocean – they identified huge geometrical structures at a depth of 120 feet. Debris recovered from the site – including construction material, pottery, sections of walls, beads, sculpture and human bones and

4 http://www.s8int.com/water1.html
5 http://news.nationalgeographic.com/news/2002/05/0528_020528_sunkencities_2.html

teeth – has been carbon dated and found to be nearly 9,500 years old.

"However, archaeologist Justin Morris from the British Museum says more work will need to be done before the site can be said to belong to a 9,000 year old civilization, since there can be errors in carbon dating.

" 'Culturally speaking, in that part of the world there were no civilizations prior to about 2,500 BC. What's happening before then mainly consisted of small, village settlements', he says.

"Strong tides make investigations in the Cambay difficult. Marine scientists led by the Madras-based National Institute of Ocean Technology are solving this problem by taking acoustic images off the sea-bed and using dredging equipment to extract artifacts.

"The Indian Minister for Ocean Technology, Murli Manohar Joshi, says the images indicate symmetrical man-made structures and also a paleo-river, with banks containing artifacts, such as pottery. Carbon dating on a block of wood brought up from the depths suggests it dates back to 7,595 BC. "We have to find out what happened then ... where and how this civilisation vanished," he says.

"The city is believed to be even older than the ancient Harappan civilisation, which dates back around 4,000 years and is the oldest on the subcontinent. Although Palaeolithic sites dating back around 20,000 years have been found on the coast of India's western state of Gujarat before, this is the first time that man-made structures as old as 9,500 years have been found deep beneath the ocean surface."[6]

If you look at human history scientifically, Homo sapiens sapiens has been around for 50,000 to 100,000 years according to the boffins. Yet the entire history of our species is compressed so that we went from caveman to spaceman in only 8,000 years. If we can do it in 8,000 years, it is possible that humans reached some form of high civilization *before* the last Ice Age. The person walking around Times Square today clutching a Blackberry has the same intellectual capacity as the guy slugging a saber-tooth with a stone ax did 10,000 years ago. Genetically and mentally we are identical to them. They thought, loved and debated as we do, albeit with a far lower knowledge of technology than we now enjoy.

Is it possible that we have reached high civilization before, only to lose it? Yeah, it's certainly possible, but it doesn't figure in orthodox history books where the assumption – based on modern-centric evolutionary principles of advancement – is that we are the crème of the human crop.

Maybe we are. Then again maybe we are not. For example, it is now well-

6 http://www.unknowncountry.com/news/?id=1176

documented that ancient civilizations appear to have developed electric batteries, similar to the ones powering your radio or flashlight today. What were the Mesopotamians or Egyptians doing with the equivalent of a Duracell battery?[7]

For more than a few readers, these opening pages will rekindle memories of the legend of Atlantis, the advanced civilization that supposedly sank beneath the waves in a massive cataclysm at some point in ancient times, possibly 11,000 years ago. The only record we have that specifically names "Atlantis" is Plato's writing in *Critias* and *Timaeus,* published around 355 BC:

"For many generations, as long as the divine nature lasted in them, they [the Atlanteans] were obedient to the laws, and well-affectioned towards the god, whose seed they were; for they possessed true and in every way great spirits, uniting gentleness with wisdom in the various chances of life, and in their intercourse with one another. They despised everything but virtue, caring little for their present state of life, and thinking lightly of the possession of gold and other property, which seemed only a burden to them; neither were they intoxicated by luxury; nor did wealth deprive them of their self-control; but they were sober, and saw clearly that all these goods are increased by virtue and friendship with one another, whereas by too great regard and respect for them, they are lost and friendship with them.

"By such reflections and by the continuance in them of a divine nature, the qualities which we have described grew and increased among them; but when the divine portion began to fade away, and became diluted too often and too much with the mortal admixture, and the human nature got the upper hand, they then, being unable to bear their fortune, behaved unseemly, and to him who had an eye to see grew visibly debased, for they were losing the fairest of their precious gifts; but to those who had no eye to see the true happiness, they appeared glorious and blessed at the very time when they were full of avarice and unrighteous power."

Sounds like a description that could equally apply today.

Plato wrote that Atlantis was situated beyond "the pillars of Hercules [in modern terms, the Straits of Gibraltar where the Mediterranean meets the Atlantic Ocean]", and that Atlantis formed "the way to other islands [the Caribbean?], and from these you might pass to the whole of the opposite continent [presumably America] which surrounds the true ocean [the Atlantic, as indeed America does]."

Now regardless of whether you believe Plato was trying to record a real place, or merely painting an allegorical picture for the sake of making

---

7 http://news.bbc.co.uk/go/pr/fr/-/1/hi/sci/tech/2804257.stm

a point, he certainly struck the jackpot in describing how the Atlantic Ocean was encircled by a landmass on the other side. I mean, how would he know? For what it's worth, a century earlier, Herodotus was calling that ocean the "*Atlantis* ocean".

According to Plato, an Egyptian priest with access to the ancient library records (later destroyed by invading Romans) told the Greek traveler Solon the story of Atlantis and how a cataclysm that hit Greece also took out Atlantis, more than 1,600 km to the West.

"But afterwards there occurred violent earthquakes and floods; and in a single day and night of misfortune all your [Greek] warlike men in a body sank into the earth, and the island of Atlantis *in like manner* disappeared in the depths of the sea."

Plato timed this destruction around 9,000 BC, which was another lucky strike given that it coincided with the end of what we now know (but he didn't) was the last Ice Age, and during which the sea level worldwide rose 150 metres.[8]

I raise the Atlantis legend only to illustrate that no matter how much we think we know through science, we probably don't even know the half of it.

So when modern authors like Dawkins, or Lloyd Geering, try and build a picture of primitive ancients worshipping tree spirits and gradually "evolving" to a higher form of religious belief, it should be remembered that these claims are based on presumptions that human civilization has no surprises, that we have all merely "evolved" from peasant to physicist, from simple beliefs to a 'modern, enlightened, scientific view' of the world.

Pontificates Geering:

"The ancient storytellers saw nothing odd in attributing creation to the utterance of words. Language fascinated the ancient mind. Although words could be heard they could never be seen or touched; yet the uttering of them seemed to be very powerful."

Oh really? Was he there, then? I'm sure mere "uttering" wasn't half as impressive as hooking up the ancient Duracell battery and conducting experiments with electricity.

Geering, like many pseuds before him, harks back to this storybook view of ancient cultures and has evidently watched *One Million Years BC* (featuring the iconic Raquel Welch as cavewoman "Loana") far too many times. Geering forgets that the ancient Hebrews were as clever as he is, and the ability to speak was no more wondrous to them than the ability to whack doddery old tribesmen over their heads in a bid to ease their dotage

---

8 Rising sea levels are not the only determinant involved. As the sunken remains 700 metres below the Caribbean suggest, tectonics can play a definitive role

before they started spouting daft theories about words and drove the rest of the tribe insane.

Long assumed to be brutes, and erroneously portrayed by Hollywood and graphic artists in science departments[9] as part man/part ape, even Neanderthals apparently had no trouble talking[10] – scientists have discovered a Neanderthal hyoid bone (essential for human speech) "identical" to that of modern humans. Speech has a long heritage[11], and it's a fair bet that when Moses opened his mouth to lecture the Israelites, the last thing they were wondering was how clever he was, being able to speak and all that!

Of course, Geering isn't the only one with a dodgy perspective on the origins of religion. The vogue theory among a small group of vocal liberals is called "the Axial Period", and if you've read books by former nun Karen Armstrong, you'll recognize the term.

It was actually coined by a German philosopher, Karl Jaspers, in 1949, and refers to the period between 800 BC and 200 BC when, Jaspers claims, similar ideas allegedly arose in religions around the world – apparently independently of each other. He points to developments in religion and philosophy in ancient Greece mirroring the ideas emerging in Buddhism and Confucianism, Zoroastrianism, Hinduism and Judaism.[12]

"The spiritual foundations of humanity were laid simultaneously and independently," Jaspers says, "and these are the foundations upon which humanity still subsists today."

It was not divine revelation, Axialists like Geering or Armstrong or John Shelby Spong argue, but growing wisdom among the ancients responding to changes in their societies that led to the new ideas.

Lloyd Geering, for example, waxes lyrical in the assumption that older religions played a major role in influencing Christianity. One of his assertions in *Christianity Without God* is that Zoroastrianism is the origin of "such ideas as the Last Judgment (preceded by a general resurrection), an afterlife with rewards and punishments, the concept of a personal Devil,

---

9 These "artists" pulled the same stunt with the 2004 discovery of the 'hobbit skeletons' on Indonesia's Flores Island, by drawing them as small humans with chimpanzee heads, even though the skulls are so close to ours in style that there is a heated dispute in the scientific community about whether the hobbits are indeed a different species or just a dwarf race of modern humans. Every time artists draw ancient humans as part-ape, they are guessing, based entirely on their own belief in Darwinism
10 http://en.wikipedia.org/wiki/Neanderthal
11 http://www.nytimes.com/2007/10/18/science/19speech.html Another discovery late October 2007 confirms Neanderthals had the FOXP2 gene necessary for human speech, identical to the one the rest of us have, and apparently they had it from about 350,000 years ago, throwing evolutionary theory into disarray, again
12 http://en.wikipedia.org/wiki/Axial_Age

the writing of our life story in a heavenly book of life and the naming of angels with specific functions."

Once again I am forced to say, 'Oh really?'.

Zoroastrianism, the Persian religion, supposedly gave these ideas to the Jews during their Babylonian captivity around 500 BC. But if the idea of God judging the world only emerged in Judaism in 500 BC, how do we explain a verse like this, written around 1400 BC:

"Will not the Judge of all the Earth do right?" asked Abraham in Gen. 18:25.

And doesn't this Psalm, written around 900 BC, give hope of an eternal afterlife beyond the grave?[13]

"You will not abandon me to the grave, nor will you let your Holy One see decay. You have made known to me the path of life; you will fill me with joy in your presence, with eternal pleasures at your right hand." Psa. 16:10-11.

If you want it more explicit, Psalm 1, also from around 900 BC, talks at verse 5 of "the wicked will not stand in the Judgment, nor sinners in the assembly of the righteous".

If it's a personal Devil you seek, look no further than the Book of Job (pronounced 'Jobe'), which records events that scholars attribute to as far back as 1800 – 2000 BC because of its cultural nuances and archaic language.[14] The entire book is about Job's sustained attack at the hands of a very personal Satan.

In truth, this is one of the frustrating things about books written by skeptics: they offer unsourced anecdotal tales and claims that make persuasive soundbites but which are utterly untrue.

We will return in detail to which religion borrowed from which, later in this book. But regardless of the sport that Geering, Armstrong, Spong, Dawkins, Hitchens and others will provide us (and trust me, we will have fun doing it), there is no escaping the reality that humans and a belief in

---

13   The answer from Axialists will initially be that the earliest records of a written Book of Psalms date to the sixth century BC, which means the ideas could have been borrowed from Zoroastrianism during the captivity. The answer is simplistic however. With Jerusalem captured, the temple destroyed and its inhabitants bundled off to a foreign land, it is easy to see why we no longer have physical copies of manuscripts dating back to the time of Moses or King David. However, there is ample circumstantial evidence to suggest the older books of the Old Testament were well known to Jews at the time of the captivity, and that they were not changed. Firstly, the Jews held fast to their Jewishness and what little they had been left with. Rather than widely integrating into Persian society they were mindful of the previous great captivity in Egypt nearly a thousand years earlier, and the need to preserve their beliefs and culture through this time. Having been warned by their prophets repeatedly about the dangers of worshipping false gods, and that the captivity was a punishment for Jewish disobedience, it stretches credulity to believe that the Jews then would further anger their God by importing foreign religious beliefs into what was left of Judaism. Secondly, portions of the Psalms are quoted in other pre-Exile books like 1 and 2 Samuel. Thirdly, the internal evidence in many of the earliest psalms – the words used and events referred to – clearly place them between 1000 BC and 900 BC in origin.
14   *Survey of Old Testament Introduction*, Gleason Archer, Moody, 1994, pp. 503-515

the supernatural go hand in hand. Always have, always will.

Opinion polls in the West consistently show anywhere in the region of 80% to 90% of people believe in a divinity of some kind.

A *Fox News* poll in 2004, for example, found 92% of Americans say they believe in God, 85% in heaven and 82% in miracles. Surprisingly, support for New Age beliefs was a lot lower, with 34% belief in the existence of ghosts, 34% in UFOs, 29% in astrology, 25% in reincarnation and 24% in witches.[15]

"Young people are much more likely than older Americans to believe in both hell and the devil," noted *Fox News*. "An 86% majority of adults between the ages of 18 to 34 believe in hell, but that drops to 68% for those over age 70."

You would think that older people would be more likely to believe in hell and the devil and orthodox Christian theology, until you realize that most of those people grew up in churches who'd been hit by a crisis of faith in the late 19th/early 20th centuries. The liberal view, that ideas of hell or miracles were merely "quaint" stories which science had disproved, poisoned the mainstream churches through the first three-quarters of the 20th century, until fresh scholarship overturned that lukewarm Christianity. Seen in that light, it is no surprise that young people have a stronger faith – the growing churches today are those that have returned to the basics of Christian doctrine, such as the existence of a real God, a real hell and a real Resurrection.

Intriguingly, there's not just an age gap, there's a political gap as well. Left-wingers are more likely (an additional 14%) to believe in New Age ideas than conservatives. As for the state of religion in society, the poll turned up a figure that is an undoubted source of fury to atheist fundamentalists like Dawkins and Hitchens: a staggering 69% of Americans believe religion needs to play a bigger role in people's lives, with only 15% arguing it should play a smaller role.

Another poll, from 2003[16], found that more than a quarter of those who say they are *not* Christian nonetheless believe in the resurrection of Christ and the virgin birth.

A Gallup poll in May 2007 showed a slight drop in belief in God, down to 86%, although when the question was rephrased to include belief in a higher power it bounced back to nearly 90%.

But we all know Americans are the most "religious" westerners. What about the rest of us in the English-speaking world?

A UMR research poll in New Zealand in September 2007[17] that directly

15 www.foxnews.com/story/0,2933,99945,00.html
16 www.harrisinteractive.com/harris_poll/index.asp?PID=359
17 http://www.umr.co.nz/Media/FinalMorality-Religion-Evolution-NZ_USComparison-Sep07.pdf

compared the May 07 US Gallup poll shows only 56% downunder believe in God, and only 48% believe in Heaven, compared with 81% of Americans. Seventy percent of Americans believe the Devil exists, while only 26% of New Zealanders buy into that.

When researchers broke down the "God" question the same way Gallup had, 46% of New Zealanders professed a belief in "God", while a staggering 31% opted to believe in the New Age concept of "a universal spirit or higher power".

Then there is the question of 'Why?'. *Why* do we believe in God?

Time magazine put it another way:

"Which came first, God or the need for God? In other words, did humans create religion from cues sent from above, or did evolution instill in us a sense of the divine so that we would gather into the communities essential to keeping the species going?"[18]

Examine the last part of that statement for a moment. It's the idea that *evolution* created the idea of God in our heads. Yet evolution is supposed to be purposeless and randomly-caused. How could a single-celled organism *know in advance* that in order to succeed it needed to believe in an imaginary friend called 'God'?

The idea seems more farcical and fraught with contradictions than simply believing in God himself, but it has led to what some scientists are calling their theory of "the God Gene" – the idea that humans are programmed to believe in God.

"Even among people who regard spiritual life as wishful hocus-pocus, there is a growing sense that humans may not be able to survive without it," says *Time*. "It's hard enough getting by in a fang-and-claw world in which killing, thieving and cheating pay such rich dividends. It's harder still when there's no moral cop walking the beat to blow the whistle when things get out of control. Best to have a deity on hand to rein in our worst impulses, bring out our best and, not incidentally, give us a sense that there's someone awake in the cosmic house when the lights go out at night and we find ourselves wondering just why we're here in the first place. If a God or even several gods can do all that, fine. And if we sometimes misuse the idea of our gods – and millenniums of holy wars prove that we do – the benefits of being a spiritual species will surely outweigh the bloodshed."

These, then, are some of the questions this book sets out to answer. Is there a rational basis for believing in God? Did humans simply invent the concept of God? Is belief in God, whether fiction or fact, scientifically

---

18 http://www.time.com/time/magazine/article/0,9171,995465,00.html

necessary for us as a species in order for us to avoid slaughtering each other? Are all gods and religions created equal, or is it possible that some are either better or closer to the truth than others? Can belief in God be reconciled with scientific discoveries?

Perhaps the biggest question of all, though, is this: If God exists, is that 'just another news story', or the most significant piece of information in human history?

As you can see, it promises to be an intriguing journey.

CHAPTER 2

IN THE BEGINNING

"I am attacking God, all gods, anything and everything supernatural, wherever and whenever they have been or will be invented"
Richard Dawkins, *The God Delusion*

I F YOU READ OR LISTEN to the Karen Armstrongs of this world, you'll be familiar with the theory that religions "evolved" from a primitive belief in many gods, to the modern, monotheistic belief in just one Creator. Now, of course, Armstrong, John Shelby Spong, Don Cupitt and Lloyd Geering are arguing we have evolved to the next stage of religion: a non-belief in a Creator or the supernatural which, they argue, reflects our growing scientific "wisdom".

It is said, by these writers, that the Genesis creation story featuring one God is a late development rather than an authentic representation of early Jewish belief. The Jews, argue these writers, "borrowed" their creation story from the older Babylonian civilization.

I guess, if this was all true, we would see evidence in various creation stories of this *evolution* of thought and belief, from primitive to sophisticated. So forget everything you've ever heard about creation – I'm going to take you back through history to a range of creation myths from around the world. The purpose is simple: is there evidence of common themes from different cultures all over the planet? If so, what are those common themes?

SUMERIA circa 2000 BC
When heaven had moved away from the earth,
And earth had separated from heaven,
And the name of man was fixed;
When the Sky God, An, had carried off the heavens,
And the Air God, Enlil, had carried off the earth …

THEMES: No full text of the Sumerian myth still exists, so historians have pieced together fragments of what they know. The earth, it turns out, was born of sexual intercourse between the gods, out of water. It emerged from water, and the heavens had to be separated from land. There are multiple gods involved. As *creation ex nihilo*, or creation from nothing, is a foreign concept to the Sumerians, they believed earth must have emerged from something.

BABYLON (Enuma Elish, written circa 1200 BC)
When there was no heaven,
no earth, no height, no depth, no name,
when Apsu was alone,
the sweet water, the first begetter; and Tiamat
the bitter water, and that
return to the womb, her Mummu,
when there were no gods-

When sweet and bitter
mingled together, no reed was plaited, no rushes
muddied the water,
the gods were nameless, natureless, futureless, then
from Apsu and Tiamat
in the waters gods were created, in the waters
silt precipitated,

Lahmu and Lahumu,
were named; they were not yet old
not yet grown tall
when Anshar and Kishar overtook them both,
the lines of sky and earth
stretched where horizons meet to separate
cloud from silt.

THEMES: OK. What are the themes in this? Firstly, a time when no heavens and no earth existed. Just a character called Apsu, translated as "the sweet water" and later "the father of the gods" and his bride Tiamat. By their intercourse, in a watery realm, child gods were created and silt to make earth. The myth talks in its last verse here of separating sky from earth. Anshar being a longer form of the Sumerian sky god An, and Kishar likewise a longer form of Ki. The Babylonian myth, like the Sumerian, involves creation via sex and multiple deities.

THE BIBLE circa 1400 BC

1 In the beginning God created the heavens and the earth. 2 Now the earth became formless and empty, darkness was over the surface of the deep, and the Spirit of God was hovering over the waters. 3 And God said, "Let there be light," and there was light. 4 God saw that the light was good, and He separated the light from the darkness. 5 God called the light "day," and the darkness he called "night." And there was evening, and there was morning – the first day. 6 And God said, "Let there be an expanse between the waters to separate water from water." 7 So God made the expanse and separated the water under the expanse from the water above it. And it was so. 8 God called the expanse "sky." And there was evening, and there was morning – the second day. 9 And God said, "Let the water under the sky be gathered to one place, and let dry ground appear." And it was so. 10 God called the dry ground "land," and the gathered waters he called "seas." And God saw that it was good.

THEMES: Creation from nothing. God creates the heavens and the earth, which remains covered by water. God then creates light, then day and night, then he separates the atmosphere (sky) from the land. It is obvious that the Jews, Babylonians and Sumerians all tell a similar story (leaving aside the mechanism of creation – sex vs divine word – and the number of 'gods' involved). At one level, the Hebrew story seems more ancient. It begins, after all, with a divine act of creation, followed by the emergence of earth from water. The Babylonians and Sumerians appear to begin their stories, really, with the earth emerging from water.

EBLA circa 2600 BC

Lord of heaven and earth:
the earth was not, you created it,
the light of day was not, you created it,
the morning light you had not [yet] made exist.

THEMES: Here's where our journey gets interesting. The Ebla civilization is a very recent discovery,[19] dating back only to the 1960s when thousands of clay tablets were unearthed at Tell Mardikh in northern Syria. Many were written in a previously unknown language, and dated from a time

---

19 http://en.wikipedia.org/wiki/Ebla.

that was contemporary with the previous oldest known civilization in the area, the Sumerians. Yet, from the text above, here is a creation story that sounds remarkably close to Genesis in the Bible. It talks of one God, the "Lord of heaven and earth" (a phrase also used in the Bible a thousand years later[20]). It talks of a sequence of events, the creation of Earth, the creation of day and night, then the creation of the morning light (the Sun). As you'll see, this sequence bears striking parallels to Genesis, even though the Jews would not set their own creation story down in writing for at least a thousand years after Ebla had been buried by desert sands.

***

It is Ebla that strikes a fatal blow to Karen Armstrong and the Axial Age theory, because it shows primitive belief in monotheism – one creator God – right back in earliest times and long before the Babylonians resurrected the old Sumerian polytheistic myths. It is also the first corroboration of the Genesis version from outside the Bible, and what makes it even more significant is that the Ebla tablets are the oldest written tablets in existence, far older than the ones retrieved from nearby Mari or the Babylonian records.

For this reason, it also spikes the guns of those who try to deny the significance of the Ten Commandments purely because similar ideas had already been expressed in King Hammurabi's Babylonian Code of Laws from around 1760 BC. Do the math: the Ebla tablets with their Genesis-type theology and names of Hebrew patriarchs pre-date Hammurabi by around 800 years.

You would think, more than three decades after Ebla's discovery and the translation of key tablets, that liberals would make some attempt to explain the anomaly. But they don't. They simply ignore its existence. In her bestselling 2004 reprint of her book, *The History of God*, Armstrong makes no reference to Ebla, even though academic research papers on the tablets had been published over the preceding 27 years. Yet Armstrong's book is being held up as "definitive" on the history of God!

Her refusal to even address it backfires with a statement on one of the opening pages of her book, when she says "There was no creation out of nothing, an idea that was alien to the ancient world."

How can Armstrong make a statement like that? Remember Ebla: "Lord of heaven and earth, the earth was not, you created it."

The earth was *not*, you created it.

Another who shows no appreciation of Ebla is Lloyd Geering.

---

20 Gen 14:22, Eza 5:11

"Let us now summarise the history of god [sic]," writes Geering in *Christianity Without God*. "The concept originated in mythology and referred to a class of powerful but unseen beings, created by the human imagination in the ancient past to explain the mysterious phenomena of what today we call the natural world.

"Then came the time, in the Axial period [800BC – 200BC], when these gods were rejected in favour of one basic concept to which everything else could be related. In both the Jewish and Greek traditions the concept of 'god' was retained but underwent a distinct change in meaning and usage. What became the classical understanding of God in the Christian tradition was a synthesis of both the Jewish and Greek traditions."

Geering might be right in the relevance of the Axial period to Greek moves away from polytheism (Zeus, Hera, Apollo, Athena and the whole shebang of 'gods') towards Christian monotheism as preached by the apostle Paul throughout Greece, but Geering is way off beam, as you've just seen, in trying to explain away the Jewish concept of God. The Eblaites, 1,800 years before the much-hyped Axial period, have a creation story that talks of *one* God. The Hebrews, consistently, told the same story. There is good archaeological evidence to suggest that belief in one God might in fact be a pure strain of religious truth that other civilizations simply forgot. Alternatively, given that most ancient cultures still recognized one supreme god, isn't that evidence that monotheism was the starting point to which extra deities were added as people met new tribes. Perhaps it was easier for cultures to recognize their own supreme god but keep the peace by also recognizing the supreme gods of other tribes and cultures, thus building a polytheistic pantheon over time.

Yet the Jews, who held always to their own spiritual purity (albeit with some slip-ups), were able to keep loyalty to their own single God alive.

One who subscribed to the idea that monotheism was the original, and polytheism the later, evolution, was Father Wilhelm Schmidt, whose 1912 book on the point was used by Karen Armstrong to set up a strawman introduction in her own *History of God*.

"In the beginning, human beings created a God who was the First Cause of all things and Ruler of heaven and earth," Armstrong begins, paraphrasing Schmidt. "He was not represented by images and had no temple or priests in his service. He was too exalted for an inadequate human cult. Gradually, he faded from the consciousness of his people. He had become so remote that they decided that they did not want him anymore. Eventually he was said to have disappeared.

"That, at least, is one theory...Schmidt suggested that there had been primitive monotheism before men and women started to worship a number of gods. Originally they had acknowledged only one Supreme Deity, who had created the world and governed human affairs from afar. Belief in such a High God (sometimes called the Sky God since he is associated with the heavens) is still a feature of the religious life in many indigenous African tribes. They yearn toward God in prayer; believe that he is watching over them and will punish wrongdoing."

Over time, Schmidt argued, belief in the one was replaced by belief in the many. Karen Armstrong largely shies away from this, arguing it as "impossible to prove one way or the other", and heads off down her Axial path instead.

But it is not "impossible to prove". Ebla has shown that. Little wonder, however, that Armstrong and Geering steer clear of the inconvenient truth that is Ebla. There is strong evidence to illustrate that the people of Ebla in 2600 BC knew a similar creation story to the Hebrews. Archaeologists have uncovered tablets featuring the names "Adam" (Adamu), "Eve" (H'à-wa), "Abraham" (Abarama), Ishmael, Isûra-el ("Israel"?), Esau, Mika-el, Mikaya, Saul, David and even Noah.[21]

The evidence is not clear whether these are direct references to Adam and Eve from Genesis, but they do show for the first time outside the Bible that these names existed and were written down at least a thousand years before ink was first drawn on a scroll for the Bible (possibly 2000 years if you believe the liberals who think Genesis wasn't transcribed until 600 BC).[22]

---

21 http://en.wikipedia.org/wiki/Ebla
22   There has been enormous debate about whether the Old Testament books of the bible are historically authentic, or whether they are merely myths written between 600 and 400 BC and projected backwards in time to give the Jewish people a "backstory" that they could believe in. This came to the fore earlier this decade with the publication of archaeologist Israel Finkelstein's book, *The Bible Unearthed.* In it, he claimed that a review of the archaeological evidence led him to believe that ancient Israel did not, in fact, exist, and that most of the OT was therefore entirely myth. This led William Dever, another leading archaeologist and agnostic, to deliver a stinging rebuke of this theory in his own book, *What Did The Biblical Writers Know?* In it, Dever points out massive errors made by what he calls "the revisionists". They include that the Hebrew used in the Old Testament is genuine Iron Age Hebrew, not the later dialects in use closer to the time of Christ. "Finally, we must confront the dilemma that the revisionists pose, but have never acknowledged. If the writers of the Hebrew Bible living in the 4th to 1st centuries BC, and they succeeded in producing a 'story' that was artificially and deliberately projected back into the Iron Age, several conclusions must be drawn. a) They did so without trace of any anachronisms that would have given them away, that is, implicit or explicit references to conditions of their own day. b) They wrote this purportedly historical account without any of the historical records that we take for granted, since most of these had disappeared with the end of the Iron Age (i.e., Assyrian, Babylonian and Egyptian records) and were not recovered until the 19th-20th centuries AD. The biblical writers simply 'invented' the story of an ancient Israel in the Iron Age and got right virtually every detail that we can now confirm. c) Finally, if the revisionists' view of the nature and origins of the literary traditions of the Hebrew Bible were correct, the biblical 'fiction story' of an ancient Israel would constitute the most astonishing literary hoax of all time and the most successful, too, since it fooled almost everyone for 2000 years. Possible? Yes: but not very likely." – WDTBWK?, p. 276-277

In another crushing blow to Armstrong, Geering and others, Ebla also blows holes in the theory that ancient cultures in the area were too primitive to have written traditions capable of being passed down.

It is staggering that people described as "learned theologians" by the popular media can get away with interview after interview without being challenged about what *Time* magazine described as the "20th century's third great breakthrough in biblical archaeology [after discoveries at Ugarit and the Dead Sea Scrolls]…perhaps the most complete record of an ancient civilization ever recovered".[23]

The *Time* article, from 1981, carries some important commentary on the Ebla discoveries, including the bombshells it contains for liberal scholarship.

"Findings from Ebla may have an even broader impact. Many liberal Bible scholars treat Abraham not as a historical figure but as a sort of Semitic King Arthur. Their view is that the stories about Abraham and the other Patriarchs must have been written down more than 1,000 years later than the events they purport to describe. Now, in the area of the world that produced the Bible, Ebla has established that sophisticated and extensive written culture existed well before Moses and even Abraham, as early as the middle of the 3rd millennium B.C. According to the ebullient [scholar Mitchell] Dahood, "After Ebla, we've got to take the Bible much more seriously as a historical document. The people who wrote those books had a long literary tradition behind them."

"Especially tantalizing," reports *Time*, "was the appearance of two names which later appear in the Hebrew tradition: Abraham, the spiritual forefather of Jews, Christians and Muslims, and his biblical ancestor Eber (whose name formed the root of the term Hebrew)… [scholar Giovanni] Pettinato… proposed that Abraham was a native of northern Syria. An intriguing Ebla text shows a town named Ur near Haran, the biblical town in Syria from which Abraham moved into the promised land. Genesis, however, says that Abraham grew up in "Ur of the Chaldees," understood by both the biblical and Islamic traditions to be the famous Ur in lower Mesopotamia. Ebla aside, the Israelites were instructed in Deuteronomy 26: 5 to recite that Abraham was "a wandering Aramaean." In other words, the Bible labeled him a *Syrian*.

"The merest suggestion that the Eblaites might have been the ancestors of today's Israelis fell into Middle East politics like a missile. Israeli archaeologists shuddered. The Syrians detected Zionist designs in the notion and persuaded Matthiae and Pettinato to warn other scholars

---

23   http://www.time.com/time/magazine/article/0,9171,953100-1,00.html

publicly against making ethnic linkages between the 3rd millennium B.C. and the 20th century."

Nonetheless, regardless of how politically incorrect they are, or how much liberal scholars try to ignore them, those linkages are there, written in stone. Hauntingly, the names of the cities of Sodom and Gomorrah, once considered fictional by liberal scholars, are listed on Ebla's clay tablets – a voice from 4,600 years ago now reverberating around the halls of biblical research.

From this much, it should now be apparent that the ancients in the Middle East shared some very similar views on the creation of Earth, and that there is now independent support for the Genesis version of creation, from a civilization that pre-dated Moses by more than a thousand years. At the stage Moses led the Israelites out of Egypt, the civilization of Ebla was a dusty, abandoned mound in the desert, its original inhabitants and greatness long forgotten, the tablets long buried in the sand. The idea that two civilizations, separated in time by more than ten centuries and hundreds of kilometres, could both share the same creation story, lends weight to those who argue the stories might be the same because they are true.

To see whether belief in creation is a peculiarly Middle Eastern phenomenon, or whether it is widespread, we need to study the myths of other cultures. If all are singing a similar song, is it possible that humanity may have a collective mythic memory of those first events?

To understand the creation myths, you have to see them firstly for what they are – stories handed down from generation to generation to explain the origin of humankind. As we've already seen from the Middle East, it is possible for a pure story to become more and more corrupted over time as wilder and more fantastic bits are added to it. Recognising the clearly mythical aspects, then, is the first step towards finding the kernel of truth that may lie at the heart of each creation story.

JAPAN (Translated by Yaichiro Isobe)
"Before the heavens and the earth came into existence, all was a chaos, unimaginably limitless and without definite shape or form. Eon followed eon: then, lo! out of this boundless, shapeless mass something light and transparent rose up and formed the heaven. This was the Plain of High Heaven, in which materialized a deity called Ame-no-Minaka-Nushi-no-Mikoto (the Deity-of-the-August-Center-of-Heaven). Next the heavens gave birth to a deity named Takami-Musubi-no-Mikoto (the High-August-Producing-Wondrous-Deity), followed by a third called Kammi-Musubi-no-Mikoto (the Divine-Producing-Wondrous-Deity). These three

divine beings are called the Three Creating Deities.

"In the meantime what was heavy and opaque in the void gradually precipitated and became the earth, but it had taken an immeasurably long time before it condensed sufficiently to form solid ground."[24]

THEMES: An infinite void exists prior to the creation of the heavens and earth. But the deity of High Heaven appears to be created as part of the process. In the end, three gods rule heaven (a primitive allusion to the Trinity concept, perhaps?)

APACHE

"In the beginning nothing existed – no earth, no sky, no sun, no moon, only darkness was everywhere.

"Suddenly from the darkness emerged a thin disc, one side yellow and the other side white, appearing suspended in midair. Within the disc sat a small bearded man, Creator, the One Who Lives Above. As if waking from a long nap, he rubbed his eyes and face with both hands.

"When he looked into the endless darkness, light appeared above. He looked down and it became a sea of light. To the east, he created yellow streaks of dawn. To the west, tints of many colours appeared everywhere. There were also clouds of different colours…"[25]

THEMES: Creation from nothing. One supreme deity.

CHELAN (native American)

"Long, long ago, the Creator, the Great Chief Above, made the world. Then he made the animals and the birds and gave them their names – Coyote, Grizzly Bear, Deer, Fox, Eagle, the four Wolf Brothers, Magpie, Bluejay, Hummingbird, and all the others.

"When he had finished his work, the Creator called the animal people to him. "I am going to leave you," he said. "But I will come back. When I come again, I will make human beings. They will be in charge of you."

"The Great Chief returned to his home in the sky, and the animal people scattered to all parts of the world."[26]

---

24 http://www.wsu.edu:8080/~wldciv/world_civ_reader/world_civ_reader_1/kojiki.html
25 http://www.indians.org/welker/creation.htm
26 http://www.ilhawaii.net/~stony/lore59.html

THEMES: One supreme deity. Animals created first.

DIGUENOS (Native American)

"When Tu-chai-pai made the world, the earth was the woman, the sky was the man. The sky came down upon the earth. The world in the beginning was a pure lake covered with tules. Tu-chai-pai and his younger brother, Yo-ko-mat-is, sat together, stooping far over, bowed down by the weight of the sky.

"...All of this time the Maker knew what he was about to do, but he was asking his brother's help. Then he said, "We-hicht, we-hicht, we-hicht," three times. He took tobacco in his hand. and rubbed it fine and blew upon it three times. Every time he blew, the heavens rose higher above their heads.

"...We are going to dig in the ground and find mud to make the first people, the Indians." So he dug in the ground and took mud to make the first men, and after that the first women. He made the men easily, but he had much trouble making women. It took him a long time.

"After the Indians, he made the Mexicans...At last he told them that they must travel toward the East, where the sun's light was coming out for the first time. The Indians then came out and searched for the light, and at last they found light and were exceedingly glad to see the Sun. The Maker called out to his brother, "It's time to make the Moon.""[27]

THEMES: No separation between earth and sky. Humans fashioned from mud. Similar to Genesis in these two aspects.

MIK'MAQ (Native Canadian)

"After the Mik'Maq world was created and after the animals, birds and plants were placed on the surface, Gisoolg caused a bolt of lightning to hit the surface of Ootsitgamoo. This bolt of lightning caused the formation of an image of a human body shaped out of sand. It was Glooscap who was first shaped out of the basic element of the Mik'Maq world, sand."[28]

THEMES: A main Creator, Gisoolg, and humans made from sand.

---

[27] http://www.ilhawaii.net/~stony/lore63.html
[28] http://www.dreamscape.com/morgana/cordelia.htm

MAORI

"Io is known as the Supreme Being and ex nihilo (out of nothing) creator of the entire universe. He creates Ranginui (Rangi) and Papatuanuku (Papa), Sky Father and the Earth Mother, respectively. The sky and earth produce numerous offspring while they are physically, "cleaved together in a procreative embrace." The children are forced to live in the darkness since their parents block all the rays from the sun. They soon become restless and worn out from the living conditions and gather to question whether to separate their parents or to kill them for more room and light.

"The fiercest of the offspring, Tumatauenga (Tuma) voices his opinion for death, while Tanemahuta (Tane) wishes to just separate the mother and father so that the earth will "remain close as our nursing mother." Most of the sons, including Tuma, finally agree with the plan for separation with a major dissenting vote from only one sibling, Tawhirimatea. As the guardian of winds and storms, he fears that his kingdom will be overthrown if the parents are torn apart. In the minority, Tawhirimatea remains silent and holds his breath.

"The children begin to divide Rangi and Papa, and they soon realize their task is very difficult to accomplish. After many siblings attempt to separate the parents, Tane finally succeeds as he places his shoulders against the earth and his feet against the sky. He pushes slowly with both his upper and lower body with great strain. "Soon, and yet not soon, for the time was vast, the Sky and Earth began to yield." The Earth Mother and Sky Father bleed and this gives rise to ochre (red clay), the sacred color of the Maoris. As the parents cry out for Tuma to stop, he only presses on harder. Sky Father and Earth Mother's blood spills on his head, known as the kokowai, the sacred red earth that is created when the first blood spills at the dawn of time. Now that the separation is complete, there is a clearly defined sky and earth.

"One of the offspring, Urutengangana, states that there is one element still missing, and he urges his siblings to find the female element, ira tangata, to enable the creation of woman. The search spans both land and sea, and Tane finally consults his mother, Papa, for her advice and knowledge. The earth takes pity on Tane and tells him to search an area named Kura-waka. Tane returns to his siblings with the new insight and they travel to the location. The children find the element in the Earth and dig it out to contribute in the creation of woman and her form. The elder siblings shape the body and the younger siblings add the flesh, fat, muscles, and blood. Tane then breathes life into it, and creates Hine-ahu-one, the earth formed maiden."[29]

THEMES: As one commentator has noted, the Maori creation myth has some strong similarities with others in the world, particularly the recurring theme of the sky and earth needing somehow to be physically separated – an element that even Genesis 1:7 refers to. But let's return for a moment to the brief mention of Io, the supreme creator being, and a more detailed extract pertaining to his involvement in the process:

> Io dwelt within the breathing-space of immensity.
> The Universe was in darkness, with water everywhere.
> There was no glimmer of dawn, no clearness, no light.
> And he began by saying these words,-
> That He might cease remaining inactive -
> 'Darkness become a light-possessing darkness.'
> And at once light appeared.
> (He) then repeated those self-same words in this manner.
> That He might cease remaining inactive:
> 'Light, become a darkness-possessing light.'
> And again an intense darkness supervened.
> Then a third time He spake saying:
> 'Let there be one darkness above,
> Let there be one darkness below.
> Let there be one light above,
> Let there be one light below,
> A dominion of light,
> A bright light.'
> And now a great light prevailed.
> (Io) then looked to the waters which compassed him about,
> and spoke a fourth time, saying:
> 'Ye waters of Tai-kama, be ye separate.
> Heaven, be formed.' Then the sky became suspended.
> 'Bring forth thou Tupua-horo-nuku.'
> And at once the moving earth lay stretched abroad.[30]

29 http://www.laits.utexas.edu/doherty/plan2/liangcreation.html
30 http://www.mircea-eliade.com/from-primitives-to-zen/011.html

This account, again, bears a spooky resemblance to Genesis. Intriguingly, few ordinary Maori were ever permitted to hear the full stories of Io. According to researchers working with Maori in the 1840s, the legend of Io was something only the tohunga, or shaman priest, was permitted to know or talk about. More often than not, they refused to talk, with one document now held in New Zealand's National Library recording, "The presence of the Christian God has silenced the Maori gods, but the gods of the Maori still hold us in their power, and if I break their laws they will punish me with death."

In other words, the tohunga movement was guarding its own secrets from perceived corruption by Christianity. They couldn't protect it forever, though, as "Io" or "Iho" was close enough to the Maori word for Jehovah, "Ihowa", to allow Maoridom's supreme deity to easily be absorbed into Christianity. This may have been one of the reasons the Maori, unlike many other tribal nations around the world, took to Christianity like ducks to water: instinctively, it felt to them that Christ was a reconnection with the creator God.

Explorer and anthropologist Elsdon Best, writing in the *Transactions and Proceedings of the Royal Society of New Zealand* comments:

"All ritual and ceremonial pertaining to Io was retained in the hands of the superior priesthood, by no means a numerous body. It may be described as an aristocratic cultus, known only to such experts and the more important chiefs. It is quite probable, indeed, that this superior creed may have been too exalted for ordinary minds, that such would prefer to depend on more accessible and less moral deities.

"It is interesting to note that no form of offering or sacrifice was made to Io, that no image of him was ever made, and that he had no aria, or form of incarnation, such as inferior gods had."[31]

These are just some of the creation stories assembled from around the world. So much for the Axial period and the theory that primitive humans believed in polytheistic creation before evolving towards monotheism. This then is what ancients across the globe believed about the creation of the earth and heavens. How does it compare to scientific knowledge?

---

31 Elsdon Best, *Some Aspects of Maori Myth and Religion*, p.20

CHAPTER 3

THE MOMENT OF CREATION

"In China, we can criticize Darwin, but not the government; in America,
you can criticize the government, but not Darwin"

Jun-Yuan Chen, paleontologist

ONE OF THE INTRIGUING THINGS about the world's creation myths is how many of them evoke a time when there was just an empty void. *Creation ex nihilo* may have been a foreign concept to the Babylonians, but it wasn't to the New Zealand Maori, or America's Apache Indians, or the Japanese. What made all of these primitive peoples, and many others besides, conceive the idea of a timeless, limitless void, out of which both the heavens (stars) and earth emerged? Why did these tribes, from right across the planet, not take the much simpler view – as the Hindus and Buddhists did – that the earth had always existed or that it endlessly recycled itself?

An early Tahitian creation myth, recorded by a passing ship's captain in 1855 and published the following decade, reads: "In the beginning, there was nothing but the god, Ihoiho, afterwards there was an expanse of waters which covered the abyss."[32] Similar, again, to the Maori legend and the supreme being Io. The creation myths across the Pacific, again, go much deeper and further back than the cultures that now remember them.

What, then, is the picture that science paints for us of the moment of creation? According to cosmologist Stephen Hawking, the event that kicked off the Big Bang was so incredibly powerful that the entire universe went from being the size of a grain of sand to filling the void of space in literally milliseconds. Now *that's* a feat that matches the poetry of "he spread out the heavens with his hands".

---

32 M. de Bovis, Annuaire des Etablissements Francais de l'Oceanie, Papeete, 1863, p. 95.

The idea that something so insignificantly tiny could explode with such intensity beggars belief. As a point of trivia, there's a good chance the watch on your wrist is powered by a lithium battery. What you probably don't know is that you are wearing material as old as the universe itself. All of the lithium in existence was produced during *the first four minutes* of the Big Bang explosion. If God indeed exists, his signature is written on the battery powering your wristwatch, or notebook computer.

Does science know why it went Bang? No, we don't have a clue. Sure, there are theories. Scientists like Edward Tryon have tried to argue that the universe is the result of what he called "a vacuum fluctuation". Although this sounds suspiciously like what happens when you accidentally suck a sock up the hosepipe, in fact he was talking about a quantum event. Scientists studying quantum physics have long known that particles seem to miraculously appear and disappear, sometimes with quite spectacular energy effects. Could the universe, wonders Tryon, simply be a quantum event that popped into existence and didn't disappear again?[33] Another to theorise along these lines more recently is British physicist Paul Davies in his book, *God and the New Physics*.

The argument seems quite tempting, until you crunch the numbers. Quantum events are happening all over the place, even as you read this. But the universe is an incredibly large place. There must be quadzillions of quantum events happening every second throughout the universe. There are 86,400 seconds per day, or nearly 32 million seconds a year. And according to science the Big Bang happened nearly 15 *billion* years ago.

Now, we know from history that if any one of the quantum events happening all around us turned into a Big Bang, it would wipe the slate clean and destroy the universe as we know it. Yet, despite the enormous, incalculable opportunities for a new Big Bang originating somewhere in the universe in the past 15 billion years, the event has never happened again.

Tackling Paul Davies specifically, astrophysicist Hugh Ross argued on his website[34] that Davies had been caught in his own trap. In one part of *God and the New Physics*, Davies argues that God did not cause the Big Bang because causing, by definition, can only happen within a time-bound realm, not a timeless one. Davies overlooks the transcendence of God, however – virtually all religions argue that a Deity capable of creating the universe is just as capable plunging his hand into it from outside to stir the mix. I digress, however. Hugh Ross pinged Davies on the theory that the universe may be a quantum event:

---

33 Tryon, Edward P. "Is the Universe a Vacuum Fluctuation," in *Nature*, 246(1973), pp. 396-397
34 http://www.reasons.org/resources/apologetics/quantummech.shtml

"Noting that virtual particles can pop into existence from nothingness through quantum tunneling, Davies employs the new grand unified theories to suggest that in the same manner the whole universe popped into existence. Ironically, his argument against God's creating can now be turned against his hypothesis. Quantum mechanics is founded on the concept that quantum events occur according to finite probabilities within finite time intervals. The larger the time interval, the greater the probability that a quantum event will occur. Outside of time, however, no quantum event is possible. Therefore, the origin of time (coincident with that of space, matter, and energy) eliminates quantum tunneling as 'creator'."

In simple language, there's still no natural explanation for the Big Bang.

To his credit, Paul Davies has conceded the weakness of the argument and now grudgingly concedes there is an apparent design in the universe.

In a column written for Britain's *Guardian* this year,[35] he addresses the problem.

"Scientists are slowly waking up to an inconvenient truth – the universe looks suspiciously like a fix. The issue concerns the very laws of nature themselves. For 40 years, physicists and cosmologists have been quietly collecting examples of all too convenient "coincidences" and special features in the underlying laws of the universe that seem to be necessary in order for life, and hence conscious beings, to exist. Change any one of them and the consequences would be lethal. Fred Hoyle, the distinguished cosmologist, once said it was as if "a super- intellect has monkeyed with physics".

"To see the problem, imagine playing God with the cosmos. Before you is a designer machine that lets you tinker with the basics of physics. Twiddle this knob and you make all electrons a bit lighter, twiddle that one and you make gravity a bit stronger, and so on. It happens that you need to set thirtysomething knobs to fully describe the world about us. The crucial point is that some of those metaphorical knobs[36] must be tuned very precisely, or the universe would be sterile.

"Example: neutrons are just a tad heavier than protons. If it were the other way around, atoms couldn't exist, because all the protons in the universe would have decayed into neutrons shortly after the big bang. No protons, then no atomic nucleuses and no atoms. No atoms, no chemistry,

---

35 http://www.guardian.co.uk/comment/story/0,,2111345,00.html
36 Here's another example of how Richard Dawkins is selective in his book *The God Delusion*. Paul Davies quotes here "thirtysomething" knobs that need to be set "just so" for life to occur. Dawkins, quoting atheist physicist Martin Rees, talks of only "six knobs". As astrophysicist Hugh Ross points out in *The Creator and the Cosmos*, by 2001 there were 128 different knobs that each had to be set correctly. The picture is far, far more complex than the mere six constants that Dawkins and Rees discuss in their books

no life. Like Baby Bear's porridge in the story of Goldilocks, the universe seems to be just right for life. So what's going on?

"The intelligent design movement has inevitably seized on the Goldilocks enigma as evidence of divine providence, prompting a scientific backlash and boosting the recent spate of God-bashing bestsellers.

"Fuelling the controversy is an unanswered question lurking at the very heart of science – the origin of the laws of physics. Where do they come from? Why do they have the form that they do? Traditionally, scientists have treated the laws of physics as simply "given", elegant mathematical relationships that were somehow imprinted on the universe at its birth, and fixed thereafter. Inquiry into the origin and nature of the laws was not regarded as a proper part of science."

Davies looks at some options, such as the theory of an infinite number of multiple universes, and perhaps we just happen to live on the universe capable of supporting life. It's not a truly scientific theory, because it can never be tested, and Davies recognizes this:

"The multiverse theory...falls short of a complete explanation of existence. For a start, there has to be a physical mechanism to make all those universes and allocate bylaws to them. This process demands its own laws, or meta-laws. Where do they come from? The problem has simply been shifted up a level from the laws of the universe to the meta-laws of the multiverse.

"The root cause of all the difficulty can be traced to the fact that both religion and science appeal to some agency outside the universe to explain its lawlike order. Dumping the problem in the lap of a pre-existing designer is no explanation at all, as it merely begs the question of who designed the designer. But appealing to a host of unseen universes and a set of unexplained meta-laws is scarcely any better."

Having abandoned the quantum theory, debunked the multiverse theory, and rejected Intelligent Design because, well, it implies a Designer, Davies searches for a replacement theory and comes up with a belief that the universe miraculously (but entirely naturally) altered its own laws during the Big Bang to ensure a life-friendly outcome.

"In the first split second of cosmic existence, the laws must therefore have been seriously fuzzy. Then, as the information content of the universe climbed, the laws focused and homed in on the life-encouraging form we observe today. But the flaws in the laws left enough wiggle room for the universe to engineer its own bio-friendliness.

"Thus, three centuries after Newton, symmetry is restored: the laws explain the universe even as the universe explains the laws. If there is an ultimate meaning to existence, as I believe is the case, the answer is to be found within nature, not beyond it. The universe might indeed be a fix, but if so, it has fixed itself," concludes Davies.

Are you convinced? To me, he sounds desperate, conjuring up a universe that thinks for itself. It's probably a reflection of the desperation he himself expressed in his book, *The Cosmic Blueprint*.

"There is for me powerful evidence that there is something going on behind it all ... it seems as though somebody has fine-tuned nature's numbers to make the Universe ... The impression of design is overwhelming."

Rather than go into all the technical jargon about which atomic elements are crucial for life as we know it, I'll paint a broader picture of the "monkeying" that has taken place, and why it is so significant that atheists like Richard Dawkins and Christopher Hitchens are now feeling seriously threatened by the latest scientific discoveries.

One aspect of the Big Bang is that the energy and timing of its explosion were incredibly precise. If this allegedly random event had fluctuated by even a nano-second in its crucial first minute, the whole showboat would have sunk without trace on the spot: no universe, period. If the acceleration forces of the Big Bang had been a mere nano-fraction stronger, the material needed to form stars and galaxies would have been flung too far and spread out too much to coalesce into stars and galaxies. If the Big Bang had been a nano-fraction slower, the gravitational pressures would have caused it to implode back in on itself.

Luckily, in this random scientific world where God does not exist, Goldilocks won the day and the universe was born. What you are about to read will, however, give you a new appreciation for how incredibly lucky you actually are. You don't even know the half of it!

CHAPTER 4

THE IMPROBABILITY OF EARTH

"Banishing the One Creator God, they would then end up with what has been described as the ultimate in polytheism – a universe in which every particle has god-like capabilities"
Professor John Lennox, *God's Undertaker*

GALILEO'S DISCOVERY THAT THE EARTH revolves around the sun is often cited as a turning point, the moment that science trumped religious belief for the first time. Its significance, according to atheists, is that it showed the Earth was not the centre of the solar system, let alone the universe, and that really we inhabit an insignificant speck of rock, three planets out from the sun, in a forlorn and minor arm of an inconsequential galaxy in a far-flung corner of the cosmos.

Some scientists – the late Carl Sagan, for example – are so certain that we are not unique, and that the universe must be teeming with life that they set up projects like SETI, the Search for Extra-Terrestrial Intelligence, which harnesses the power of millions of home computers over the internet to number crunch radio telescope data in the hunt for intelligent messages from outer space.

As anyone who has seen *Star Trek* or *Star Wars* knows, the appeal of other civilizations in far off places is at the core of modern science fiction, touching as it does on the deep human need to explore, seek out new frontiers and to boldly go where no man has gone before![37] Well, you get the picture. In a sense, our search for aliens is a reflection of our deeper search for meaning and truth in the universe. What is life for, if not to seek out the unknown?

---

37 One wit has even postulated that science fiction is really nothing more than the Christian *Left Behind* series for atheists: apocalyptic writing where aliens, rather than gods, come to save humanity from themselves. http://www.brucebethke.net/leftbehind_4_atheists.html

What most people don't appreciate, however, is that our location appears to make us unique in the universe. If the earth was not placed precisely where it is in space, none of you would be here, let alone reading this book.

Romantic as science fiction is, there are growing signs that the universe is *not* teeming with life, and that we may indeed be alone. Part of this is because of the brick wall evolutionary biology has hit in trying to find out how life arose on earth. As I explained in my earlier book, *Eve's Bite*, experiments to create life from scratch have failed. The best that science appears able to do is cobble together components of existing life forms to create new hybrid organisms. Creating life from a puddle, even with the best amino acids, electricity surges and ideal conditions, has flopped. Various alternative theories have been put forward, such as life arising elsewhere in the universe and arriving here either on a comet or via aliens "seeding" Earth (panspermia theory); or alternatively the "RNA World hypothesis", which suggests that RNA molecules might have powered primitive life forms on our planet before evolving into DNA life.

The problem with panspermia theory is that if life is too complex to have arisen on the planet most suited to sustaining life (Earth), then how likely is it to have arisen somewhere else in the universe and survived millions of years of cosmic radiation while being transported here on a comet? And how did it survive the journey from its own planet onto a comet in the first place?

Christopher Hitchens, in *God Is Not Great*, says "Francis Crick even allowed himself to flirt with the theory that life was 'inseminated' on earth by bacteria spread from a passing comet."

Not so fast, Hitch. In an interview with *Bible Code* author Michael Drosnin, Crick denies the comet idea:[38]

"I called," writes Drosnin, "the most eminent authority in the world, Francis Crick, the Nobel laureate biologist who discovered the double helix, the spiral structure of DNA. It was one of the greatest scientific discoveries of all time. As Crick himself declared in the first moment of revelation, 'We've discovered the secret of life'.

" 'Is it possible,' I asked Crick, when I reached him at the Salk Institute in San Diego, California, 'that our DNA came from another planet?'

" 'I published that theory twenty-five years ago,' said Crick. 'I called it 'Directed Panspermia.'

" 'Do you think it arrived in a meteor or comet?' I asked.

---

38 *The Bible Code 2*, Michael Drosnin, W&N Publishing, 2002, p. 144. Interview of Crick by phone on October 27, 1998. Incidentally, don't be fooled by *The Bible Code* – the book itself is rubbish in my view

" 'No,' said Crick. 'Anything living would have died in such an accidental journey through space.'

'Are you saying that DNA was sent here in a vehicle?' I asked. 'It's the only possibility,' said Crick.

"I asked him to explain his theory of the genesis of DNA. The DNA molecule, Crick said, was far too complex to have evolved spontaneously on Earth in the short time between the formation of this planet 4 billion years ago and the first appearance of life 3.8 billion years ago.

" 'But it is unlikely,' said Crick, 'that living organisms could have reached Earth as spores from another star, or embedded in a meteorite.' Therefore, said Crick, there was only one possibility:

" 'A primitive form of life was planted on the Earth by an advanced civilization on another planet – deliberately...all life on Earth represents a clone derived from a single extraterrestrial organism.

" 'We know very little about the origins of life,' said Crick, 'but all of the new scientific discoveries support my theory and none disprove it.

" 'There has been one big change since our theory was first published', he told me. 'We now know that other stars do have planets. So it certainly is possible that an advanced technological civilization existed elsewhere in the galaxy even before the Earth was formed'.

"Crick was more certain than ever. 'DNA was sent here in a vehicle,' he said. 'By aliens'."

Three things emerge from this fascinating discussion between Crick and Drosnin. Firstly, suggestions in some quarters that Crick had backed away from his "aliens theory" appear to be wrong. Secondly, Crick destroys any possibility of random life traveling here on a comet. Thirdly, his thesis requires there not only to *be* aliens, but for the aliens to *specifically choose Planet Earth* on which to seed new life. Anyone care to run the probability calculations across *that* one?

RNA theory has difficulties too, such as RNA's vulnerability to breaking down in sunlight and water. RNA life forms would find it hard to go outside on a fine day, or a rainy day, and probably any day in between.

As acclaimed DNA chemist Robert Shapiro noted earlier this year, RNA is not what many are still cracking it up to be.[39]

"The hypothesis that life began with RNA was presented as a likely reality, rather than a speculation, in journals, textbooks and the media. Yet the clues I have cited only support the weaker conclusion that RNA preceded DNA and proteins; they provide no information about the

---

39   http://sciam.com/article.cfm?chanID=sa004&articleID=B7AABF35-E7F2-99DF-309B8CEF02B5C4D7&pageNumber=1&catID=4

origin of life, which may have involved stages prior to the RNA world in which other living entities ruled supreme. Just the same, and despite the difficulties that I will discuss in the next section, perhaps two-thirds of scientists publishing in the origin-of life field (as judged by a count of papers published in 2006 in the journal *Origins of Life and Evolution of the Biosphere*) still support the idea that life began with the spontaneous formation of RNA or a related self-copying molecule."

Citing the 1986 study by Nobel Laureate Walter Gilbert that ushered in the RNA hypothesis, Shapiro now says:

"Enormous obstacles block Gilbert's picture of the origin of life, sufficient to provoke another Nobelist, Christian De Duve of Rockefeller University, to ask rhetorically, 'Did God make RNA?'"

Some scientists, he notes, still appeal to the "prebiotic soup" idea, that enough amino acids existed on primitive earth that can be forced in the lab to combine.

"It mattered little if kilograms of starting material were required to produce milligrams of product," remarks Shapiro wryly of the experiments. "The point was the demonstration that humans could produce, however inefficiently, substances found in nature. Unfortunately, neither chemists nor laboratories were present on the early Earth to produce RNA."

He describes in his paper the huge lengths scientists are still going to in a bid to make the base ingredients bind in the lab, and the ridiculous claims they then make in science journals like *Nature* about how it might have happened on primitive earth.

"The exceptionally high urea concentration was rationalized in the *Nature* paper by invoking a vision of drying lagoons on the early Earth. In a published rebuttal, I calculated that a large lagoon would have to be evaporated to the size of a puddle, without loss of its contents, to achieve that concentration. No such feature exists on Earth today.

"The drying lagoon claim is not unique. In a similar spirit, other prebiotic chemists have invoked freezing glacial lakes, mountainside freshwater ponds, flowing streams, beaches, dry deserts, volcanic aquifers and the entire global ocean (frozen or warm as needed) to support their requirement that the "nucleotide soup" necessary for RNA synthesis would somehow have come into existence on the early Earth.

"The analogy that comes to mind is that of a golfer, who having played a golf ball through an 18-hole course, then assumed that the ball could also play itself around the course in his absence. He had demonstrated the possibility of the event; it was only necessary to presume that some combination of natural forces (earthquakes, winds, tornadoes and floods, for example) could produce the same result, given enough time. No physical law need be broken for spontaneous RNA formation to happen, but *the chances against it are so immense, that the suggestion implies that the non-living world had an innate desire to generate RNA*. [Author's emphasis] The majority of origin-of-life scientists who still support the RNA-first theory either accept this concept (implicitly, if not explicitly) or feel that the immensely unfavorable odds were simply overcome by good luck.

"Many chemists, confronted with these difficulties, have fled the RNA-first hypothesis as if it were a building on fire. One group, however, still captured by the vision of the self-copying molecule, has opted for an exit that leads to similar hazards. In these revised theories, a simpler replicator arose first and governed life in a "pre-RNA world." Variations have been proposed in which the bases, the sugar or the entire backbone of RNA have been replaced by simpler substances, more accessible to prebiotic syntheses. Presumably, this first replicator would also have the catalytic capabilities of RNA. Because no trace of this hypothetical primal replicator and catalyst has been recognized so far in modern biology, RNA must have completely taken over all of its functions at some point following its emergence.

"Further, the spontaneous appearance of any such replicator without the assistance of a chemist faces implausibilities that dwarf those involved in the preparation of a mere nucleotide soup," warns Shapiro.

"The chances for the spontaneous assembly of a replicator in [such a nucleotide soup] can be compared to those of [a] gorilla composing, in English, a coherent recipe for the preparation of chili con carne. With similar considerations in mind Gerald F. Joyce of the Scripps Research Institute and Leslie Orgel of the Salk Institute concluded that the spontaneous appearance of RNA chains on the lifeless Earth "would have been a near miracle." I would extend this conclusion to all of the proposed RNA substitutes that I mentioned above."

Shapiro's 'solution' to this dilemma is a relatively new theory called metabolistic evolution based on small molecules. This is the idea that chemicals can metabolise in rocks or similar compartmentalised structures that might, just might become self-replicating by virtue of environmental actions like heat, tides, rock-falls etc that allow the chemicals to leach from one compartment to another. These would be entirely different lifeforms to those on earth today. Experiments have so far failed to produce these either, and Shapiro concedes that even if it can be done, that would not explain the emergence of RNA and then DNA and the path to life as we know it. In short, there's no guarantee that such a process would throw up DNA lifeforms at all.

Yet, if such an explanation for origin of life were credible, wouldn't we be seeing rival life forms on earth all around us, based on non-DNA structures? We don't, of course, and I suspect it is simply more clutching at straws. If Shapiro and the leading biochemists have to redefine the search for life to include rocks, then frankly it is not that inspiring.

"A highly implausible start for life, as in the RNA-first scenario, implies a universe in which we are alone," he acknowledges. In short, none of the scientific theories about life's origin are anywhere near remotely convincing, so from a biological point of view the possibility of meeting wise and advanced aliens is getting more unlikely by the day.

When you take into account what you saw in the previous chapter – that scientists are now admitting the universe seems mysteriously fine-tuned to support life – what you're about to read is, frankly, stunning. You see, whilst the universe is finely tuned for life, *it appears to be finely tuned specifically to support life on Earth.*

It is not until you see the astrophysics evidence, about the conditions necessary for life on Earth, that you begin to appreciate why our third rock from the sun is anything but insignificant.

Take the moon. Contrary to popular belief, the moon has not always been in our skies. According to the best scientific theories to date,[40] the moon was formed during a gigantic game of cosmic skittles that was crucial to giving us a breathable atmosphere. As astronomer Dr Hugh Ross points out, the general "rule of thumb in planetary formation is that the greater a planet's surface gravity and the greater a planet's distance from its star, the heavier and thicker its atmosphere." Earth, he says, "departs dramatically from that rule".

In theory, our atmosphere should be even heavier and thicker than Venus', but instead it is forty times thinner. The solution, says Ross, lies with the moon. As he points out, the moon is 250 million years younger than Earth, based on the composition of moon rocks brought back for analysis. It is made from a different kind of rock to those found on Earth, meaning the two bodies could not have been formed together. Furthermore, we know from measuring the moon's orbit that it was once much closer to Earth than it now is.

"The moon's movement away from Earth and the measured slowing of Earth's rotation imply some kind of collision or near collision more than 4 billion years ago," writes Hugh Ross.

"Only one collision scenario fits all the observed Earth-moon parameters

---

40 A New Zealand born scientist named Ross Taylor, working for NASA during the Apollo missions, was given the task of analyzing moon rocks to determine their origin. Taylor is widely regarded as the father of the "giant impact" theory that is now considered the most likely explanation of lunar creation and dynamics: a body at least the size of Mars (nine times the mass of the moon and one ninth the mass of Earth) and possibly twice as large made a nearly head-on hit and was absorbed, for the most part, into the Earth's core.

"Such a collision would have blasted almost all of Earth's original atmosphere into outer space. The shell of cloud or debris arising from the collision would orbit Earth and eventually coalesce to form our moon."

It was this singular, unrepeated event (our very own, localized 'Big Bang'), scientists argue, that stripped the dangerous gases out of our atmosphere and left us with air and water vapour. With the atmosphere now much thinner, light could reach the surface of the planet for the first time, and the absorbtion of the rogue planet into Earth's core increased our gravity enough that we could hold onto the water vapour in our atmosphere (molecular weight 18), but not so much that it would keep dangerous levels of the lighter ammonia (molecular weight 17) or methane (mw 16) in the atmosphere. Both of those gases now eventually dissipate off into space (methane in the atmosphere takes about 8.5 years to go, partly by reacting with oxygen and hydrogen to create water vapour, and partly by stratospheric loss).

Putting this known scientific event up against the creation story in Genesis, there is a remarkable harmony.

"1 In the beginning God created the heavens and the earth. 2 Now the earth became formless and empty, darkness was over the surface of the deep, and the Spirit of God was hovering over the waters."

While most modern Bibles translate Genesis 1:2 as "the earth *was* formless", the nuance of the original Hebrew is "became". The sequence then is clear: Earth and the heavenly bodies were initially created, *then* something happened that made the planet "formless and empty" which – you could easily argue – would certainly be the result of a Mars-sized object slamming into us. The huge explosion of debris into near-Earth orbit would certainly account for the "darkness". The moon, of course, had not yet been formed (being 250 million years younger than Earth).

"3 And God said, "Let there be light," and there was light. 4 God saw that the light was good, and He separated the light from the darkness. 5 God called the light "day," and the darkness he called "night." And there was evening, and there was morning—the first day."

The significance of Genesis 1:3-5 can easily be overlooked, but when you examine the scientific effect of the collision, you may see the biblical passage in a new light (no pun intended). Day and night are relative to an observer, they only exist if a planet rotates on its axis. Mercury, for example, does not rotate, and one side of the planet is continually burning in the sun's heat while the other side is perpetually in the dark and cold. The moon, likewise, does not rotate relative to us. Earth, on the other hand, was left spinning like a top after the collision – we know this because the Earth is now slowing down.[41]

Thus, the collision that led to the eventual creation of the moon also set Earth spinning,[42] thereby creating the effect of "day" and "night" and providing inspiration for the poetry in Genesis.

Significantly, it is not until a few verses later (Gen 1:16) that the moon is officially "made" – the Hebrew word implying 'formed from existing materials' rather than "created" from nothing, which is used in Genesis 1:1. The scientific theory – that the moon formed from the debris left orbiting Earth – dovetails with the language used in this passage. The creation of the moon *after* the Earth is something the ancient Hebrews could not have known scientifically – it is a recent discovery.

All of this is merely an aside, however, setting the scene for the scientific evidence about the unique events that allow life to exist on earth.

Had the Mars-sized object *not* slammed into Earth, we wouldn't be here. According to Dr Ross, the collision between the mystery planet and Earth also "boosted the iron content of Earth's crust [so much] as to permit a huge abundance of ocean life", iron being crucial to biological life, particularly in the marine food chain.

The collision created a phenomenon known as plate tectonics. You probably learnt about this in school or on the Discovery Channel – it's the theory that continental plates float on a sea of volcanic magma, occasionally releasing the tension when they collide with another plate, creating volcanoes and earthquakes. No other planet in the solar system has active plate tectonics like Earth. Instead, the predominant form of crust renewal involves entire continental plates tipping up and sinking back into the magma[43] in their entirety. Such destruction on Earth would take all life with it. In contrast, earthquakes and volcanoes seem a small price to pay for our relative stability.

---

41 Scientific studies such as Scrutton and Wells' work in 1963 and 1964 on fossil corals suggest the Earth had a 22 hour day 370 million years ago, and may originally have had a 14 hour day. As a rule of thumb, the steady-state Atomic Clock requires the insertion of a 'leap second' roughly every 1.5 years to keep pace with the slowdown in the Earth's rotation
42 In sharp contrast, the planet Venus is rotating so slowly that it takes nearly a Venusian year to have just one day and night there. The slow spin makes Venus utterly hostile to life, and the surface temperature (because of the thick atmosphere and long day in the sun) is a blisteringly fatal 480 C
43 It is a process known as stagnant lid convection. Because the crust is thicker than Earth's (our crust is thin thanks to the collision), it builds up heat underneath that eventually flips the continent like a lid on a boiling pot. Venus, again, is a good example. Its surface totally regenerates over a period of time.

Astrophysicist Guillermo Gonzalez sums it up pretty succinctly:

"Earthquakes destroy property and kill many people every year; nevertheless, they benefit both our planet's habitability and scientific discovery. Without earthquakes, we probably wouldn't even be here and, if somehow we were, we would know far less about Earth's interior structure," he writes in *The Privileged Planet*.

Through measuring the pressure waves created by earthquakes, which reverberate around the planet "like a hammer hitting a bell", says Gonzalez, scientists have been able to create a map of the type of rock the waves are passing through, "like a geological CAT scan". It is this data, recorded by seismographs, that allowed scientists to figure out the boundaries of the various continental plates.

Of course, the current layout of the world is a relatively recent phenomenon. Originally, it appears all land existed in one giant mass, the most recent manifestation being "Pangaea" around 1.1 billion years ago through to 200 million BC.[44]

Pangaea was surrounded on all sides by one giant ocean that covered the whole planet. Again, purely as an aside, Genesis (written about 3,500 years ago) records that on the primeval Earth there was one place for all the land, and the rest was ocean:

"9 And God said, "Let the water under the sky be gathered to one place, and let dry ground appear." And it was so. 10 God called the dry ground "land," and the gathered waters he called "seas." And God saw that it was good."

Pangaea eventually broke up, the southern half forming Gondwana – the prehistoric continent that included modern Australia, New Zealand, India, Africa, Arabia, South America and Antarctica.

It was through one of the earthquake wave "CAT scans" just mentioned that scientists were able to confirm that a core of liquid iron is still spinning inside the planet, independent of the planet's own rotation. It is this spinning iron core that creates Earth's magnetic field. And by measuring the impact of that magnetic field on rocks, this has allowed science to trace the positions of the various continents over hundreds of millions of years.

We wouldn't have a spinning iron core, however, if the mystery planet had not collided with Earth just after it was created. And without a spinning iron core, you and I wouldn't be here.

The reason for this is actually quite simple. It is Earth's strong magnetic field that shields the planet from much of the most damaging cosmic radiation. The field holds in place what scientists call the "Van Allen

---

44 http://en.wikipedia.org/wiki/Pangaea

belts" – a series of highly charged energy fields.[45] In essence, the Earth's magnetism traps these radioactive particles and energy streams before they can hit the planet. Without the magnetic field, life on Earth would be nuked, day in, day out. Venus, again, is a good example. It is spinning so slowly that it has almost no magnetic field. The solar radioactivity rips into Venus 24/7 like a hot knife into butter.

So far in this chapter, then, you've seen how a cosmic road accident had to happen in order for you to live: it ripped away the thick, poisonous primitive atmosphere and left us with air and water vapour, it gave us the mineral iron essential for life to grow, it gave the planet a spinning iron core which generates magnetism to protect us from lethal radiation, it gave us night and day to balance out temperatures, and it gave us relatively gentle earthquakes and volcanic activity rather than the wholesale destruction of entire continents. This is on top of the unknown series of coincidences that fine-tuned the universe to support life.

Critics will no doubt argue that it doesn't support the idea of God, because if God existed he could have done it right first time. Yeah, he could. But the ability to sling the occasional lightning bolt or play ten-pin bowling with planets might actually have given the deity some enjoyment – which is surely as good a motive as any other. It is also entirely possible that God did it this way deliberately to leave his fingerprints visible – to help scientists come to the conclusion Paul Davies reached in that extract last chapter when he said, "Scientists are slowly waking up to an inconvenient truth – the universe looks suspiciously like a fix..."

Strongly agnostic cosmologist Stephen Hawking agrees that the universe does indeed have this appearance.

"The laws of science, as we know them at present, contain many fundamental numbers, like the size of the electric charge of the electron and the ratio of the masses of the proton and the electron .... The remarkable fact is that the values of these numbers seem to have been finely adjusted to make possible the development of life."

Agnostic scientist Robert Jastrow summed up the views of many of his peers a few years ago in his book, *God and the Astronomers*:

"For the scientist who has lived by his faith in the power of reason, the story ends like a bad dream. He has scaled the mountains of ignorance; he is about to conquer the highest peak; as he pulls himself over the final rock, he is greeted by a band of theologians who have been sitting there for centuries."

But wait, as the TV hucksters say, there's more!

---

45 http://en.wikipedia.org/wiki/Van_Allen_radiation_belt

Let's return to the role of the moon in all this. There is no other grouping in the solar system, or indeed the known universe so far, that is similar to Earth and its moon. Unlike the relatively tiny moons of other planets, our moon is effectively a sister planet to Earth. Without the moon, you wouldn't exist either.

Our moon is big enough to create a tidal pull on Earth. It is the motions of the tides on the world's oceans that allowed life to survive. Without tides, the oceans would be dead, stagnant millponds. The smashing of waves on the shore releases oxygen and in turn releases shorebound nutrients and minerals into the oceans. Much of our planet's life exists in that complex intertidal region of the seashore.

The moon generates around two thirds of the total tidal energy on Earth (the sun being responsible for the final third). The tidal currents in the ocean also impact on Earth's weather patterns.

"If Earth lacked such lunar tides," says Gonzalez, "Seattle would look more like northern Siberia than the lush, temperate, 'Emerald City'."

Nor is it just tides. Because of its size, the moon has been able to hold the Earth in a steady 23.5 degree tilt on its axis. If you look at a globe of the Earth, the tilt is what puts the planet slightly on its side as it orbits the sun. It is the tilt that gives us summer or winter.

Twenty-three degrees is, according to Guillermo Gonzalez, pretty much the optimum number for sustaining life on Earth.

"A larger tilt would cause larger climate fluctuations, [hotter summers, colder winters]" he writes in *The Privileged Planet*. "At present, Earth tilts 23.5 degrees and it varies from 22.1 to 24.5 degrees over several thousand years. To stabilize effectively, the moon's mass must be a substantial fraction of the Earth's mass. Small bodies like the two potato-shaped moons of Mars, Phobos and Deimos, won't suffice. If our moon were as small as these Martian moons, Earth's tilt would vary not 3 degrees but more than 30 degrees.

"That might not sound like anything to fuss over," says Gonzalez, "but tell that to someone trying to survive on Earth with a 60 degree tilt. When the North Pole was leaning sunward through the summer half of the year, most of the Northern Hemisphere would experience months of perpetually scorching daylight. High northern latitudes would be subjected to searing heat, hot enough to make Death Valley in July feel like a shady spring picnic. Any survivors would suffer viciously cold months of perpetual night during the other half of the year."

A smaller tilt would reduce seasonal differences and produce less rain, creating drier, desert areas.

You know the drill by now: In other words, without the moon, you would not be here to read this.

Up until now we have dealt only with the Earth/moon dynamic. It isn't the only one. Earth is thundering around the sun at an incredible 110,000 km/h.[46] During a 24 hour day, while you work, eat, sleep and read this book, all of us have traveled a further 2.5 million kilometres through space. It has been this way since Earth began, a silent, epic mission through the darkness as the planet carries its valuable cargo around the sun.

According to Einstein's Theory of General Relativity and its subsequent modifications, the sun acts like a fat guy sitting in the middle of a trampoline, and creates a big "dip" in the fabric of space time. Earth is circling around the edge of the dip at speed, never getting close enough to fall in or far enough to fly away. It just so happens that our planet exists in what astrobiologists call "the Goldilocks zone" – the narrow orbit band around a sun where a planet is capable of sustaining liquid water, and hence life. Too close, and the water burns off in the heat, like Venus. Too far away and it becomes ice, like Mars. Just right, however, and water becomes the backbone of life.

Atheist fundamentalist Richard Dawkins, in his recent book *The God Delusion*, tries to address some of these problems by disarmingly conceding the point. Yes, he admits, we appear to live on a unique planet. Yes, the moon is crucial for the existence of life. Yes, we inhabit the Goldilocks zone.

"Earth's orbit," he agrees, "is so close to circular that it never strays out of the Goldilocks zone."

Faced with all of this, Dawkins tries to convince readers that despite everything having to be "just right", science still has a natural answer.

"The great majority of planets in the universe are not in the Goldilocks zones of their respective stars, and not suitable for life. None of that majority has life. However small the minority of planets with just the right conditions for life may be, we necessarily have to be on one of that minority, because here we are thinking about it."

Simple, really. Using Dawkins' logic you can wave all the unlikely pre-conditions aside, put it down to blind chance, and say 'well, here we are then, so it must have happened naturally'.

Richard Dawkins' fatal mistake here is the assumption that his very

---

46   At this blistering speed – around 50 times faster than a bullet from a gun – the chances of a Mars-sized object just happening to collide with Earth by accident in this huge expanse of space are even more remote. And to give you some idea of relativity here, our galaxy, the Milky Way, is screaming through space at 600km per second, or 52 million km a day, fuelled by the force of the Big Bang 15 billion years ago. Some other bodies in the universe are moving much faster again, still speeding away from the centre of the Big Bang at a mind-ripping 48,000 km per second – which is fast enough to travel from Earth to the Sun in less than an hour

existence and ability to ponder the probability of it all, proves in itself a natural first cause. He offers no hard evidence in *The God Delusion* to support this, and instead wades deeper into error when he tries to link it to the origin of life issue.

Readers of my earlier book, *Eve's Bite*, will remember I tackled Dawkins on this in the chapter, "The Dawkins Delusion". It is worth a brief expansion here.

"Just as we did with the Goldilocks orbits," writes Dawkins, "we can make the point that, however improbable the origin of life might be, we know it happened on Earth because we are here.

"Again, as with temperature, there are two hypotheses to explain what happened – the design hypothesis and the scientific or 'anthropic' hypothesis. The design approach postulates a God who wrought a deliberate miracle, struck the prebiotic soup with divine fire and launched DNA, or something equivalent."

The scientific approach, argues Dawkins, is statistical. "Scientists invoke the magic of large numbers." So Dawkins himself plucks a large number out of the air – declaring a "one in a billion" chance of life arising on a planet like Earth naturally. Based on his own guesstimate that there are a billion billion planets in the Universe, he proudly states that "even with such absurdly long odds, life will still have arisen on a billion planets – of which Earth, of course, is one."

This argument, incidentally, is also at the heart of Dawkins' previous bestseller, *The Blind Watchmaker*.

Using that logic, Dawkins tells his readers the science is settled. Clearly Earth is one of those billion planets in the universe where life has arisen, no need to invoke God. Case closed.

He would be right, if the probability was truly a one in a billion chance. It isn't.

Israeli biophysicist Dr Lee Spetner, in his book *Not By Chance*,[47] tackled Dawkins on this soon after *The Blind Watchmaker* was released.

"[Dawkins] noted that the origin of life may be highly improbable at any one place at any one time. Yet, it had a lot of time and space going for it, and that would be enough to make it more likely than not. He, therefore, advised us to try to change the way we look at probabilities. We must stop thinking of the relatively large probabilities with which we are used to dealing. We should, instead, try to think of the very small probabilities that might suit a hypothetical alien being who lives millions of years.

---

[47] Endorsed as "extremely thorough and compelling" by the late Nobel Prize winning biologist, Professor Christian Anfinsen. See pages 164-166

"Dawkins' advice," continues Spetner, "shows that he didn't understand probability."

Dawkins suggestion was that an alien who lived for a hundred million years and played many hands of the card game, bridge, may well live long enough to see a 'perfect' bridge hand where each player was dealt thirteen cards of the same suit.

"They will expect to be dealt a perfect bridge hand from time to time, and will scarcely trouble to write home about it when it happens," Dawkins says in his book.

"He's wrong," states Spetner. "One can easily calculate the chance of Dawkins' alien experiencing a perfect bridge hand at least once in his lifetime. The chance of getting such a hand in one deal is 4.47×10^{-28}. If the alien plays 100 bridge hands every day of his life for 100 million years, he would play about 3.65×10^{12} hands. The chance of his seeing a perfect hand *at least once in his life* is then 1.63×10^{-15}, or about one chance in a quadrillion."

Based on the known requirements for the Goldilocks factor, scientists have been able to factor more than a hundred critical factors that allow life to exist on Earth. If any one of those factors was missing, we wouldn't be here. They ran those factors through the probability computations. The chance of life spontaneously arising on any planet in the universe is not one in a *billion*, as Dawkins offhandedly suggests. It is in fact one chance in a trillion, trillion, trillion, trillion, trillion, trillion, trillion, trillion, trillion, trillion, trillion, trillion.[48] In the high stakes card game between scientists "invoking large numbers", Dawkins lost.

Do you now see the dangers of Dawkins' throwaway "Suppose…"?

Dr Lee Spetner simply shakes his head, sadly.

"Dawkins' error is one that evolutionists often make. Many of them have fallen into that trap. They think the Earth's age [only 4.5 billion years] is long enough for anything to have happened.

"The events necessary for cumulative selection [Darwinian evolution] are much too improbable to build a theory on. The events needed for the origin of life are even more improbable.

"Dawkins did not make a convincing case for the spontaneous origin of life… but his failure to convince is not surprising. Even the army of research scientists working on the problem for the past generation have not succeeded."

Another whose voice has been heard on the odds against life arising spontaneously is former Yale professor Harold Morowitz, described by his peers as "one of the world's seminal thinkers about the origin of

---

48   *The Creator and the Cosmos*, Hugh Ross, Ph.D. Navpress, 2001. p. 195

life within the context of the physics of our universe".[49] A specialist in molecular biophysics and biochemistry, Morowitz once ran the numbers on the "shake and go" theory of generating life: that you can throw a whole bunch of amino acids together under the right conditions and, hey presto, you've created Frankenstein's Amoeba.

As Morowitz pointed out, if you broke open the simplest living cell known to exist today, and broke every chemical bond within it so that you were left with its individual ingredients, the odds in favour of that cell putting itself back together again would be only one chance in $10^{100,000,000,000}$. To put that figure in perspective, there haven't even been that many nano-seconds on the clock since the dawn of time nearly 14 billion years ago.

With odds this remote, explains Hugh Ross,[50] "the time scale issue becomes completely irrelevant. What does it matter if the earth has been around for 10 seconds, 10 thousand years or 10 billion years? The size of the universe is of no consequence either. *If all the matter in the visible universe were converted into the building blocks of life, and if assembly of these building blocks was attempted once every microsecond (1 millionth of a second) for the entire age of the universe, then instead of the odds being 1 in $10^{100,000,000,000}$ they would be 1 in $10^{99,999,999,916}$.*" [my emphasis]

Now for the sake of scientific accuracy, that's not an estimation about the spontaneous generation of life randomly, but it is an estimation of whether the known chemical ingredients of a living cell – every ingredient needed – could re-combine from scratch. Clearly the answer is an emphatic no, never, not in a billion universes.

As Morowitz himself wrote in his study, "A number of authors on the origin of life have missed the significance of vanishingly small probabilities. They have assumed [like Richard Dawkins] that the final probability will be reasonably large by virtue of the size and age of the system. The previous paragraph shows that this is not so: calculable values of the probability of spontaneous origin are so low[51] that the final probabilities are still vanishingly small."[52]

Picking up on the theme is the aforementioned Robert Shapiro, an

---

49 http://gazette.gmu.edu/articles/8808/

50 Ibid., p. 204

51 Interestingly, Richard Carrier of the website Infidels.org has tried to suggest that Morowitz was not talking about the origin of life: "This statistic is laughable not only for its outrageous size, but for the mere absurdity of anyone who would bother to calculate it – but what is notable is that it has nothing to do with the origin of life." (http://www.infidels.org/library/modern/richard_carrier/addendaB.html#Morowitz). Having read Carrier's attempts to evade the issue, however, I don't think he has factored in Morowitz's very explicit comments above. Nor does Carrier appear to have understood the science in Morowitz's paper, as he misquotes it.

52 *Energy Flow in Biology*, Harold Morowitz, Ox Bow Press, 1979, p. 12

Emeritus Professor of Chemistry, specialising in DNA, at New York University:

"The answer computed by Morowitz reduces the odds of Hoyle [1 in $10^{40,000}$] to utter insignificance: 1 chance in $10^{100,000,000,000}$.... This number is so large that to write it in conventional form we would require several hundred thousand blank books. We would enter '1' on the first page of the first book, and then fill it, and the remainder of the books, with zeros. ... The Skeptic will want to rewrite Professor Wald's conclusion: Improbability is in fact the villain of the plot. The improbability involved in generating even one bacterium is so large that it reduces all considerations of time and space to nothingness. Given such odds, the time until the black holes evaporate and the space to the ends of the universe would make no difference at all. If we were to wait, we would truly be waiting for a miracle," says Shapiro.[53]

A molecular biophysicist by profession, Morowitz, is pretty clear on what the science tells him:[54]

"Life is too intricate to have random origins. There are laws of physics and chemistry at work that governed the process. We may not yet know all of the hows, but for a scientist, answering these questions is a continuum of discoveries."

On the basis of the evidence in front of scientists at present, the chances of life arising naturally anywhere in the universe, without divine intervention of some kind, are currently statistically classed as "impossible".

There are other factors however, that suggest the universe was designed deliberately for us to discover it, now, at this precise moment in history. These are factors that go beyond the Goldilocks conditions necessary to preserve or nurture life. What I'm talking about is the difference between spending your life in a cave, or being sufficiently inspired to fly to the moon.

In *The Privileged Planet*, Guillermo Gonzalez and his co-author Jay Richards make the striking suggestion that Earth has deliberately been given a birds-eye view of the Cosmos, solely so that humanity can discover the fingerprints of God. We are the only planet we know of with a fully transparent atmosphere. Since the first humans wandered the Earth, we

---

53 *Origins: A Skeptic's Guide to the Creation of Life on Earth*, Robert Shapiro, Summit: New York NY, 1986, pp.125-128. Shapiro argued that protein must be the answer, protein must be capable of generating RNA and both RNA and protein work together to create DNA. Except, this provides no explanation as to how random chemicals could assemble in such a way as to encode intelligent crucial information capable of being read and understood by humans the same way we read an encyclopedia.
54 http://gazette.gmu.edu/articles/8808/ Morowitz describes his own beliefs as 'pantheist' – that God is Nature. He currently theorises that Nature *requires* life to arise in order to soak up excess energy in our biosphere. The process remains frustratingly elusive, however

have had the chance to look at the stars and the sun and wonder. We take it for granted, but in a random universe it could easily have been different. We could have been on a planet with massive cloud cover and never seen the moon or the stars. Think of the impact on our human culture. Would we have built rockets to fly to the moon if we didn't know it even existed? Would we even have flight, if it was too cloudy for planes to land and take off safely?

Excessive cloud cover and reduction in sunlight would reduce agriculture and plant activity, meaning less food for humans and animals and consequently a more peasant-like existence – hardly the kind likely to develop high technology solutions.

The stability of our orbit and clear atmosphere allowed the ancients to tell the time with sundials, mark off the seasons, keep accurate records of historical events, and navigate by the stars – critical for any attempt to cross and explore the oceans successfully.

Most of our major modern scientific discoveries owe their existence to scientists who were able to use unique attributes of the Earth/moon relationship (eclipses, planetary motion, gravitational pull) to test theories against. No other planet in our solar system, and indeed no other planet that we know of in the universe, is such an ideal lab for scientific discovery as Earth is.

The significance of this is quite simple. Earth could just as easily be a barren rock, and all of its great features for scientific experimentation and observation would be wasted. Not only is it the ultimate all-round viewing platform, but it happens to have exactly the people on board who can make the most of it.

Perched on the outer arm of the Milky Way, Earth has a unique window on the universe. Because of our positioning, our telescopes and equipment have been able to discover fundamental secrets of the universe, looking back through time itself to see light left over from the Big Bang 15 billion years ago. Had Earth been positioned closer to the centre of the Milky Way, there would be too much light pollution from other stars for us to see that far into the past. Only here, where we now speed through space, is it possible.

"If you're religious, it's like looking at God," exclaimed Nobel Prize winning astrophysicist and cosmologist George Smoot at the 1992 news conference to announce his team had photographed the background radiation from the Big Bang for the first time.

And here's how the science journal, *Discover*, described the fallout of that news conference and the chaos of the Big Bang that our scientists have only been able to study because of Earth's unique location:

"Some 15 billion years ago, everything in the known universe was crowded into an infinitely dense and hot point that violently exploded. At that time the four forces of nature that govern the universe today – gravity, electromagnetism (which sparks lightning bolts and directs compass needles), and the strong and weak forces which hold atoms intact – were welded together by the unimaginable heat into a single unified force.

"By 10^{-43} second[55] the universe had cooled to 100 million trillion trillion degrees. Gravity became a distinct force, but matter remained an indistinguishable soup of collisions more energetic than anything witnessed in the universe today.

"After a mere 10^{-34} second the temperature had dropped to a billion billion billion degrees – cool enough for the first wisps of matter to coalesce. Quarks (black), the building blocks of protons and neutrons, emerged, as did electrons (pink) and similar indivisible particles. As the first pieces of matter formed, the charged conditions also created their antimatter counterparts. At this point the strong force, which holds protons and neutrons together, split off. Three distinct forces – gravity, the strong force, and the electroweak force – began pulling and pushing at the primordial bits of matter.

"By 10^{-10} second the electromagnetic and weak forces had separated. From that moment on, the four forces began shaping the universe.

"At 10^{-5} second the universe had cooled to a trillion degrees. When quarks crashed into one another now, they stuck together. At the lower temperatures, particles that rammed into the newly formed protons (blue) and neutrons (green) could no longer knock them apart. Antiquarks also came together and formed antiprotons. For every 10 billion particles of antimatter, the universe contained 10 billion and 1 bits of matter. In the still-dense broth of the early universe, flecks of anti-matter and matter collided, annihilating each other in a flash of particles of light called photons (purple). By now the energy level of the universe was too low to build new quarks and antiquarks, so virtually all antimatter was destroyed, leaving only a fraction of the original mass of the universe. The resulting photons ricocheted around, unable to escape the dense environment.

"One *second* after the Big Bang, electrons and their antimatter counterparts, positrons, similarly annihilated each other; because electrons slightly outnumbered positrons, only electrons were left.

"One *minute* after creation, the now relatively sluggish neutrons and protons banged into each other, stuck together, and formed the nuclei of helium, lithium, and heavy forms of hydrogen. After this brief instant in

---

55 The '-' indicates this is a fraction of a second, in this case a one million trillion trillion trillionth of a second after the Bang began, or thereabouts

time, the temperature fell below a billion degrees and the density of the ever-expanding universe was too low for such nuclei-forming collisions to occur again. (Billions of years would pass before stars forged helium into heavier elements such as carbon and oxygen – the building blocks of life.)

"When the universe was 300,000 years old and 3,000 degrees hot, the assembled nuclei captured electrons as they whizzed past and formed the first atoms. As electrons were constrained to orbiting atoms, the photons that the electrons had once interacted with began to streak the universe with light. Because the atoms were unevenly scattered throughout the expanding cosmos, the photons emerged in a rather spotty pattern seen today as slight variations in the microwave background radiation – the afterglow of the decoupling of energy from matter.

"After one billion years or so, the pull of gravity had caused atoms to coalesce into clouds of gas. Galaxies formed as the nascent clouds continued to swirl together, perhaps around bits of very dense but undetectable dark matter. In another billion years the galaxies themselves began to group together into superclusters and gigantic structures – bubbles of space with walls of thousands of galaxies surrounding voids millions of light-years across.

"After 3 billion years the stars began to shine. Earth and our solar system formed 10.4 billion years after the Big Bang. After basking for another 2 billion years in the light of our nearest star, our planet sprouted its first traces of life."[56]

You'll recall how many ancient tribes believe the earth emerged from water, and Genesis talks about the spirit of God hovering above the waters. What science now knows is that those gas clouds that congealed to become our solar system were comprised of hydrogen, helium and a large amount of "water vapour".

Little wonder that Nobel Laureate George Smoot was overcome when asked to describe the significance at the news conference to announce all this.

"If you look at what most cosmologists were saying, about half or two-thirds were in some sense mystical or religious: it's the Holy Grail of cosmology, it's the birth of the universe, the handwriting of God. It's the natural description," he told *Discover* magazine.

In his book, *The God Delusion*, Richard Dawkins tries to suggest that scientists don't really mean 'God' when they mention him: "Einstein was using 'God' in a purely metaphorical, poetic sense. So is Stephen Hawking, and so are most of those physicists who occasionally slip into the language of religious metaphor."

---

56 http://discovermagazine.com/1992/oct/thefingerprintof136

Much as Richard Dawkins would hate it, George Smoot couldn't avoid the overtly Christian analogy.

"There is no doubt that a parallel exists between the big bang as an event and the Christian notion of creation from nothing," says Smoot.

Stephen Hawking was equally impressed, calling it "the most important discovery of the century, if not of all time."

Robert Wilson, one of the pioneers on Big Bang work, told an interviewer, "Certainly there was something that set it all off. Certainly, if you are religious, I can't think of a better theory of the origin of the universe to match with Genesis."[57]

Allan Sandage, an award winning cosmologist who even has an asteroid named after him, says God is definitely part of the scientific equation.

"We can't understand the universe in any clear way without the supernatural."

Henry Schaeffer III, recognized as one of the world's leading computational quantum chemists,[58] says the evidence reinforces his belief in Intelligent Design theory:

"A Creator must exist. The Big Bang ripples (1992) and subsequent scientific findings are clearly pointing to an *ex nihilo* creation consistent with the first few verses of Genesis."[59]

As if to reinforce the claim that our entire universe is geared towards giving humans a bird's-eye view of the majesty of God, here's one other point: Not only are we living in a particular place that makes observation of all this possible, we are living in a particular time that makes it possible. The history of the universe will only be visible in space for a brief period. On current scientific data, the expansion of the universe is mysteriously accelerating, instead of slowing down, throwing many previous assumptions and calculations out the window. If humanity had come into existence a million years from now, there's a very good chance future scientists could never discover what we are currently observing. In other words, we have ringside seats to a one-time-only performance.

Regardless of what Richard Dawkins tries to tell you, a growing number of scientists are getting that gnawing suspicion that the God of Genesis did indeed build the universe and is having a little fun at their expense by gently reminding them who's boss.

And speaking of building, think about this. Roughly 70% of the human body is composed of water, which itself is a molecule combining two

57   http://www.veritas-ucsb.org/library/origins/quotes/universe.html
58   http://en.wikipedia.org/wiki/Henry_F._Schaefer,_III
59   *God's Undertaker: Has Science Buried God?* by John Lennox, Lion, 2007, p29 cited

hydrogen atoms and one oxygen atom. All the hydrogen in your body – all of it – was created in that first minute of the Big Bang. We're not talking 'descendants' of those original hydrogen atoms – we're talking the very same atoms you just read about. You, I and everyone else are built from 15 billion year old bricks forged in the fire of the most unique event in history.

We are, indeed, children of the universe.

CHAPTER 5

HOW WRONG IS HITCH?

"They are wrong, they are reliably, verifiably and factually incorrect. Richard Dawkins is wrong. Daniel C. Dennett is wrong. Christopher Hitchens is drunk, and he's wrong. Michel Onfray is French, and he's wrong. Sam Harris is so superlatively wrong that it will require the development of esoteric mathematics operating simultaneously in multiple dimensions to fully comprehend the orders of magnitude of his wrongness"

Vox Day, *The Irrational Atheist*

THERE ARE MANY THINGS I agree with Christopher Hitchens on – the rise of radical Islam being one. But when this curmudgeonly atheist stepped up to the plate this year to publish *God is Not Great: How Religion Poisons Everything*, I fell all over the place laughing. Not for long, admittedly, because enough people were gullible enough to shell out the $35 and make Hitchens a millionaire on the proceeds…but I still chortle over the content.

The book, like Dawkins' *The God Delusion*, is riddled with false assumptions and dodgy examples. Except with Hitchens his lack of scientific knowledge does him even more harm.

"Investigation of the fossil record and the record of molecular biology shows us that approximately 98% of all the species that have ever appeared on earth have lapsed into extinction," he writes in an unsourced claim on p88 of his book.

Given that there are up to 100 million species on earth currently,[60] presumably they account for the remaining 2% according to Hitchens' math. So that's 50 million species per 1%.

On that basis, Hitchens is asking you to believe that earth has hosted

---

60 http://news.nationalgeographic.com/news/2002/03/0305_0305_allspecies.html

five billion species. Oh really? Alternatively, if he's measuring from the number of *known* [i.e., catalogued] species today (about two million) then the total historic figure becomes 100 million, which is not really that different from the total estimate today. Species come, species go, other species move in to fill gaps in the market.

Hitchens must have conducted a pretty demanding "investigation of the fossil record", given that only 250,000 fossil species have been discovered.[61]

He devotes an entire chapter to "Arguments from Design", but apart from skittering lightly over the surface offers no cutting edge information whatsoever. In fact, the pinnacle of his entire chapter 'demolishing' Intelligent Design is this:

"In early April 2006 a long study at the University of Oregon was published in the journal *Science*. Based on the reconstructions of ancient genes from extinct animals, the researchers were able to show how the non theory of 'irreducible complexity' is a joke."

Again, one sighs, mutters the words, 'Oh really?' and checks in with the godfather of Irreducible Complexity theory, Michael Behe, to see if he's quaking over the *Science* article.

"The study by Bridgham et al (2006) published in the April 7 issue of *Science* is the lamest attempt yet — and perhaps the lamest attempt that's even possible — to deflect the problem that irreducible complexity poses for Darwinism.

"The bottom line of the study is this: the authors started with a protein which already had the ability to strongly interact with three kinds of steroid hormones (aldosterone, cortisol, and "DOC" [11-deoxycorticosterone]). After introducing several simple mutations the protein interacted much more weakly with all of those steroids. In other words, a pre-existing ability was decreased.

"That's it! The fact that this extremely modest and substantially irrelevant study is ballyhooed with press releases, a commentary in *Science* by Christoph Adami, and forthcoming stories in the mainstream media, demonstrates the great anxiety some folks feel about intelligent design."[62]

Behe added that the system *Science* tested wasn't even irreducibly complex in the first place.

"The authors (including Christoph Adami in his commentary) are conveniently defining "irreducible complexity" way, way down. I certainly would not classify their system as IC. The IC systems I discussed in *Darwin's*

61   http://gpc.edu/~pgore/geology/historical_lab/preservationlab.php
62   http://www.idthefuture.com/2006/04/the_lamest_attempt_yet_to_answ.html

Black Box contain multiple, active protein factors. Their "system", on the other hand, consists of just a single protein and its ligand. Although in nature the receptor and ligand are part of a larger system that does have a biological function, the piece of that larger system they pick out does not do anything by itself. In other words, the isolated components they work on are not irreducibly complex."

I was reminded of just how misleading much of the evolutionary hype actually is, when a news release hit my in-tray from the Botanic Gardens in Sydney, Australia:

"An example of the genius of Charles Darwin's theory on evolution is currently in flower in the guise of an orchid, the Star of Bethlehem, at Sydney's Royal Botanic Gardens.

"Botanic Gardens Trust Executive Director, Dr Tim Entwisle said Darwin predicted 41 years before its discovery that a pollinator had to exist to ensure the survival of the orchid.

"The Star of Bethlehem was discovered in Madagascar in the 1860s. It's unique because it stores nectar at the bottom of a tube up to 30 centimetres (12 inches) long," Dr Entwisle said.

"Darwin saw the extraordinary flower with its very thin and long tube and believed an animal had to have evolved to enable it to reach the nectar and ensure the plant's survival.

"In 1903, 21 years after Darwin's death, the mysterious pollinator was found – supporting Darwin's theory of evolution. The pollinator was a hawk moth with a proboscis long enough to reach the bottom of the orchid's nectar tube or 'spur'. It was named Xanthopan morganii praedicta – to honor Darwin's prediction.

"It's clear the moth and orchid evolved together, starting with an orchid with a small tube and a moth with a small tongue and over time they both grew longer and longer," he said. "It's all about competition for food and pollination."

That's how evolutionists see it, and tell it. Quite confidently, as you can see. Now let's deconstruct it. They would have you believe that a plant somehow knew how to co-evolve with an equally mindless moth, until both became incredibly specialised. There are many such examples in nature, incidentally.

Because these "teams" are specialised, evolutionists are convinced that they must have "evolved" that way. The other way of looking at it, however, is that the organisms were created that way.

If evolutionists could point to fossil orchids in the smaller transitional states, and equally provide fossilised examples of smaller moths with those fossil orchids, then we would have hard scientific evidence. But of course, we don't have that. We have only a guess, and frankly it could just as easily be an example of Intelligent Design.

I don't have an intrinsic problem, by the way with the kind of microevolution illustrated above, in the sense that there is plenty of evidence that organisms adapt to local environmental pressures. This is change *within* a species, though, not a change that magically creates a new species. I retain my skepticism however at the claim two non-sentient organisms instinctively "evolve" together. I really think that is pushing probability theory way too far. It could take millions of generations of moths for one to be born with a longer snout capable of reaching deep inside the orchid – how does the orchid stay alive, unfertilised, until such a serendipitous event? It seems to me the orchid is on a negative natural selection path if it becomes too deep for insects to pollinate – hardly a trait likely to secure the birth of more baby orchids.

This is not a book about the Intelligent Design debate. I laid that information out in *Eve's Bite* earlier this year. But it does go to show the desperation of atheism's rock stars – people like Hitchens and Dawkins – as they clutch straws in a bid to persuade the public that evolution is still credible.

A poll in New Zealand's biggest newspaper, the *NZ Herald*, suggests otherwise.[63] Only 30% of New Zealanders believe in thoroughly naturalistic evolution, and that was *before* Intelligent Design hit the news. People don't believe evolution in a monkey-to-man sense because instinctively they can see the huge gaps in the scientific evidence. The scientific argument directed at the public these days by evolutionists reminds me of those old-time pantomimes where the character sticks his head in a box, or a bucket, or whatever, and yells out to the audience, "You can't see me!". Yes, we can all see Darwin's choirboys like Hitchens and Dawkins desperately hamming it up for public consumption.

Few ordinary members of the public seriously believe in the macro-evolution myth anymore. Yes, we all believe in micro-evolution (change within a species) that gives us racial differences, strange-looking dogs or antibiotic resistance within bacteria, but few intelligent people still believe in weasels becoming cats, whales becoming cows or T-Rex evolving into a turkey. The evidence for species-hop is virtually non existent.

The problem really seems to be that biologists and atheists absolutely love the word, "evolution", but they can't even explain it themselves, and

---

63 http://www.nzherald.co.nz/section/1/story.cfm?c_id=1&objectid=3371

spend most of their high-brow conferences fighting behind closed doors over how evolution "might work".

Even Hitchens begrudgingly concedes the point.

"There are many disputes between evolutionists as to *how* [his emphasis] the complex process occurred, and indeed as to how it began."

Yes. They seize on the word "evolution" because they need the word to mean something important, but they don't actually have a blind clue about any of the detail of this alleged natural process, despite 150 years of study. Any time a critic comes close they shriek "evolution" with one voice, to illustrate 'unity', then go back behind closed doors to beat each other up over the lack of evidence.

"We do not hold our convictions dogmatically," suggests Christopher Hitchens in what must be the ultimate piece of self-deprecating mickey-taking by an atheist fundamentalist I've ever seen in print. "The disagreement between Professor Steven Jay Gould and Professor Richard Dawkins, concerning 'punctuated evolution' and the unfilled gaps in post-Darwinian theory, is quite wide as well as quite deep, but we shall resolve it by evidence and reasoning and not by mutual excommunication."

Oh really? That would be why it is OK for evolutionists to rubbish each other, but Intelligent Design scientists are not permitted to write articles for scientific journals proving their case, lest science be 'corrupted'. If you dare to laugh at the evolutionary Emperor wearing no clothes, you are indeed "excommunicated". Only as long as you pay homage to the word 'evolution' can you stay in the tent. In fact, as the new movie "Expelled" makes clear,[64] a number of top scientists who dared to support further investigation into Intelligent Design have suddenly found themselves without jobs. Excommunicado and ex-employed.[65]

Before leaving this section, it is worth examining what another of atheism's "rock stars", Richard Carrier at Infidels.org, has to say about the cosmological scientific evidence for God. Carrier, a historian studying for his Ph.D. and currently working as a librarian's assistant, is a strident opponent of any claims that God had a hand in anything. Naturally, this fine-tuning issue is like swallowing a sea-urchin intact for Carrier, and he argues strongly that we shouldn't leap to conclusions.[66]

"While the creationist thinks God explains the "fine tuning" of the universe, he fails to see that every possible universe which can contain intelligent life will appear "fine tuned" no matter what its cause."

---

64 http://www.expelledthemovie.com
65 http://www.worldnetdaily.com/news/article.asp?ARTICLE_ID=57974
66 http://www.infidels.org/library/modern/richard_carrier/ten.html

I don't know that I accept his reasoning. Look at it another way. The reason science is increasingly getting excited about the "fine tuning" is because we appear to be alone. A universe teeming with life on every planet would not raise suspicions about fine tuning; if life arose here, there and everywhere then there would appear to be nothing particularly special about the residents of Planet Earth.

Carrier's argument is only valid if the "every possible universe" he talks of turns out to have just one planet with life on it. In that case, I agree, the residents of every universe would have reason to feel suspicious and 'fine-tuned'. But employing the multiple universe theory is the scientific equivalent of reaching for an old alchemy textbook, or perhaps *Hogwart's Invisible Book of Invisibility*. We can't see any other universes. We can't reach any other universes because, by definition, the laws that govern this universe prevent that. Nor is there a shred of evidence that any other universe can, or does exist. And even if it does, as cosmologist Paul Davies notes, it only pushes the first cause problem back from "who created *the* universe?" to "who created *all* these universes?"

Carrier, funnily enough, doesn't want to admit that he has a problem here.

"We already have evidence that universes exist (we live in one), and so we already have some grounds for positing multiple universes to explain the parameters of ours, e.g. there may be a million universes with different parameters and only one has life (and thus we are in it, since that is the only place we could be). This is no more ad hoc than positing God, and is arguably less so, since there is less reason to invoke an unknown type of entity (a god) than a known one (a universe)."

Again, sounds plausible. For a nano-second.

We know "universe*s* exist", he says, because "we live in *one*" [my emphasis, really it should be "we know *a* universe exists because we live in *it*", because there is not the slightest piece of scientific evidence that *universes* exist, or are even capable of existing] therefore it is reasonable to assume millions of universes exist. On that logic, my clone could be God. After all, I exist so there could be billions of me and, using Dawkins' dodgy math, one of the other Ian Wisharts is actually quite likely to be God. Or maybe I'm a "universe" in one of my other lives. Do I hear faint yelps of "Flying Spaghetti Monsterism"[67] in the darkness? There is a point

---

67 A favourite atheist argument is to claim the universe could equally have been created by a "flying spaghetti monster", which is really an appeal to the absurd to make the idea of a divine Creator sound equally daft. Appealing to invisible, undetectable other universes, however, is equally a question of belief, not science. Anyone who appeals to multiverse theory is explicitly admitting the need for a Creator to explain the Big Bang. It is, in essence, an appeal to "Science of the Gaps"

when atheists, too, must face the reality that their own religious beliefs transcend scientific evidence and begin to make a mockery of true science. That's fine, if Richard wants to call his god "Multiverse Theory", that's his business. But let's not pretend it is "science" in any accepted definition of the term.

Carrier instinctively knows that the cosmological evidence for the fingerprints of God is getting stronger by the day. He can feel it. That's why his essays are peppered with escape clauses:

"Maybe one day we will end up with God at the end of our investigations, but right now there is little encouraging news…"

"…In his 1999 debate with Phil Fernandes, Jeff Lowder made an equally crucial point: if the actual parameters of the universe *do* require an explanation, God is not necessarily the most probable option, since to give such an option greater weight than others which do not include a god we must have additional evidence that something like a creator-god actually exists."

So let me get this straight: if a farmer, living on a small island known to be inhabited only by sheep and rabbits, were to come out of his house each morning for a week, and find all of his sheep slaughtered and giant animal tracks nearby, along with half-metre high piles of dung, the farmer would be wrong in assuming that something very, very big was attacking his sheep? Because, using Carrier and Lowder's logic, it would be wrong to postulate the existence of something not conclusively proven to exist. Instead, the farmer should assume the culprits are rabbits.

The truth is, as Socrates once said, science should "follow the evidence where it leads". Darwinists often accuse Christians and other religious believers of "appealing to a God of the gaps" – meaning that when something can't be explained it is weak to immediately postulate God as the reason, when there may be perfectly good natural reasons.

This is true, but in turn there is a big difference between that, and the new situation where scientists are not finding "gaps", but instead seeing clear evidence of what appears to be design in the universe. I can't stress this point enough: using God as an explanation for disease, in the days before science knew about bacteria, was using God to fill a gap. But finding something closely resembling a Mazda rotary engine inside a bacterial flagella cell, or discovering massive evidence of fine-tuning of both the universe and the earth/moon system (on separate unique occasions), is *positive* evidence of God, not merely a negative inference from a gap. It demands explanation, in and of itself.

Take the experience of geneticist Francis Collins, "the man who cracked the human genome", as the *Times of London* put it. Like many others,

Collins was stunned to find enough intelligent code in one human cell to fill more than an entire set of *Encyclopedia Britannica*. All this time, the late Carl Sagan's SETI project has been scouring space for signs of a simple Morse code, while genetic engineers have been decoding what Collins regards as a direct message from the Creator of the universe and life itself:[68]

"When you have for the first time in front of you this 3.1 billion-letter instruction book[69] that conveys all kinds of information and all kinds of mystery about humankind, you can't survey that going through page after page without a sense of awe. I can't help but look at those pages and have a vague sense that this is giving me a glimpse of God's mind."

Richard Carrier and other atheists would have us ignore the positive evidence, and instead reach for any other possible theory, including that the universe itself "wished" these things into existence. At the end of the day, the best argument Carrier can muster on the Infidels website comes down to either that, or a variation on deism – a deceased god:

"In fact, it gets worse when we consider the possibility that the creator no longer exists – imagine a lonely god who has a choice, to live alone, or to die, and in dying create a universe from his exploding "corpse" which will have populations of people who can then live the god's lost dream of knowing love and never being alone. Perhaps the god stays alive, so he can share in this love, but is powerless, having given up his body for the creation of a universe.

"This is plausible, coherent, logical, and actually better explains things – it perfectly explains how god can be good and yet silent and inactive, how the universe can function so cold and mechanically and deterministically, how humans can be so confused, divided, and uncertain about god's nature or thoughts, etc. Indeed, this theory explains *everything*, [Carrier's

---

68   http://www.timesonline.co.uk/tol/news/uk/article673663.ece
69   Permit me, while I'm at it, to deal with a frequent misconception about the commonality of DNA across the life spectrum. As Collins points out in his book, *The Language of God*, there are vast swatches of genome where the DNA structure across a number of animals, including humans, is pretty much identical. To Collins and many biologists, this is proof that life descended from a common ancestor. I don't find their arguments persuasive. When your child plays with Lego, they do not usually totally disassemble a toy before building another. Thus, what was part of a plane becomes part of a truck in the reassembly, but the original blocks the child used are still locked in sequence. DNA is the "building block" of life. Given that God knows the code, it seems fairly logical that if he knows the sequence, "gtttcacatggca" results in creatures with two legs, then you would expect that code to run in the appropriate places for those creatures, albeit with minor alterations peculiar to the organism. Do you see my point? A common DNA structure, rather than indicating a common ancestor, may simply mean that God simply plugged in that DNA structure to different creatures as required. An analogy is found in the IT industry: most of the world's computers run on the same software and hardware systems, but that doesn't mean all the computers descended from each other. Human designers simply ran the same code across a number of machines

emphasis] far better than any actual creationist theory proposed today.
"By all sense and reason, this theory should be adopted by creationists –
yet they adhere to a weaker theory, oblivious to the self-refuting character
of declarations like that of Mr. Walker when he writes "when I look at the
wondrous universe that surrounds me, I have no problem in accepting a
being that I can't fully explain" and yet fails to see how the atheist, with
just as much right if not more, can and does say exactly the same thing
– but the "being" the atheist sees and can't fully explain is the universe
itself. How much simpler this is – it requires adding nothing to what we
see or know. Instead, creationists refuse to accept "a being that they can't
fully explain" (the universe) and because of their refusal are compelled to
invent a god to provide the explanation that they insist is necessary. They
don't notice that they then do a complete about-face, and act in an exact
opposite manner when it comes time to explain their god. Inconsistency
is the creationist's hobgoblin."

Not really; it appears to be an equal-opportunities hobgoblin. We've
now discovered that the intellectual grunt behind one of the world's
main atheist websites lurks in boltholes named "deism" and "pantheism",
because even *he* can see the writing on the wall. He just doesn't want that
writing to be in Hebrew.

Perhaps the final proof needed for this chapter however comes from
Richard Dawkins himself. It turns out he *does* believe in God, he just
hasn't come out of the closet yet. Here's the clue, in his words:

"There is no limit to the explanatory purposes to which God's infinite
power is put. Is science having a little difficulty explaining X? No problem.
Don't give X another glance. God's infinite power is effortlessly wheeled
in to explain X (along with everything else), and it is always a supremely
simple explanation." [his emphasis].

Now look at Dawkins as he invokes exactly the same simplicity to get
himself out of a tight spot on the Big Bang:[70]

"It is tempting to think (and many have succumbed) that to postulate a
plethora of universes[71] is a profligate luxury which should not be allowed.

---

70   *The God Delusion*, Richard Dawkins, Bantam, 2006, p. 146
71   The multiverse theory took an even more Daffy Duck turn in late September, when its
proponents at Oxford University (where Dawkins works, incidentally) suggested that perhaps
every time there is a physical change anywhere in this universe, it creates a parallel universe.
Thus, if you have a car crash and die, somewhere in another universe you pranged your car and
lived, while in a third universe you didn't prang at all. I kid you not. Apparently, everything you
touched today created a new universe somewhere, as did everything everyone else touched
and every tree leaf blown by the wind. "Given a number of possible alternative outcomes,
each one is played out — in its own universe," reported the study, http://www.breitbart.com/
article.php?id=paUniverse_sun14_parallel_universes&show_article=1&cat=0 Do you have
any idea how many quadzillion universes are created every single day, just because we touch

If we are going to permit the extravagance of a multiverse, so the argument runs, we might as well be hung for a sheep as a lamb and allow a God.

"Aren't they both equally unparsimonious ad hoc hypotheses, and equally unsatisfactory? People who think that have not had their consciousness raised by natural selection. The key difference between the genuinely extravagant God hypothesis and the apparently extravagant multiverse hypothesis is one of statistically improbability. *The multiverse, for all that it is extravagant, is simple.*" [my emphasis]

Hey presto! Scientific atheist has big problem explaining away X (Big Bang), wheels in natural selection's alleged infinite power (multiple universes exist, and we just *happen* to live in the one with life), and best of all, the explanation is supremely *simple*.

Dawkins believes in God. He can't escape the scientific evidence for Creation staring him in the face. So he too, like Richard Carrier,[72] has named his deity "Multiverse".

Now that even the world's most vocal atheist fundamentalist has been sprung endorsing a God argument and/or a "Sky Fairy" named "Multiverse", I think it is safe to declare that "a" God exists. The question now turns to this: which God that might be...?

things? Of course, there's no proof. The scary thing is these guys are on public salaries. Which is more likely, that one God created the heavens and the earth, or that by turning the 320 pages of this book you personally created 320 new universes? 321, if you count the possible universe where a rampaging T-Rex survived the extinction, burst into your bedroom and ate you while you were reading this book. According to Oxford University, that universe *must* exist somewhere. Halfwits.

72 Carrier suffered huge disappointment at the end of 2004 when Professor Antony Flew, a man he had described as "one of the most renowned atheists of the 20th Century, even making the shortlist of "Contemporary Atheists" at About.com", publicly revealed he no longer believed atheism was a rational belief. Flew, having studied the arguments in favour of Intelligent Design, and the arguments of Richard Dawkins and others, is now convinced that science has no natural explanation for the origin of the first lifeform, nor can science explain how the first random lifeform managed to acquire reproductive ability before dying. On that basis, Flew now calls himself a "theist", saying a God must have intervened, although he does not believe in the Christian God as such because he does not believe the Creator God interacted with humanity

CHAPTER 6

THE PROBABILITY OF GOD

"God, though not technically disprovable, is very very improbable indeed"
Richard Dawkins, *The God Delusion*

I F YOU HAVE READ THIS book right through to this point, you'll have found the evidence tells a pretty compelling story. You have seen how belief in one Creator God is deeply embedded into the ancient race memories of virtually every human culture on the planet. So deeply embedded, in fact, that some scientists actually think humans are "hard wired" to believe in God.

You have seen that you owe your life today to a huge string of unprecedented coincidences that took place. You have discovered the incredible fine-tuning of the Big Bang, a never-repeated explosion of such intensity that it brought into operation the dimension of Time and created scientific laws that the world's best scientific brains believe have been "monkeyed with" to allow human life to exist. You have seen that after beating the odds with the Big Bang, planet Earth then had to be hit with a Mars-sized planet in a cosmic car crash in order for life to exist. You have seen that the car-crash had to create a moon the size of ours, or life would not exist. And you have seen that because of our unique positioning in space, we have been able to make major scientific and technical discoveries that make life more comfortable for all of us, some of which have led scientists to declare they are seeing "the fingerprints of God".

But who, exactly, is this 'God'?

Richard Dawkins, for all his many faults, unwittingly points out a fundamental truth when he says that scientists invoking 'God' do not necessarily mean the God of the Christian Bible. As we saw earlier many of them do, but Dawkins is correct that many do not. He sets out a series of thumbnail 'definitions' of the various 'gods' that people may be invoking.

"Let's remind ourselves of the terminology. A *theist* believes in a supernatural intelligence who, in addition to his main work of creating the universe in the first place, is still around the oversee and influence the subsequent fate of his initial creation. In many theistic belief systems, the deity is intimately involved in human affairs. He answers prayers; forgives or punishes sins; intervenes in the world by performing miracles."

A theist, then, is one who believes in one supreme God. Christians, Jews and Muslims are all theists.

"A *deist*, too, believes in supernatural intelligence," writes Dawkins, "but one whose activities were confined to setting up the laws that govern the universe in the first place. The deist God never intervenes thereafter, and certainly has no specific interest in human affairs."

A deist, then, is someone who still believes in a Creator God, but this god did not create life, does not answer prayer, does not judge personal behaviour or morality, does not intervene in the world in any way, and basically watches dispassionately from afar, not caring one way or the other. Some of the founding fathers of the US, like Thomas Jefferson, were deists, not Christians. Scientists are more willing to accept a deist god than the Christian one, primarily because a deist god can still be first cause of the universe, but allows evolution and random natural forces to do what they will. In short, a deist god allows science to give meaning to human life, rather than religion, and a deist god allows humans to effectively become gods themselves – anything is permissible, subject only to the limits of science or the will of society. Miracles beyond the creation event itself are impossible, they argue, because a deist god has too much respect for the immutable laws of nature and science. Stephen Hawking, together with his academic partner Thomas Hertog, begrudgingly suggested in a 2002 scientific paper that a deist god may indeed have rolled the dice to kick start the universe off.[73]

As Dawkins admits, deism is the kind of god you have when you don't actually want a god, but need one for appearances.

But there are a couple of other concepts of God that are relevant to the search for the divinity code. According to philosopher Norman Geisler, there are seven basic 'worldviews' or beliefs about the meaning of life, that exist in all of humanity. Whilst there are sub-groups from these, they all trace back to one of the Big-7. They include, theism, deism, atheism, pantheism, panentheism, polytheism, and another you've probably never heard of, finite godism. Big words, but easily explained.

---

73 http://www.worldnetdaily.com/news/article.asp?ARTICLE_ID=27721

The first three we pretty much already understand. *Atheism*, contrary to what some try to argue, is a definite belief that there is no God of any kind. Some self-proclaimed 'atheists' try to suggest that atheism is merely *a lack of belief* in God based on a lack of evidence (rather than a positive affirmation on their part that God does *not* exist). These people are not really atheists in the educated, academic sense, but "hard agnostics" – which is one of those sub-groups I mentioned.

Pantheists ["Everything is God"] are your traditional Hindu/Eastern mystic/New Age believers. Many modern Buddhists have adopted it, as have Scientologists, the Unity movement and the religion known as Christian Science. They believe that 'God' is a part of everything, that God didn't make the universe as such – he *is* the universe and everything in it. For this reason, much Eastern and New Age teaching focuses on telling followers to "get in touch with the god within you", in the belief that in our weakness as humans we have simply forgotten that we are also divine, and need to rekindle that memory and link in order to transcend to the next stage.

Die-hard pantheists go so far as to insist that the universe and everything in it is merely an elaborate illusion, and that until we accept and act as if reality is an illusion we cannot get in touch with the divine.

By definition, in true pantheism, miracles are impossible, because there is no reality to miraculously intervene in. Conversely, if everything – good or bad – is God, what motivation would God have to miraculously intervene against himself?

The only sense of intervention is the law of karma, where the universe (God) eventually corrects you if you create negative ripples. Karma is God's way of restoring equilibrium. Reincarnation is fundamental to the pantheistic belief system, because it allows followers to come back and try again if they get it wrong the first time.

Panentheism ["Everything is the body of God and heaven is his mind"] is a variation on the above. These people still believe that God is part of every rock, fish, tree, human, star etc, but they also believe God is bigger than the universe, and has a transcendent, bipolar dimension. Norman Geisler describes it in these terms:

"Rather than viewing God as the infinite, unchanging sovereign Creator of the world who brought it into existence, panentheists think of God as a finite, changing, director of world affairs who works in cooperation with the world in order to achieve greater perfection in his nature.

"Theism views God's relation to the world as a painter to a painting. The painter exists independently of the painting; he brought the painting into existence, and yet his mind is expressed in the painting.

"By contrast, the panentheist views God's relation to the world the way a mind is related to a body. Indeed, they believe the world is God's 'body' (one pole) and the 'mind' is the other pole."

The physical aspect of God, they argue, is constantly changing as the world and its inhabitants change. God's mind, on the other hand, is regarded as unchanging.

Plato's dualism advocated an earlier form of panentheism.

Polytheism is a belief in many different gods. The Romans and Greeks, for example, were polytheists. Most native tribes are polytheistic (although many like the Maori still had myths of a supreme original creator).

Finite Godism. What a name. It means, however, belief in a God who has limited power in some way. By definition, the gods in polytheism are finite – they did not have the individual power to create the universe; one might be the god of storms, another the god of the sun and so on. In modern terms, some people who struggle with the apparent inaction of the Christian God in the face of evil choose to believe that perhaps God may be all good, but he is not all powerful, that God is limited in what he can do in the face of human rebellion and natural forces.

Most believers in this worldview believe that God did not create the world out of nothing, but merely shaped existing material into a new universe. This is an example of his limits – that God was incapable of a pure creation event. Because he didn't have full power over the universe, his ability to intervene in it remains limited. The belief really hinges on God vs Evil, however. The argument, as Geisler phrases it, goes like this:

1. If God were all powerful, he could destroy evil.
2. If God were all good, he would destroy evil.
3. But evil has not been destroyed.
4. Therefore, there cannot be an all-powerful, all-good God.

There are answers to these challenging claims, but they'll be dealt with later in this book in the chapter on Evil. The lessons of science can probably allow us to dispel a couple of the other candidates straight away. Up until the discovery of the Big Bang in the 1960s, the prevailing scientific view of origins was that we lived in "a steady state universe" – one that had always existed and always would. In this sense, scientific discovery was undermining the Christian version of creation. Together with the Theory of Evolution, the Steady State Theory was a strong tool for science to rubbish Christian beliefs during the early 20th century.

By proposing the steady state model, scientists were in fact lending a lot of credibility to the pantheistic religions like Hinduism, Buddhism and the like. That's because both rely on either an infinite universe or an infinite succession of universes (reincarnations of the universe) as the basis for their beliefs. If God *is* the universe, then he cannot have been created from nothing. He must always have existed and the universe must always have existed.

At a scientific level, however, the Big Bang has destroyed that option. We now know there was a singular creation event – the universe had a beginning, it is not infinite. Further studies suggest the universe will have an ending as well. It is not infinite.[74]

Where does this leave the Eastern religions? Well, they may have workable moral codes, but they cannot be objectively true. Because the very concept of God in pantheism and panentheism is tied so tightly to the universe being part of God, the spiritual foundations for Hinduism, Buddhism and the New Age movement crumble under scientific attack. Whatever the alleged errors may be in the Christian Bible, they are nowhere near the scale of the problem now facing followers of Eastern traditions.

By nailing their god so firmly to the mast of the natural world, they have made their concept of God much more vulnerable to being contradicted by scientific discoveries. Of course, there is a get-out-of-jail-free card that pantheists can use, and that is a retreat to the belief that the universe is all just an illusion anyway. Such a statement would only be true, however, if their concept of God was correct, so it becomes a vicious circle.

As potential candidates left standing as we pursue the divinity code, then, we are left with Theism, Deism, Polytheism (including Wicca) and Finite Godism (Atheism and its cousin Agnosticism are being continually tested all the way through this book).

Logically, Deism remains a perfectly valid explanation for the first cause of the universe. It is entirely possible that a deist god kicked the event off and then left us to it. But this doesn't answer the bigger question, Why?

If God went to the trouble of creating the universe and specifically engineering it so that life on a specific location, Earth, was sustained, is

---

74 It was common scientific belief, up until the 1960s, that the Universe had somehow always existed. But the Second Law of Thermodynamics is the major problem for this scientific belief: if the Universe has existed forever, then chaos should have been reached, as the 2nd Law says available energy will eventually be used up. Expressed alternately, things left to themselves fall to disorder, and anything infinitely old would have flatlined long ago. The evidence for the Big Bang knocked the infinite universe, or "Steady State" theory, out of the sky. A variation on this is the so-called "rebounding universe – the idea of a Big Bang followed by a Big Crunch and then a new Big Bang. But the Second Law is still a problem. As Stephen Hawking put it, a yo-yo will eventually come to a stop, therefore a rebounding universe still had to have had a first cause

it logical to really believe that the same God would just walk off into the distance without any further curiosity over the outcome? Critics of the deist worldview, like Norman Geisler, argue that belief in deism has more to do with human pride and the desire to put God on a leash, than any serious analysis of God himself.

"A being who could bring the universe into existence from nothing could certainly perform lesser miracles if he chose to do so," points out Geisler.

"A God who created water could part it, or make it possible for a person to walk on it. The immediate multiplication of loaves of bread and fish would be no problem to a God who created matter and life in the first place.

"A virgin birth or even a physical resurrection from the dead would be minor miracles in comparison to the miracle of creating the universe from nothing. It seems self-defeating to admit a great miracle like creation and then to deny the possibility of lesser miracles."

As Richard Dawkins puts it, "Deism is watered-down theism".

Finite godism, the belief that God is not all-powerful, is tempting but still struggles in the face of the latest scientific evidence. The creation event that kicked off the Big Bang with pinpoint accuracy is a mind-boggling show of strength, and hardly the act of an entity with limited powers. Probably the only reason to give finite godism the time of day is because of the questions it raises about God's ability to deal with evil, which we'll deal with later in this book. For now, then, finite godism is wounded, but not fatally. Like deism, it remains in the hunt, just.

Polytheism, which includes the resurgence in neopaganism, the Goddess movement and Wicca (although these can also be pantheistic), and also the many millions of lesser spirit beings worshipped by ordinary Hindus, is making its presence felt again in the West, but suffers heavily from the science as well.

The scientific explanation of the creation event more closely matches the events in Genesis than any other religious book or belief. Therefore, if competing religions are going to stake a claim to being the ultimate source of the divinity code, they'll need to make a compelling case on their theology, rather than their claims to factually explain the universe.

Critics, particularly non-churchgoers, are often heard saying that "all religions are equal", that each religion is basically saying the same thing and which one you pick depends on your mood, or "whatever works for you".

Is this true? We're about to find out.

CHAPTER 7

ARE ALL RELIGIONS EQUAL?

"Truth, in matters of religion, is simply the opinion that has survived"
Oscar Wilde

IT IS OFTEN SAID THAT all paths lead to God. Indeed, it is the ethos behind much of what drives modern society, the belief that all religions are basically the same, so it doesn't matter which one you believe or whether in fact you believe any at all. At best, 'religion' is said to be a private matter. At worst, 'religion kills', as atheist fundamentalist Christopher Hitchens puts it.

With such a throwaway approach, it is easy to see why religious discussion has been marginalized in wider society. Unlike American talk show hosts, radio talk hosts in New Zealand and Australia, largely godless themselves, simply don't understand 'religion' in any of its nuances and struggle with debate on the matter from their callers. It is very hard to offer intelligent comment on a subject you are ignorant about. Rather than rectify their ignorance, many public domain commentators wallow in it, wearing it like a badge of pride, erroneously assuming that their audience is as ignorant as they are. They are not, of course. One *New Zealand Herald* poll[75] found two thirds of the population believe in the Christian God, even if the majority darken a church doorway only once in a blue moon.

The only people who usually respond to a radio talkhost's aggressive ignorance on religion are other – even more fundamentally mentally-challenged individuals. You can generally hear it in their voices, they'll start quoting passages from Dan Brown's *The Da Vinci Code* as if they're true, and while caller and host pat each other on the back for being so clever, the rest of the audience are falling all over the floor in guffaws of laughter.

---

75 http://www.nzherald.co.nz/section/1/story.cfm?c_id=1&objectid=3371

So having established that many talk hosts don't have the foggiest about such issues, let's clear up some of the misconceptions that exist about the world's various religions, outside Christianity.

Sometimes, you have to rise above the forest in order to see its majesty, and appreciate it for what it is. I remember, during my career as a TV news journalist, choppering up north one day to cover the search for a missing hunter, deep inside New Zealand's giant and primitive Waipoua Forest. It is here that some of the most massive trees on earth reside, the ancient kauri. Down underneath the forest canopy, moving amid these monsters, your perspective of the bush is very up-close-and-personal. You see the wood, yes, but the trees are actually so large it's pretty hard to discern one from another.

Rising out of a clearing in a twin-engined Squirrel in the late afternoon sun, however, gave me a whole new take on Waipoua. Suddenly, I could see the primeval vegetation rolling away beneath me as far as the eye could see, whilst every 100 metres or so the crest of a massive kauri broke through this tempest of green, its branches clawing upwards as if scouring the very heavens. Pools of water, glistening in the dying rays of the day, as well as flaxes and tree ferns, gathered in the cavernous crowns of these 1,500 year old creatures, like airborne ponds, nearly 60 metres above ground. It was magic, and as the pilot gunned it for faraway Auckland city, I simply reveled in the vista.

They say familiarity breeds contempt, and to suggest residents of the West have become contemptuous of the religion at the centre of our civilization would be an understatement. In many parishes of the traditional churches, the mice outnumber the parishioners, while eastern religions and New Age beliefs are enjoying rapid growth. The irony of all this is that the reverse is happening in the East: there, Hindus, Buddhists and Confucians are converting in record numbers to Christianity.

Indian theologian Ravi Zacharias straddles two very different worlds. Descended from a family of Brahmin caste Hindu priests, Zacharias had a troubled childhood, failing to live up to family expectations, and attempted suicide as a teenager. The trigger to his downward spiral was ultimately spiritual:

"I was cycling past a cremation site and stopped to ask the Hindu priest where that person, whose body was nothing more than a pile of ashes, was now.

" 'Young man,' he said, 'that is a question you will be asking all your life, and you will never find a certain answer.'

"*If that is the best a priest can do*, I thought, *what hope is there for a novice like me?*

"As the months went by, without the further explanation that I needed, the continued loss of meaning led me to a tragic moment. Had I read the atheistic philosopher Jean Paul Sartre at that stage of my life, he would have confirmed every sense of isolation that I felt. Two of his bestselling books, *Nausea* and *No Exit*, exactly described my state. Sartre went so far as to say that the only question he could not answer was why he did not commit suicide. Is it not amazing that when life seems meaningless, the poets and artists are unafraid to plead guilty while the rationalists denounce that posture and wax eloquent with little reason?

"My decision was firm but calm. A quiet exit would save my family and me any further failure. I put my plan into action. As a result I found myself on a hospital bed, having been rushed there in the throes of an attempted suicide.

"In that hospital room, a Bible was brought to me, and in the desolation of my condition, a passage of Scripture was read to me...I was being read the fourteenth chapter of John about God's purpose.

"The words in that chapter were spoken to the apostle Thomas, who [had traveled to and been murdered in] India. His memorial exists to this day, just a few miles away from where I was born. Remember that Jesus had said to him, 'I am the way, the truth and the life. No man comes to the Father except through Me.'

"But my attention was captured by a few words farther along, when Jesus said to his disciples, 'Because I live, you shall live also'. Again, I was not sure of all that it meant. I knew it meant more than just biological life.

"On that hospital bed I made my commitment to give my life and my pursuits into his hands. The struggles of my relationships, my origin and my destiny were all addressed in that conversation Jesus had with his disciples 2000 years ago."

Thirty years after that event, Zacharias and his wife were back in India and happened to be in the area where his grandmother had lived and died, when he was a child. They made a detour to the local cemetery and, after much assistance from the registrar, finally located her grave.

"With the help of a gardener, we walked through the accumulated weeds and dirt and rubble in the cemetery until we found the large slab of stone marking her grave, No one had visited her grave for thirty years.

"With his little bucket of water and a small brush, the gardener cleared off the caked-on dirt and, to our utter surprise, under her name, a verse gradually appeared. My wife clasped my hand and said, 'Look at the verse!'

"It read, 'Because I live, you shall live also'."

Zacharias has made it his life's work to study and spell out the major differences between the Eastern religions of his homeland, and the Middle Eastern religion embraced by the West. There are, he argues, major misconceptions that nobody wants to talk about for fear of offending someone, misconceptions that make it impossible for all religions to be equal.

To understand his comment, consider for a moment the statement from the Hindu American Foundation:

"A true Hindu knows that his own path, whether it is that of bhakti, karma, gyana, or raja-yoga, is but one of many and has equal respect for all the winding paths that lead to the same Truth called by different names. The true Hindu recognizes that individual souls are like raindrops falling along their own unique path to the same ocean. The true Hindu does not need to judge the path taken by others as being good or bad, right or wrong, because he knows that the destination is the same, that all paths lead to the same goal."[76]

If one God created all religion, and all religions are a valid path to God as Hindus believe, how do we explain the different moral values in each faith?

As it turns out, the biggest single difference in this area between the Western (Christianity, Judaism and Islam) and Eastern (Buddhism, Hinduism, Confucianism) faiths is the issue of objective truth. The Easterner believes each person finds "their own truth", while the religious Westerner believes God has revealed a code of right and wrong, regardless of our own personal views. In other words, murder is wrong no matter what culture you come from. How would a Hindu approach the human sacrifices of the Aztecs, where children were strapped to a slab and had their beating hearts carved out of them? Were the Aztecs, as Hinduism argues, following the same path to enlightenment as Hindus? Is there nothing "bad" about child sacrifice?

As if to answer the question, *The Hindu* newspaper in India reported this year that a tantric priest and the parents of two children had been arrested after the discovery the couple had slaughtered and sacrificed their two sons on the priest's recommendation:[77]

BHUBANESWAR: In search of prosperity, a couple reportedly killed two of their sons on being misguided by a tantrik in Mayurbhanj district.

The gruesome incident had occurred at Tilapada village under Kaptipada Police station in Mayurbhanj district, police said.

The district police had taken the couple, Padmalochan Gan and

76 Aditi Banerjee & Pawan Deshpande, Executive Council, Hindu American Foundation, India Abroad, July 9, 2004
77 http://www.hindu.com/2007/01/04/stories/2007010417500300.htm

ARE ALL RELIGIONS EQUAL?

Tuni, and the tantrik, Jagannath Tudu, into custody.

The couple had killed two sons Harish (9) and Dipu (7). They have another two-month-old girl.

``Villagers came to know only when the foul smell emanated from the decomposed bodies. Police soon rushed to the village and arrested the couple on charges of culpable homicide,'' Mayurbhanj Superintendent of Police Ravi Kant told The Hindu on Wednesday.

He said the modus operandi of the 'sacrifice' was not yet known. The younger son was killed first and then the elder one, police sources said. ``As per version of the couple, their sons were not keeping well. The children had stopped talking. They were performing special puja for last eight days and were told by the Pujari that the children would get rebirth,'' the SP said.

Mr. Kant said the couple was not in good terms with other villagers.

However, residents of Tilapada were being interrogated and a case has been registered in this connection.

Now that India has a westernized political and justice system, courtesy of British colonization, the government there is doing what it can to stamp out events like these, but they are still far more common than you think:[78]

HORROR OF INDIA'S CHILD SACRIFICE
BBC Correspondent Navdip Dhariwal reporting:
In India's remote northern villages it feels as if little has changed. The communities remain forgotten and woefully undeveloped, with low literacy and abject poverty.

They are conditions that for decades have bred superstition and a deep-rooted belief in the occult.

The village of Barha in the state of Uttar Pradesh is only a three-hour car drive from the capital Delhi. Yet here evil medieval practices have made their ugly presence known.

I was led by locals to a house that is kept under lock and key. They refuse to enter it.

Peering through the window bars you can see the eerie dark room inside, with peeling posters of Hindu gods adorning the walls and bundles of discarded bed clothes.

---

78 http://news.bbc.co.uk/1/hi/world/south_asia/4903390.stm

In one corner is the evidence we had come to find: blood-splattered walls and stained bricks.

It is the place where a little boy's life was ritually sacrificed.

Those who tortured and killed Akash Singh did so in a depraved belief – that the boy's death would offer them a better life.

"The woman who did this was crazed," the villagers say. "Akash was friends with all our children... We still cannot believe what happened here."

Akash's distraught mother discovered her son's mutilated body. The family was told he was lured away with sweets and begged his captors to set him free.

"First they cut out his tongue," his grandmother Harpyari told me. "Then they cut off his nose, then his ears. They chopped off his fingers. They killed him slowly."

The woman who abducted Akash lived just a few doors away. She claimed to be suffering from terrible nightmares and visions.

It was then she turned for guidance to a tantric, or holy man. It was under his instruction that she brutally sacrificed the boy – offering his blood and remains to the Hindu goddess of destruction.

There are temples across India that are devoted to the goddess. Childless couples, the impoverished and sick visit to pray that she can cure them.

Animal sacrifice is central to worship – but humans have not been temple victims since ancient times.

We were met with a hostile reception at the temple in Meerut. The high priest did not want us to see the ritual slaughter.

Tantrics like him clearly have an overwhelming grip on their followers. Often they are profiting from people's fears. In extreme cases others have instructed their followers to kill.

S Raju is a journalist for the *Hindustan Times* and has been reporting on child sacrifice cases since 1997 in western Uttar Pradesh. He has reported on 38 similar cases.

In one incident he says a tantric told a young man that if he hanged and killed a small boy and lit a fire at his feet the smoke from the ritual could be used to lure the pretty village girl he had his eye on.

He has been campaigning for a crackdown on the practice of tantrics, alarmed at what he has seen.

"The masses need to be educated and dissuaded from following these men," he said. "They play on people's fears and superstitions – it is crazy."

We visited the jail where those accused of murdering Akash were being held.

The prison warden told us of over 200 cases of child sacrifice in these parts over the last seven years.

He admitted many of the cases go unreported because the police are reluctant to tarnish the image of their state. He told us incidents of child sacrifice are often covered up.

Many of those killers are behind bars – but, chillingly, others poisoned by the same sinister beliefs remain at large.

If you worship a Hindu "goddess of Destruction", what do you expect? Whilst this is by no means the practice of all Hinduism, as a religion, Hinduism spiritually has no ability to combat evil, as all paths are "valid". These child sacrifices are carried out in the name of Hindu deities. Up until 1948 many Hindu temples maintained a pool of child prostitutes as part of their worship facilities, because the religion promoted sex with a temple prostitute as a means of getting enlightenment. The practice was outlawed after World War 2, but only because the State intervened.[79]

Nor is it just Hinduism. At the heart of pure Tibetan Buddhism, according to the woman who became a secret consort to one of Tibet's holiest "celibate" lamas, is sex, as this extract from a report in Britain's *Independent* makes clear:[80]

What happened was that, having become a Buddhist in her native Scotland in the hippie Sixties, she travelled to India where she became a nun. She spent 10 years in a Tibetan monastery and penetrated more deeply than any other Westerner into the faith's esoteric hierarchy. Eventually she became personal translator to the guru as, during the Seventies, he travelled through Europe and America. It was after that, she said, that "he requested that I become his sexual consort and take part in secret activities with him".

Only one other person knew of the relationship – a second monk – with whom she took part in what she described as a polyandrous Tibetan-style relationship. "It was some years before I realised that the extent to which I had been taken advantage of constituted a kind of abuse".

The practice of Tantric sex is more ancient than Buddhism. The idea goes back to the ancient Hindus who believed that [it] made

79 *Eve's Bite*, Ian Wishart, Howling At The Moon, 2007, p. 141
80 http://www.trimondi.de/EN/deba02.html

men live longer. The Tibetan Buddhists developed the belief that enlightenment could be accelerated by the decision "to enlist the passions in one's religious practice, rather than to avoid them". The strategy is considered extremely risky yet so efficacious that it could lead to enlightenment in one lifetime.

Monks of a lower status confined themselves to visualising an imaginary sexual relationship during meditation. But, her book sets out, the "masters" reach a point where they decide that they can engage in sex without being tainted by it...

More than that, he is said to gain additional strength from absorbing the woman's sexual fluids at the same time as withholding his own. This "reverse of ordinary sex", said June Campbell, "expresses the relative status of the male and female within the ritual, for it signals the power flowing from the woman to the man".

The imbalance is underscored by the insistence by such guru-lamas that their sexual consorts must remain secret, allowing the lamas to maintain control over the women. "Since the book was published, I've had letters from women all over the world with similar and worse experiences".

So why did she stay for almost three years? "Personal prestige. The women believe that they too are special and holy. They are entering sacred space. It produces good karma for future lives, and is a test of faith". The combination of religion, sex, power and secrecy can have a potent effect. It creates the Catch 22 of psychological blackmail set out in the words of another lama, Beru Kyhentze Rinpoche:

"If your guru acts in a seemingly unenlightened manner and you feel it would be hypocritical to think him a Buddha, you should remember that your own opinions are unreliable and the apparent faults you see may only be a reflection of your own deluded state of mind...

"If your guru acted in a completely perfect manner he would be inaccessible and you would be able to relate to him. It is therefore out of your Guru's great compassion that he may show apparent flaws... He is mirroring your own faults".

The psychological pressure is often increased by making the woman swear vows of secrecy. In addition June Campbell was told that "madness, trouble or even death" could follow if she did not keep silent. "I was told that in a previous life the lama I was involved with had had a mistress who caused him some trouble, and in order to get rid of her he cast a spell which caused her illness later resulting in her death.

So much for the enlightenment and journey to nirvana of Tibet's holiest monks. The philosophy behind this manipulative behaviour is the Buddhist doctrine of karma – you get what you deserve.

"From a purely secular point of view," writes Tom Grunfeld in his book, *The Making of Modern Tibet*, "this doctrine must be seen as one of the most ingenious and pernicious forms of social control ever devised. To the ordinary Tibetan, the acceptance of this doctrine precluded the possibility of ever changing his or her fate in this life. If one were born a slave, so the doctrine of karma taught, it was not the fault of the slaveholder but rather the slaves themselves for having committed some misdeeds in a previous life. In turn, the slaveholder was simply being rewarded for good deeds in a previous life. For the slave to attempt to break the chains that bound him, or her, would be tantamount to a self-condemnation to a rebirth into a life worse than the one already being suffered. This is certainly not the stuff of which revolutions are made..."

But it gets much worse. While the human face of Buddhism in the West is the exiled Dalai Lama, a number of critical studies have been published of life in Tibet under the Lama's rule, before the Chinese invasion, as Michael Parenti reports:[81]

In the Dalai Lama's Tibet, torture and mutilation – including eye gouging, the pulling out of tongues, hamstringing, and amputation of arms and legs – were favored punishments inflicted upon thieves, runaway serfs, and other "criminals." Journeying through Tibet in the 1960s, Stuart and Roma Gelder interviewed a former serf, Tsereh Wang Tuei, who had stolen two sheep belonging to a monastery. For this he had both his eyes gouged out and his hand mutilated beyond use. He explains that he no longer is a Buddhist: "When a holy lama told them to blind me I thought there was no good in religion."[82] Some Western visitors to Old Tibet remarked on the number of amputees to be seen. Since it was against Buddhist teachings to take human life, some offenders were severely lashed and then "left to God" in the freezing night to die. "The parallels between Tibet and medieval Europe are striking," concludes Tom

---

81   http://www.swans.com/library/art9/mparen01.html
82   Gelder and Gelder, *The Timely Rain*, 113

Grunfeld in his book on Tibet.[83]

Some monasteries had their own private prisons, reports Anna Louise Strong. In 1959, she visited an exhibition of torture equipment that had been used by the Tibetan overlords. There were handcuffs of all sizes, including small ones for children, and instruments for cutting off noses and ears, and breaking off hands. For gouging out eyes, there was a special stone cap with two holes in it that was pressed down over the head so that the eyes bulged out through the holes and could be more readily torn out. There were instruments for slicing off kneecaps and heels, or hamstringing legs. There were hot brands, whips, and special implements for disemboweling.[84]

The exhibition presented photographs and testimonies of victims who had been blinded or crippled or suffered amputations for thievery. There was the shepherd whose master owed him a reimbursement in yuan and wheat but refused to pay. So he took one of the master's cows; for this he had his hands severed. Another herdsman, who opposed having his wife taken from him by his lord, had his hands broken off. There were pictures of Communist activists with noses and upper lips cut off, and a woman who was raped and then had her nose sliced away.[85]

Theocratic despotism had been the rule for generations. An English visitor to Tibet in 1895, Dr. A. L. Waddell, wrote that the Tibetan people were under the "intolerable tyranny of monks" and the devil superstitions they had fashioned to terrorize the people. In 1904 Perceval Landon described the Dalai Lama's rule as "an engine of oppression" and "a barrier to all human improvement." At about that time, another English traveler, Captain W.F.T. O'Connor, observed that "the great landowners and the priests . . . exercise each in their own dominion a despotic power from which there is no appeal," while the people are "oppressed by the most monstrous growth of monasticism and priest-craft the world has ever seen." Tibetan rulers, like those of Europe during the Middle Ages, "forged innumerable weapons of servitude, invented degrading legends and stimulated a spirit of superstition" among the common people.[86]

---

83 A. Tom Grunfeld, *The Making of Modern Tibet* rev. ed. (Armonk, N.Y. and London: 1996), 9 and 7-33 for a general discussion of feudal Tibet; see also Felix Greene, *A Curtain of Ignorance* (Garden City, N.Y.: Doubleday, 1961), 241-249; Goldstein, *A History of Modern Tibet 1913-1951,* 3-5; and Lopez, Prisoners of Shangri-La, passim.
84 Strong, Tibetan Interviews, 91-92
85 Strong, Tibetan Interviews, 92-96
86 Waddell, Landon, and O'Connor are quoted in Gelder and Gelder, *The Timely Rain,* 123-125

In 1937, another visitor, Spencer Chapman, wrote, "The Lamaist monk does not spend his time in ministering to the people or educating them, nor do laymen take part in or even attend the monastery services. The beggar beside the road is nothing to the monk. Knowledge is the jealously guarded prerogative of the monasteries and is used to increase their influence and wealth."[87]

Another essay, in the American-Buddha online library, details how children were sacrificed just before the Chinese invaded:[88]

As signs of the lamas' power, traditional ceremonies used body parts of people who had died: flutes made out of human thigh bones, bowls made out of skulls, drums made from human skin. After the revolution, a rosary was found in the Dalai Lama's palace made from 108 different skulls. After liberation, serfs widely reported that the lamas engaged in ritual human sacrifice – including burying serf children alive in monastery ground-breaking ceremonies. Former serfs testified that at least 21 people were sacrificed by monks in 1948 in hopes of preventing the victory of the Maoist revolution.

As for the current Dalai Lama:[89]

These days, the Dalai Lama is "packaged" internationally as a non-materialist holy man. In fact, the Dalai Lama was the biggest serf owner in Tibet. Legally, he owned the whole country and everyone in it. In practice, his family directly controlled 27 manors, 36 pastures, 6,170 field serfs and 102 house slaves.

When he moved from palace to palace, the Dalai Lama rode on a throne chair pulled by dozens of slaves. His troops marched along to "It's a Long Way to Tipperary," a tune learned from their British imperialist trainers. Meanwhile, the Dalai Lama's bodyguards, all over six-and-a-half feet tall, with padded shoulders and long whips, beat people out of his path. This ritual is described in the Dalai Lama's autobiography.

The first time he fled to India in 1950, the Dalai Lama's advisors sent several hundred mule-loads of gold and silver bars ahead to

---

87 Quoted in Gelder and Gelder, *The Timely Rain*, 125
88 http://portland.indymedia.org/en/2003/12/277073.shtml
89 Ibid

secure his comfort in exile.

After liberation, Anna Louise Strong asked a young monk, Lobsang Telé, if monastery life followed Buddhist teachings about compassion. The young lama replied that he heard plenty of talk in the scripture halls about kindness to all living creatures, but that he personally had been whipped at least a thousand times. "If any upper class lama refrains from whipping you," he told Strong, "that is already very good. I never saw an upper lama give food to any poor lama who was hungry. They treated the laymen who were believers just as badly or even worse."

None of this is to poke the borax at Buddhism or Hinduism just for the mere sake of it. The failings of individual humans do not necessarily negate the principles of the religions themselves, but it does illustrate that Western fantasies about the "wisdom of the East" are just that, fantasies. The discovery that the absolute top echelons of Tibetan Buddhism have been engaging in sexual monkfoolery is the equivalent of discovering the Pope has been sneaking out to a Bondage and Discipline club. Yes, there are other branches of Buddhism and Hinduism, but they have their own skeletons. It does underline that any religion that has no real concept of good and evil – and in particular no way of combatting evil – is seriously, perhaps even fatally, flawed. It may also explain why in Asia – the home of these faiths – people are converting to Christianity in such numbers as to make it the fastest-growing faith in the world via conversion.[90]

Christians, of course, have also committed their share of atrocities – but in clear conflict with their Scriptures. The Hindu and Buddhist faiths can get away with theirs, however, because their own scriptures are – at best – indifferent to suffering because of the doctrine of karmic destiny (working through your fate) and at worst encouraging of it.

Hinduism, for example, is embedded with the belief that people exist in castes, and upper castes must not mix with the lower classes, nor help them. This is a sharp contrast to the humble servant message of Jesus, who openly defied Hebrew social class rules.

It should be abundantly clear, even to the most die-hard atheist, that the man who said, "I am the bread of life. He who comes to me will never go hungry, and he who believes in me will never be thirsty...whoever comes

---

90 It is estimated that Christianity is the fastest-growing religion overall in the world, but Islam is close behind. Much of Islam's growth, however, is being achieved via extremely high birthrates, rather than people "choosing" Islam *per se*

to me I will never drive away"[91] is not the same man who created the Hindu class of "untouchables".

It is true that modern Buddhism and Hinduism are changing, particularly branches of those faiths in the West. Ironically, Christian worldviews are rubbing off on them. But acts of charity and welcome to all are not in any way part of pure, original, Eastern faiths.

Of Christ, says Indian-born Ravi Zacharias,[92] "his life has always been regarded as the purest that has ever been lived. On numerous occasions, his antagonists were challenged to bring some contrary proof against him.

"By contrast, no other individual has ever elicited such accolades. By their own admission, this includes Muhammed, Buddha and Krishna. Their lives and their struggles are recorded within their own scriptures."

When Muslims talk of Muhammed being sinless, he says, they ignore Quranic verses like Surahs 47 and 48, where "Muhammed himself was told to ask for forgiveness for sin".

Muhammed had 11 wives, including a nine year old girl. Christ, of course, did not.

"Hinduism is not exempt from this scrutiny," says Zacharias. "The playfulness of Krishna and his exploits with the milkmaids in the Bhagavad-Gita is frankly an embarrassment to many Hindu scholars.

"How does Buddha measure up against the standard of personal purity that Jesus set? The very fact that he endured rebirths implies a series of imperfect lives. When he left his home in the palace, turning his back on his wife and son, it was in search of an answer. He did not start with the answer."

Christ, says Zacharias,[93] was not embarking on a journey where he hoped to find personal enlightenment: "That was the origin of Buddhism".

"He did not come to affirm a people who boasted in the strength of their military power, as the citizens of Rome did…He did not come to compliment the Greeks for their intellectual prowess, in fact he did not even come to exalt a culture because it was the recipient of God's moral law, a boast the Hebrews delighted in.

"His strong and unequivocal claim was that heaven was his dwelling and earth was his footstool."

Zacharias believes part of the attraction of the Eastern faiths in the West is a huge disenchantment with leadership in the Christian church.

"Of all the enterprises in which the human heart engages, none lends itself more to abuse and manipulation than the activities of religion. For

91   John 6:35-37
92   *Jesus Among Other Gods*, Ravi Zacharias, Thomas Nelson, 2000, pp. 40-41
93   Ibid, p. 42

here, sacrifice and greed can meet in the most trusting and exploiting context. The much respected scholar and one-time missionary Stephen Neill once said, 'I am inclined to think that ambition in any ordinary sense of the term is nearly always sinful in ordinary men. I am certain that in the Christian it is always sinful, and that it is most inexcusable of all in the ordained minister'.

"I believe that Neill was right. From Voltaire to Einstein, thinkers have heaped grave suspicion on institutional religion because of its chequered past. It is a tragedy that the history of religion, Christianity included, is filled with so much abuse that skeptics are often justified in their 'rational rejection' of the message.

"Jesus bore the brunt of the anger of the ecclesiastical authorities when he reminded them that their duplicity was the cause of unbelief in the masses."

And it is not just Christianity with its hypocrites. On the streets of Asian cities, you can see little streetside shrines to Buddha and other deities.

"I have watched every morning, as thousands walked by," says Zacharias. "Most would pause, bow, fold their hands, or make some kind of reverential sign to honour the deity and then move on. Many of those who ceremoniously carried out that ritual would then walk a few paces and lie in wait to see which tourists they could hoodwink that morning. From unfurling nude pictures or offering the services of a prostitute, to selling fake Rolex watches for $20, their day was spent in the illegal and the immoral…yet if anyone were to hint at desecrating that shrine, his life would be in peril."

The bottom-line claim in the Eastern faith is that when you die you have no idea whether you have attained nirvana, or whether you will be reincarnated as a beetle. This is why the Hindu priest at the cremation ceremony that a teenage Ravi Zacharias witnessed was unable to say what the fate of the deceased was.

Christianity, on the other hand, boldly declares certainty:

"I am the resurrection and the life. He who believes in me will live, even though he dies; and whoever lives and believes in me will never die," said Christ.[94]

Again, could the same God have created both the Christian message and the Eastern one? Could the God of the Bible, who said, "Your people whom you brought out of Egypt have become corrupt. They have turned away quickly from what I commanded them and have made a cast idol for themselves"[95], be the same God endorsing the streetside shrine Zacharias mentions above?

---

94 John 11:25
95 Deut. 9:12

Is the Hindu philosopher who says "all paths lead to the same goal" thereby endorsing the absolutely exclusive claim of Christ?:[96]

"For God so loved the world that he gave his one and only Son, that whoever believes in him shall not perish but have eternal life. For God did not send his Son into the world to condemn the world, but to save the world through him. Whoever believes in him is not condemned, but whoever does not believe stands condemned already because he has not believed in God's one and only Son."

The point of me raising these quotes is merely to show the massive gulf in logic that exists between Eastern and Western faiths. Only those who know little of religion would make the otherwise ignorant statement that "all religions are equal".

It is true that the Eastern religions do urge followers to work towards good (albeit that "good" does not carry the same objective weighting it has in the West). It is true that they have some redeeming features. But if the God that created the Universe exists, is he/she/it likely to recognize the Eastern faiths as true reflections of God's will, or merely shadows of the truth?

The scientific evidence goes against the Hindu/Buddhist endless universe idea, as we have already seen, and morally the Eastern faiths are far more tolerant of harm to others than Christianity is. Their messages, however, are diametrically opposed. All religions are not equal, because they are genuinely saying opposite things.

If the world is genuinely an illusion, as pure Buddhism tells us, why do we not see Buddhist monks test that theory while crossing the road? If the bus is merely an illusion, step in front of it...

The reality is, the religion may say one thing, but its followers live their lives as if the opposite were true. We all do. All of us live our lives as if trucks are real, pain is real and death is real. Failure to go through life in accordance with that would mean we would swiftly come in contact with all three.

Religions that not only conflict with scientific reality, but with the reality of life, cannot really be in tune with the precision of the creator of the Big Bang.

What of Islam? Is Allah the God of the Christian Bible?

A Dutch Catholic Bishop caused a storm of controversy late 2007 by suggesting that tensions between Muslims and Christians in Europe could be eased if Christians agreed to refer to God as "Allah".[97]

Whilst it is true that Allah is the Arabic word for God, and is therefore

96 John 3:16-18
97 http://www.worldnetdaily.com/news/article.asp?ARTICLE_ID=57178

used in Christian Bibles in the Arabic language, the character of Allah as revealed through the Qu'ran is vastly different from the character of the Christian God revealed in the New Testament.

The Sura of the Sword, 9:5 boldly tells Muslims:

"Slay the infidels wherever ye find them, and seize them, beleaguer them, and lie in wait for them in every stratagem; but if they repent, and establish regular prayers and practice regular charity, then open the way for them."

Christ, on the other hand, urged Christians to "love your enemies... turn the other cheek." By definition, the same God cannot have written both the Qu'ran as we currently know it, and the Gospels.

There is growing evidence, however, that the original Islam might, in fact, have been a form of Christianity. Not only is Jesus Christ mentioned more often in the Qu'ran than Muhammed, but an Islamic scholar living in hiding in Germany has published a thesis arguing the Arabic version of the Qu'ran has been mistranslated quite seriously, as this story from *Newsweek* shows:[98]

PROMISES RAISINS, NOT VIRGINS
By Stefan Theil, *Newsweek International*

In a note of encouragement to his fellow hijackers, September 11 ringleader Muhammad Atta cheered their impending "marriage in Paradise" to the 72 wide-eyed virgins the Qur'an promises to the departed faithful. Palestinian newspapers have been known to describe the death of a suicide bomber as a "wedding to the black-eyed in eternal Paradise." But if a German expert on Middle Eastern languages is correct, these hopes of sexual reward in the afterlife are based on a terrible misunderstanding.

Arguing that today's version of the Qur'an has been mistranscribed from the original text, scholar Christoph Luxenberg says that what are described as "houris" with "swelling breasts" refer to nothing more than "white raisins" and "juicy fruits."

Luxenberg – a pseudonym – is one of a small but growing group of scholars, most of them working in non-Muslim countries, studying the language and history of the Qur'an. When his new book is published this fall, it's likely to be the most far-reaching scholarly commentary on the Qur'an's early genesis, taking this infant discipline far into uncharted – and highly controversial –

territory. That's because Islamic orthodoxy considers the holy book to be the verbatim revelation of Allah, speaking to his prophet, Muhammad, through the Angel Gabriel, in Arabic. Therefore, critical study of God's undiluted word has been off-limits in much of the Islamic world. (For the same reason, translations of the Qur'an are never considered authentic.) Islamic scholars who have dared ignore this taboo have often found themselves labeled heretics and targeted with death threats and violence. Luxenberg, a professor of Semitic languages at one of Germany's leading universities, has chosen to remain anonymous because he fears a fatwa by enraged Islamic extremists.

Luxenberg's chief hypothesis is that the original language of the Qur'an was not Arabic but something closer to Aramaic. He says the copy of the Qur'an used today is a mistranscription of the original text from Muhammad's time, which according to Islamic tradition was destroyed by the third caliph, Osman, in the seventh century. But Arabic did not turn up as a written language until 150 years after Muhammad's death, and most learned Arabs at that time spoke a version of Aramaic. Rereading the Paradise passage in Aramaic, the mysterious houris turn into raisins and fruit – much more common components of the Paradise myth.

The forthcoming book contains plenty of other bombshells. It claims that the Qur'an's commandment for women to cover themselves is based on a similar misreading; in Sura 24, the verse that calls for women to "snap their scarves over their bags" becomes in Aramaic "snap their belts around their waists". Even more explosive are readings that strengthen scholars' views that the Qur'an had Christian origins. Sura 33 calls Muhammad the "seal of the prophets", taken to mean the final and ultimate prophet of God. But an Aramaic reading, says Luxenberg, turns Muhammad into a "witness of the prophets" – i.e., someone who bears witness to the established Judeo-Christian texts. The Qur'an, in Arabic, talks about the "revelation" of Allah, but in Aramaic that term turns into "teaching" of the ancient Scriptures. The original Qur'an, Luxenberg contends, was in fact a Christian liturgical document – before an expanding Arab empire turned Muhammad's teachings into the basis for its new religion long after the Prophet's death.

Such interpretations will undoubtedly draw the ire of many Muslims – and not just extremists. After all, revisionist scholars have been persecuted for much less; in 2001, Egypt's Constitutional Court confirmed the "apostasy" of former University of Cairo scholar Nasr Hamid Abu-Zayd, for considering the Qur'an a document written by humans.

Still, Luxenberg may be ushering in a whole new era of Qur'anic study. "Luxenberg's findings are very relevant and convincing," says Mondher Sfar, a Tunisian specialist on the historic origins of the Qur'an in exile in Paris. "They make possible a new interpretation of the Qur'an." In the West, questioning the literal veracity of the Bible was a crucial step in breaking the church's grip on power – and in developing a modern, secular society. That experience, as much as the questioning itself, is no doubt what concerns conservative Muslims as they struggle over the meaning and influence of Islam in the 21st century. But if Luxenberg's work is any indication, the questioning is just getting underway.

The implications for religious scholarship are huge, but will probably come too late to make any impact on a religion as large as Islam. After all, the Arabic version, having urged followers to slay infidels wherever they find them, then authorizes the capture and rape of infidel women as a right available to all Muslim men.[99]

Perhaps the most intriguing of all these competing religions in the West, however, is Wicca, or witchcraft, and its companion philosophy New Age. We'll focus on them in more detail later in the book, but one aspect deserves scrutiny now.

---

99 http://www.islam-watch.org/MA_Khan/ProphetCartoons.htm

CHAPTER 8

SUPERNATURAL EXPERIENCES IN THE WEST

"Thus is the New Age dawning...we are all Gods"

Alice Bailey, *New Ager*

ONE BIG GROWTH AREA IN the West is in New Age beliefs and psychic phenomena. In New Zealand, the latest survey on the subject[100] shows just how far attitudes are moving in that direction. Only 46% of those surveyed believed in the concept of a Christian God, while 31% believe in the New Age idea of "a universal spirit or higher power". In the US, 78% believe in God and only 14% in the universal spirit/higher power.

Magazines are full of psychic columnists, and TV is likewise abuzz with homegrown and visiting clairvoyants and mediums wowing audiences with their seemingly incredible talents.

In October 2007, however, TVNZ's *Breakfast* show ran this interview with the 'star' of a psychic show:

"Psychic Deb Webber may be a born and bred Australian but she says kiwis seem a lot more ready to accept her gift than people back home in Australia. Deb Webber has become a household name in New Zealand, thanks to her role helping police solve old cases in TV2's *Sensing Murder*. She joins *Breakfast*[101].

HOST: "When you say that New Zealanders are more willing to accept your talent, or gift – is it a talent or a gift, or both?

WEBBER: "Both."

HOST: "It is both I suppose."

---

100 http://www.umr.co.nz/Media/FinalMorality-Religion-Evolution-NZ_USComparison-Sep07.pdf
101 http://tvnz.co.nz/view/video_popup_windows_skin/1380062?bandwidth=128k

WEBBER: "And I have to practice at it, I have to work at it. If you don't use it you lose it…

HOST: "But when you say that about New Zealanders, what does that say about us?"

WEBBER: "I think it's more spiritually orientated, the actual land. I think the Maori energy over here is higher, it's open, they live it still. Where over in Australia you have all the aboriginal spirits and everything but they're dampened, it's like it's been squashed. But over here it's everywhere, you can feel it coming out of the earth, there's something here that's just unique and beautiful.

HOST: "I want to talk about the shows you're doing over here, but first *Sensing Murder* because it is hugely popular here, and I know that a lot of skeptics watch it, and they watch it probably because they are skeptics to start with, but you've turned a lot of skeptics around, haven't you?":

WEBBER: "I have, for many years, actually. And then you get the odd person who will never change, and that's just their belief system, they're too scared, or they don't understand it. Someone actually said to me a few weeks ago it's because they're the ones who need help, they've got something in themselves stopping them from believing in something magic or beautiful. And it is, spirit is beautiful. I wonder why they have to judge someone else when it takes one to know one so they're judging themselves first."

HOST: "Why don't police just pay you $10 million a year and just second you to solving crimes?

WEBBER: "Well the police don't pay us. I work for police in Australia and they don't pay you –

HOST: "But shouldn't they, I mean when you watch the programme, given what you are able to find, surely if you were paid, if you were used by the police force more, it would save a fortune, wouldn't it?"

WEBBER: "Yeah I think so, I think it would help them, well it does help them – I have certain police officers in Australia who ring me constantly, they get a case and they keep ringing. I've got one fellow where I actually feel like saying, 'you know, you've got to do your job, why are you always ringing me to do your job?' He's getting paid, I'm not.!

HOST: "I know sometimes you have people coming up to you asking you all the time, but you also have spirits coming up and badgering you, don't you?"

WEBBER: "Pretty much."

HOST: "Have you got any spirits badgering you now?"

WEBBER: "Well I've got someone talking to me now about you, and I just think you're going to ring the wrong Deborah for a coffee?"

HOST: "Oh? really? Alright, extraordinary, you're watching the television, the Madeleine McCann investigation…could you solve it?"

WEBBER: "I wouldn't say I could solve it, because I never say I can do anything, but I believe I could help, get them in the right direction. I've actually had dreams about that girl and I've rung the police, but the problem is the family don't want the help from a psychic. That's where our dilemma comes. I started Sensing Murder because a boy went missing where I live, for the parents to see, look I'm good at what I do so give me a go, you've got nothing to lose and you might have something to gain, which is your son. But they never came, because of their religious belief. And I think that's sad, because if I had a child missing I'd try anything."

HOST: "Do you think the parents did it?"

WEBBER: "No. I think she was smuggled, because that's what my dream was telling me. I think she was smuggled through an airport.."

HOST: "Tell me about your shows, because you're doing a lot of shows around New Zealand, and I think we've got the website on television, www.debwebber.com.au, for people to find out show dates because there are lots of them. What happens in your shows?"

WEBBER: "In my live shows I run into the audience, I don't stay on the stage because I find it very impersonal for a reading, and I tell them what I see. That's it.

HOST: "How come some people are chosen and others are not?"

WEBBER: "It's up to the spirit, not me, anyway. I find the adult spirits take over the child spirits, so I do a prayer saying I want the children to come in, I did that last night, and 15 minutes later all the children came in and I could talk to the parents."

Now what does that little interlude show? Firstly it shows the TV host on one of the country's leading news shows was totally accepting of the whole psychic/spirit/channeling idea, with no challenging questions at all.

Secondly, isn't it interesting how skeptical people are about the Christian God now, but how open and welcoming Deb Webber finds them in regard to spirit mediums, far more so than Australia, she remarks.

Thirdly, it shows she is unlikely to be right about Madeleine McCann because in these terrorist-blighted times you can't even smuggle a bottle of shampoo through an airport, let alone a missing toddler without a passport.

Fourthly, it shows that mediumship is big business. Webber recently concluded a three month tour of New Zealand with dozens of shows. Tickets for her Auckland shows were selling at $67 a head, and the venue was averaging 2500 to 3000 people a time. That's a gross financial haul of $201,000 a night in the big cities – far more than the average flash evangelical church takes in.

Webber may not be paid by police, but the TV shows and interviews give her and her fellow psychics an incredibly high, marketable profile.

There's also a health warning:

"Please Note: *Deb Webber Live* accepts no responsibility for emotional & psychological experiences that may cause injury."

Her site shows she also does private readings and workshops, presumably at a much higher fee than mere show tickets, touching on topics like these:

Understanding of Who & What We Are
Meditation & Visualisation Technique
Belief Systems
Protection from Negative Emotions
Chakra & Aura Awareness & Cleansing
Crystal
Past Lives
Spiritual Guides and Angels
Tuning into Higher Self & Communicate with Higher Beings
Self Healing: Mind, Cellular Structure & Touch
Affirmations

So let's take a look at some of the cold cases Webber has worked on, like the murder of an Auckland photographer, Simon Buis. The programme is reviewed here on the website NZRealityTV:[102]

"Both psychics [Webber and colleague Sue Nicholson] believed that there were two young men (age 16-20 years) driving a stolen car. Two men found driving a stolen car were initially charged with the murder but charges were later dropped. The descriptions provided by the psychics did not match these two individuals, however there was another pair of men joyriding in a car around the same time. They weren't investigated at the time, and this is considered a possible lead.

"During the show psychic Deb Webber gave three names which match those of someone who lived in the area at the time. These names were bleeped out by producers for legal reasons.

"The psychics describe the killers as driving an older car, possibly a light coloured 1950s DeSoto Chrysler. Witnesses saw a similar car leaving the area. Given the age of the vehicle, and its uniqueness it seems astonishing

---

102 http://www.nzrealitytv.com/2007/10/sensing-murder-simon-buis.html

that this didn't lead to the owner of the vehicle at the time of the murder, however it appears to be a loose end."

All very vague, really, and suspiciously like information that could have emerged from police news releases and media stories a year ago.[103] And it's not as if numerous books written by authors like Tony Williams[104] and Scott Bainbridge[105] [insert real-crime writer of your choice] haven't listed many unsolved cases chapter and verse.

Then there's the tragic case of missing, presumed dead, prostitute Jayne Furlong. This episode, in my view, busts the psychics as having been pre-briefed on the case before arriving in the country.

Here's what NZRealityTV said in its review[106] (publicly known facts are in bold):

"This week Australian psychic Deb Webber and New Zealand psychic Kelvin Cruickshank come up with remarkably similar statements on the physical description and personality. Without looking at the photo of Jayne, both describe a young woman and both mention that she tries to tell them **she's 16 years old.** The psychics go on to say that **she's a prostitute** and Deb says her name is Jane but that it is spelt with five letters, eventually suggesting **her name is Jane with a Y.** This is pretty impressive. Less impressive is Kelvin's statement that **she worked in K Road.** If Miss Prozac had to guess where a prostitute worked in Auckland this would be her first guess, too.

"Both Kelvin and Deb believe that Jayne was grabbed from K Road, and went with the man thinking it would be just a chat. The man was described as a balding middle-aged businessman, who possibly gave the name Clyde. They also suggest it may be someone Jayne knew, so it seems strange she didn't give his real name. Later Deb gives a name of a financial type firm that she believes could be involved. Naturally, this hot development is bleeped out leaving Miss Prozac none the wiser.

"Investigator Duncan Holland says the psychics have come up with promising new leads for the investigation. This sounds like a case of hyperbole given the analysis he provides of the "new leads". This episode was the most disappointing to date. Both psychics

103   http://www.police.govt.nz/news/release/2406.html
104   *Unsolved Murders in New Zealand,* Tony Williams, Hachette, 1999
105   *Without Trace,* Scott Bainbridge, Reed, 2005
106   http://www.nzrealitytv.com/2007/10/psychic-detectives-hunt-jayne-furlongs.html

were confident that **her body had never been recovered** and appeared to give an accurate read on her character, and similar readings on her murderer.

"However, they failed to locate her body. After the success of last week, when psychics Deb Webber and Sue Nicholson both identified Gribblehirst Park as the location of the murder, Miss Prozac expected the psychics to identify the murder site. It seems like they were suggesting that it could have been somewhere in the 75ha Auckland Domain or the Symonds St cemetery.

"In their defence the psychics can only pass on information that they receive and stated that Jayne didn't want to revisit the murder site and felt that no one cared about what happened, but the episode ended up being a bit of a non-event.

"There was also a suggestion from Kelvin that **it could be payback from a motorcycle gang.** This fitted in with existing police evidence from retired officer Dayle Candy that Jayne was going to give testimony against a motorcycle gang. **Kelvin gave the first name of a man (also bleeped) that matched the name of one of the people Jayne was going to testify against.** Miss Prozac hopes the name was something unusual like Trent or Sharif and not John or Dave…

"Kelvin also felt that **Jayne had been buried under concrete or at a construction site.** Miss Prozac was intrigued by that as she recalls hearing a similar theory from an ex-detective over the watercooler."

There was enormous publicity in the 1990s about a theory that Furlong had fallen foul of a client in the concreting industry. Police were later alleged to have fabricated evidence against the man. But my wider point is this: there are so many accurate public facts in this testimony that if it were truly a spiritual manifestation from the dead Jayne herself, the psychics should have been able to lead TV cameras right to the burial spot. Are we seriously to believe the psychics when they claim Jayne, who supposedly is now a 'higher enlightened being' according to Webber's workshops, threw a tanty and refused to provide closure for her grieving mother on the basis that "no one cared about what happened"? If no one cared, what were TV crews doing crawling all over the case? And what are we to make of "Jayne" on the one hand telling Deb she'd been done in by a middle-aged businessman named Clyde that she knew and who was involved with a finance company, and on the other hand telling Kelvin it was a hit organized by a motorcycle gang? And then where does the concrete man, who wasn't named Clyde, nor a bikie, fit into it?

Australia's Channel 7 ran a piece on Deb Webber three years ago, planting three people in the audience that Webber gave readings for. None of the details were correct:

"For example, Webber claimed to be talking to dead relatives who, it turned out, never existed. "Michelle" was one of the test subjects:

"I never had a husband," Michelle said. "She saw two large dogs, a large house and property – I have none of those things."[107]

Webber later told producers that she can only go with what the spirits tell her, and can only assume that on this particular occasion the spirits were lying to her.[108]

In Australia, local skeptics point out[109] that TV programmes like *Sensing Murder* leave a lot of videotape unseen.

"A common tactic for psychic TV-shows is to record copious amounts of film and then edit it down to the best bits – in other words throw out the mistakes and guesses that didn't "hit". Audience members for John Edward shows have reported filming going on all day, for an half hour show! We'll never know just how much has been pruned out of these *Sensing Murder* episodes. Who said "the camera never lies"?

ABC's John Stossell[110] pinged one of America's best known mediums, Kathlyn Rhea:

Rhea claims she finds missing people all the time:
HOST: "How many bodies have you found?"
RHEA: "Oh, sometimes it's three or four a week."
Rhea charges fees. We persuaded her to discount it down to US$1,800, She then explained to Cathy and the private investigator Cathy hired that Kristine had been murdered:
RHEA: "I think it's strangulation, because I felt her go choke choke, like that."

---

107 http://www.paranormal-phenomena.info/bio/psychic/deb-webber.html
108 For those remotely interested in how spirit mediums could genuinely supernaturally know details about another person's life, Christian theology explains it this way: according to Christians, the dead do not and cannot return to haunt us or tell us anything. However, just as there are "guardian angels" one is equally likely to attract what are called "familiar spirits" which can hang around families for generations (being immortal they outlast everyone). Such a familiar spirit could pose as the ghost of a loved one. Such an entity would be quite capable of rattling off old Aunt Mavis' favourite recipe, or the name of her brother etc, or telling the inquiring family member that it saw them doing such and such last week. It is precisely such an explanation that is provided in the Bible, with a reasonably harsh penalty for those who dabble in it: "A man or a woman who is a medium, or who has familiar spirits, shall surely be put to death; they shall stone them with stones. Their blood shall be upon them." Lev. 20:27
109 http://www.keypoint.com.au/~skeptics/Sensing_Murder
110 http://www.youtube.com/watch?v=hW0CbKueesA

She was very confident that she knew where Kristine's body was:
RHEA: "And it's about 30 minutes or 30 miles from here."
HOST: "But that could be anywhere?"
RHEA: "Well, that's true, so they have to draw a map around for 30 miles, and start looking for the other details that go with it."
The other details included a road that branches off like a Y, something that looks like a country church, something with the letter S. We tried to follow her instructions but there were lots of Ys in the road and signs with S's.
HOST: "Shouldn't you go with them and show them, because this is all vague?"
RHEA: "Ha, no, they need to draw a map and do the legwork. I've done my share, they need to do their share. What, do you want me to do the legwork? Ha ha ha."

Kathlyn Rhea may have found it amusing, but the idea of searching a map area 100 kilometres across – about the size of Auckland or Sydney – for a body is clearly ridiculous. She got her US$1,800 paycheck, however, and no one found a body.

Another disgruntled Rhea victim calls her "the second wave of predators".
Ten years ago Mark Klass' 12 year old daughter Polly was abducted and murdered in California. The Klass family went to psychics to try and find Polly. Kathlyn Rhea gave them a location where her body was supposed to be, and a TV show paid Rhea more than US$6000 to talk about it. Police say her information was wrong.
Rhea also said this police sketch was wrong, that he wasn't the murderer…But he was."

For the record, the FBI says psychics have never solved a single missing person case in the US. Ever.

Interestingly, a commenter on the James Randi skeptic forum picked up on Rhea's claim to recover three or four bodies a week:[111]

"Now, the United States is a pretty big country, and there sure are a lot of murders. But shouldn't we expect that a success rate like that would register somewhere in the police records? Shouldn't we expect that, with a success rate like that, Rhea would openly and frequently be consulted by

---

111   http://forums.randi.org/showthread.php?t=87952&page=10

not just the police, but also the families of the many missing persons in the United States, and the rest of the world? The press – always eager to find really truly amazing stories – haven't picked up on this?

"What the hell is going on here? Is there a world-wide conspiracy to suppress this? That can't be it, because nobody has tried to silence Rhea when she makes her claims – quite contrary.

"If she can find bodies at that rate (I doubt even the NYPD can work that fast), why isn't she employed full-time finding missing bodies – regardless of the cost?"

Valid questions, especially in light of the easy ride Deb Webber received on that TV interview I referred to earlier. Maybe there is a worldwide daily media conspiracy to take seriously anything psychics say, who knows.

Whatever the reason, it is not just spirit mediums having a tough time. The track record of celebrated seers like Jeanne Dixon has been re-examined in the light of time's passing. Here are some of her prophecies for the 21 year period between 1979 and 2000, the end of the millennium:

Predictor: JEANE DIXON
Future Predictions: For 1979-2000[112]
- We are going to experience the biggest civil war that can be imagined. It is coming in the 1980s.
- UFOs will give us the knowledge to harness the sun's energy, making the earth a better place to live. The world's top scientists will be brought together and all mankind will benefit.
- It may soon be possible to nourish ourselves on a "sun pill," a concentrated dose of solar energy with great health benefits. We may also be able to run our machines on a sun pill.
- Americans may find themselves preparing for another threatened disaster. The old civil defense air-raid shelters will be revived. The nation will return to its former policy of massive preparedness for armed conflict.
- Americans will travel less in the years ahead.
- The papacy will cease to exist.
- People will communicate through telepathy and use faith healing to cure themselves.
- Canada and Brazil, rich in food and energy, will become powerful countries.
- Formal education as we know it today will virtually disappear.

112 © 1975 – 1981 by David Wallechinsky & Irving Wallace. Reproduced from "The People's Almanac" series of books

Many children will be taught by their parents at home.

For 2000-2037 – China will start to take over the world but will ultimately be defeated.

• In 2020, the Antichrist will be revealed as evil. The Battle of Armageddon, involving millions, will take place, and the forces of good will win.

Even on her most successful prediction however, Jeanne Dixon had a bob each way. In 1956, *Parade* magazine in the US recorded her saying that the 1960 presidential election would involve the labour movement and be won by a Democrat, who would either die in office or be assassinated, "but not necessarily in his first term".

Then, in 1960, just before the election, Dixon swung the other way, definitively stating, "John F. Kennedy will fail to win the presidency." Instead, Dixon saw Republican Richard Nixon as the clear winner.

Dixon got it wrong. As history shows, Kennedy won on the day, not Nixon. Kennedy, however, *was* later assassinated. Clear win for Dixon on the dying in office prediction? Maybe not.

Statistically, for some bizarre reason, the following presidential elections were won by presidents who all later died in office: 1840, 1860, 1880, 1900, 1920, 1940. Knowing this spooky trend, one would almost expect a famous psychic like Dixon to take a punt on the upcoming 1960 date – which indeed she did. The hoodoo has continued incidentally although not fatally, with attempts on the life of Ronald Reagan (elected 1980) and George W Bush (elected 2000) via the targeting of the White House in the 9/11 attacks.

Even so, the natural odds in favour of a prediction about a dead president (remember, it was *either* dying naturally *or* assassination, so Dixon was covering her options here) are even higher than the above trend suggests. That's because, of the 31 elections between 1840 and 1960, 13 had presidents who died at some point during their terms in office, *not necessarily the first term* (remember Dixon's exact prediction had this qualifier as well?). That's odds of almost 50/50 if you want to take the gamble. In turn, 5 of the 13 involved presidents being assassinated, so in terms of natural vs unnatural, the odds are still pretty even.

It didn't matter. Dixon's prediction was sufficiently general to cover all possibilities at odds of 50/50, so the prediction was worth making even just for the hell of it.

And that was her best ever prediction.

CHAPTER 9

THE MYTH OF CHRIST

"There is overwhelming evidence that the New Testament is a reliable record composed by contemporaries and eyewitnesses of the events"
Norman Geisler, New Testament scholar

ON THE BACK COVER OF this year's bestselling book, *God Is Not Great*, Christopher Hitchens' publicist boasts, "Here he makes the ultimate case against organized religion."

That's a pretty big call. The *ultimate* case against organized religion? According to Hitchens, Christianity is a myth, the Gospels are fairy stories, and there's "no firm evidence whatever that Jesus actually *was* a 'character in history'."

I guess if he could prove all that, then Hitchens indeed would have penned a worthy tome, rather than a novel with as much intellectual merit as Dan Brown's *Da Vinci Code*. Unfortunately for Hitchens, like Dawkins before him[113], he goes for a skate when he starts to tackle the New Testament.

Now again, I make no apologies for getting stuck in here. The point I'm trying to make clearly, so that readers understand where I'm coming from, is this: the purpose of this book is to give you the level playing field of information that the media and atheist fundamentalists like Hitchens and Dawkins are depriving you of. Chances are you have never heard the information contained in these pages.

In the first part of *The Divinity Code*, I've illustrated why atheist presumptions about the non-existence of God are fatally flawed. The fact that most people in the West still believe in God is proof that the atheists have failed to convince the public with their weak, if noisy,

---

113   See *Eve's Bite* by Ian Wishart, Howling At The Moon Publishing, 2007

arguments. On the other hand, with the huge drop in attendance at organized religious services in the West over the past fifty years, two to three generations of people have now left school with little more than a vague concept of what the 'God' they tentatively believe in might actually be. They have even less familiarity with the basics of Christianity itself, let alone the more advanced concepts. On this front, the secularists have been overwhelmingly successful, muddying the waters enough that while people are not prepared to abandon belief in God, they largely no longer believe Jesus Christ is "the way, the truth and the life".

If one makes a rational decision to rubbish Christianity – the founding religion of the West – on the basis of carefully weighed evidence, well, that's one thing. But if one's decision is not based on a first-hand reading of the facts, but instead on what someone mockingly said on talk radio late one night, or on the bluster and out-of-context 'facts' of a writer like Richard Dawkins or Hitchens, then that's a tragedy.

The secularists crack jokes about a religion that they themselves do not actually either understand, nor really know. But if you think this is just a Christian conservative talking, think again. Camille Paglia is an atheist icon. Left wing, feminist, respected at all the right Manhattan parties. But even she is getting sick of people – particularly "artists" – taking the piss out of Christ or, in one celebrated case, putting him in it. American photographer Andres Serrano raised a storm of controversy nearly two decades ago by dunking a plastic crucifix of Christ in a jar of the artist's urine and photographing it (the 1989 shock-photo entitled, appropriately, "Piss Christ").

"It's always Catholic iconography, I might point out," Camille Paglia remarked in an interview[114] recently. "I am atheist, by the way. It's never Jewish. It's never Muslim. So I am saying this is a scandal. The art world has actually prided itself on getting a rise out of the people on the far right. Thinking, 'We're avant-garde'. The avante-garde is dead. It has been dead since Andy Warhol appropriated Campbell's Soup labels and Liz Taylor and Marilyn Monroe into his art. The avante-garde is dead. "Thirty years later, 40 years later, people will think they are avante-garde every time some nudnik has a thing about Madonna with elephant dung, 'Oh yeah, we are getting a rise out of the Catholic League'."

Mid-year, in another interview[115], Paglia refocused her guns on the Left's obsession with crushing Christianity.

"The only people I'm getting at my school who recognize the Bible are African-Americans," she says. "And the lower the social class of the white

114 http://www.themorningnews.org/archives/birnbaum_v/camille_paglia.php
115 http://www.thebriefingroom.com/archives/2007/07/camille_paglia.html

person, the more likely they recognize the Bible. Most of these white kids, if they go to church at all, they get feel-good social activism."

What are they left with? "Video games, the Web, cellphones, iPods – that's what's left," Dr. Paglia laments. "And that's what's going to make us vulnerable to people coming from any side, including the Muslim side, where there's fervour. Fervour will conquer apathy. I don't see how the generation trained by the Ivy League is going to have the knowledge or the resolution to defend the West."

Our cultural crisis is precisely that serious, Paglia believes, – as does Pope Benedict, one of the most cultured men on the planet – that we could well be reliving the last days of the Roman Empire.

"If the elite class sees nothing in the West to defend, we're reproducing this situation of the late Roman Empire, which was very cosmopolitan and very tolerant, but which was undone by forces from within."

Remember, Paglia is an atheist. Her concerns, however, are that a people ignorant of where they have come from and unsure of what they believe face a major disadvantage when it comes to combating a people motivated strongly by passion and belief – like Islamists are.

So if a thinking atheist can recognize the problem, maybe we should pay some attention. Paglia thinks we need to inject the Bible back in our culture to find a bit of spine. But the Bible won't provide spine unless one believes it, and Hitchens and Dawkins give great reasons not to believe it, don't they?

Let's take a closer look at what the Antichrist's rock stars say is the smoking gun evidence that the New Testament is a crock.

HITCHENS:

1. That the New Testament documents have been "tampered with"

2. That the Gospels were not published until "many decades after the crucifixion

3. That the Gospels are full of contradictions – the flight to Egypt, the Virgin Birth, the genealogy of Christ, the Crucifixion, the Resurrection

4. That the Gospels contain proven errors – the 'Quirinius problem'

5. That the Gnostic Gospels, like Judas and Thomas, are somehow significant

6. That the very existence of Jesus Christ is "highly questionable"[116]

---

116 You'll see that these points are pretty much echoed by American author and former Christian John Shelby Spong in his latest book, *Jesus For The Non-Religious*. I won't relitigate the list, suffice to say the arguments apply against both of these authors

"The contradictions and illiteracies of the New Testament have filled up many books by eminent scholars," pontificates Hitchens, "and have never been explained by any Christian authority except in the feeblest terms of 'metaphor' and 'a Christ of faith'."

Now I see Hitchens' problem, he's been reading too much of Don Cupitt and Lloyd Geering's work! So they have "never been explained"? Christopher, read on.

Rather than a point by point rebuttal, which is frankly passé, let me take you on an epic sweep, Christianity 101 if you like, through the pages of history. During this journey, Hitchens' and Dawkins' weak challenges will be answered, and many more besides. It's a story you won't hear in a fusty little Anglican church run by a twee vicar from the liberal wing. But it's a story that needs to be told.

As you would expect in the sacred book of the world's largest religion, there are some major claims being made. The biggest claim of all, undoubtedly, is that Jesus Christ is God; that the Creator of the universe and the God of the Old Testament decided to come to Earth himself in human form, and suffer life and death in our place as a sacrifice to beat the evil loose in our world. But the Bible is a book that spans nearly 1,500 years in its writings, across 39 books in the Old Testament, and 27 books in the New. Suffice to say, over that period of time, dozens of authors were involved. Yet the finished book sings a remarkably coherent song. Despite the huge timelines and individual idiosyncrasies of the authors, it tells a very clear tale of a God who created the heavens and the earth, who interacted with his people, who tried to keep them pure enough so that Mary could eventually give birth to the saviour not just of the Jews but the entire world.

It is a story that progressively unfolds, which is as it should be given the fact that the Israelites who received the 10 Commandments with Moses were primitive herders for the most part, whilst the society that Christ was born into 1,500 years later was far more sophisticated and westernized. God did not reveal his whole plan all at once, but nor did he reveal it in a way the peasants could not understand in their day. The message had to be able to be heard and followed in 1500 BC, even if layered with extra meanings that would become clearer to later generations.

The Old Testament is not a science book written for 21st century boffins – it doesn't use modern descriptions or precise calculations when they were not needed by bronze age goat farmers. The average Jewish shepherd boy needed to know the value of *pi* like he needed rocks in his head. Thus, when describing the measurement around the edge of a circle in 2 Chron.

4:2, the Bible doesn't use the precise numbering for *pi*, 3.14159265 etc, but simply rounds the number down to 3. This is not an error, it is merely being practical. Wikipedia notes that science still rounds pi down:

"While the value of pi has been computed to billions of digits, practical science and engineering will rarely require more than 10 decimal places. As an example, computing the circumference of the Earth's equator from its radius using only 10 decimal places of pi yields an error of less than 0.2 millimeters. A value truncated to 39 decimal places is sufficient to compute the circumference of the visible universe to a precision comparable to the size of a hydrogen atom."

In other words, horses for courses.

If you want to pounce on the Bible's use of round numbers (given it was written for people who had not yet invented the decimal point) and use that as proof of error, then frankly you've missed the point. Hitchens is correct when he mutters that the Bible doesn't talk about the creation of germs in Genesis. But nor does God talk about computers or mobile phones. Much of the scientific discoveries of the world would be taking place far in the future. Had God intervened and handed advanced knowledge over on a platter, the future would have been vastly altered and you wouldn't be here to read about it.

There are areas of the Bible, however, that do evoke images of modern battles, things the ancients would not be familiar with.

"And this shall be the plague with which the LORD will smite all the people that have fought against Jerusalem; Their flesh shall consume away while they stand upon their feet, and their eyes shall consume away in their holes, and their tongue shall consume away in their mouth."[117]

I doubt that such a weapon description would make any sense to an ancient Hebrew, but from residents of Hiroshima you might get an entirely different reaction. And in case you are wondering, *that prophecy is yet to be fulfilled.*

Yes, there is a bit of hellfire and smiting in the Bible, but I'll get to that in due course.

What the Old Testament does do, however, is foreshadow the future. Almost from the very beginning, Genesis onwards, there are coded phrases and double meanings, all of them pointing towards a future Messiah. At first these codewords appear to be mere hints, but like a boulder gathering speed down a hill they pick up the pace and substance as the history of the Israelites unfolds in the pages of the Bible.

---

117 Zech 14:12

You saw in the last chapter the best that 20th century psychics and mediums have been able to offer, and it isn't that impressive.

In contrast check out the detail and specificity in the following passage from the Old Testament prophet Ezekiel, dealing with the fate of the ancient Phoenician city of Tyre, now part of modern Lebanon and called Sur (not Tyre). At the time, Tyre was a powerful city, and an unusual one in the Middle East. Its settlements stretched for about 30 kilometres along the coast, and are said to have housed some 40,000 citizens. But three miles offshore, on a fortress island surrounded by 50 metre high walls, the city grew as well. The island city had the naval power in the region, while the coastal suburbs provided the peasants, the timber and the infrastructure needed.

The Tyrians had taken advantage of strife in Jerusalem by raiding for treasure and Jews they could sell to Greek slave traders. For this, said Ezekiel, God went looking for vengeance.

A PROPHECY AGAINST TYRE[118]

1 In the eleventh year, on the first day of the month, the word of the LORD came to me: 2 "Son of man, because Tyre has said of Jerusalem, 'Aha! The gate to the nations is broken, and its doors have swung open to me; now that she lies in ruins I will prosper,' 3 therefore this is what the Sovereign LORD says: I am against you, O Tyre, and I will bring many nations against you, like the sea casting up its waves. 4 They will destroy the walls of Tyre and pull down her towers; I will scrape away her rubble and make her a bare rock. 5 Out in the sea she will become a place to spread fishnets, for I have spoken, declares the Sovereign LORD. She will become plunder for the nations, 6 and her settlements on the mainland will be ravaged by the sword. Then they will know that I am the LORD.

7 "For this is what the Sovereign LORD says: From the north I am going to bring against Tyre Nebuchadnezzar [a] king of Babylon, king of kings, with horses and chariots, with horsemen and a great army. 8 He will ravage your settlements on the mainland with the sword; he will set up siege works against you, build a ramp up to your walls and raise his shields against you. 9 He will direct the blows of his battering rams against your walls and demolish your towers with his weapons. 10 His horses will

---

be so many that they will cover you with dust. Your walls will tremble at the noise of the war horses, wagons and chariots when he enters your gates as men enter a city whose walls have been broken through. 11 The hoofs of his horses will trample all your streets; he will kill your people with the sword, and your strong pillars will fall to the ground. 12 They will plunder your wealth and loot your merchandise; they will break down your walls and demolish your fine houses and throw your stones, timber and rubble into the sea. 13 I will put an end to your noisy songs, and the music of your harps will be heard no more. 14 I will make you a bare rock, and you will become a place to spread fishnets. You will never be rebuilt, for I the LORD have spoken, declares the Sovereign LORD... 19 ..."This is what the Sovereign LORD says: When I make you a desolate city, like cities no longer inhabited, and when I bring the ocean depths over you and its vast waters cover you, 20 then I will bring you down with those who go down to the pit, to the people of long ago. I will make you dwell in the earth below, as in ancient ruins, with those who go down to the pit, and you will not return or take your place [b] in the land of the living. 21 I will bring you to a horrible end and you will be no more. You will be sought, but you will never again be found, declares the Sovereign LORD."

To understand this, first let's take a look at what actually happened to Tyre. The prophecy says God is rewarding Tyre for its treachery by bringing a series of assailants against it, like "waves" hurled in by the sea. The imagery then, is of sequential hits.

The first of these is predicted to be the Babylonians, led by Nebuchadnezzar.

According to Jewish/Roman historian Josephus, Nebuchadnezzar's troops rolled in as promised and utterly destroyed the coastal mainland suburbs of Tyre, reducing them to rubble and selling the residents into slavery and prostitution. Try as they might, however, they couldn't project their landforce power three miles out to sea where the fortress city remained. The Tyrians, getting wind of the approaching Babylonian troops, had shifted all their loot across to the island before the attack got close, meaning Nebuchadnezzar's army didn't secure jewels, gold or other commercial plunder. After a 13 year siege, the Babylonian armies gave up further military action and left, allowing the island city to continue. The mainland however was now a no-go area for the Tyrians. The prophecy about tearing down the walls and tall pillars had been fulfilled. But the ghost town was not yet a place for fishnets.

Two hundred and forty years passed, the prophet Ezekiel was long dead and his book already in print, and then in 333 BC Alexander the Great brought his armies down to Tyre.

"After conquering the mighty Persians," write theologians John Ankerberg and John Weldon,[119] "he proceeded down the coast of Palestine until he reached Tyre in 333 BC.

"Strategically, he was unwilling to continue down to Egypt while such a fortified city, containing a powerful fleet of ships, was at his rear. He knew he first had to conquer Tyre before proceeding southward, and this comprises one of the most dramatic sieges in military history. Thus, with ulterior motives, he requested from city officials permission to worship their deity, Hercules, within the city walls.

"The plan was to bring in enough soldiers to capture the city. Not unexpectedly, his request was refused. But now, even more determined to take the city, he at once set about entering its gates by the only means available to him – the construction of a causeway across the ocean.

"Alexander's soldiers were ordered to throw into the sea the very rubble and remains of Nebuchadnezzar's conquests some 200 years earlier. This was a vast undertaking, and it was necessary to use everything they could find.

"According to the second century Greek historian and governor of Cappadocia, Arrian, in *History of Alexander and Indicia*,[120] the project went well at first. But the farther out the soldiers went, both the depth of the water and the harassment by the soldiers of Tyre increased."

As Ankerberg and Weldon recount the story, you can almost see it unfolding on a movie screen in front of you.

"It is hard to comprehend the difficulties faced by Alexander. For example, from the high walls the defenders of the city could do considerable damage...occasional raids were also staged against the Greek troops, which greatly hindered their progress. This literally forced them to build two tall towers directly on the causeway for protection. The citizens of Tyre countered with a fullscale raid – even using fire ships to start the towers burning. After routing the Greeks, they then swarmed over the causeway and destroyed whatever they could.

"There were other difficulties. At one point, a great storm washed away part of the causeway."

Not to be outdone, however, Alexander called in a fleet of 220 ships

119 *Ready With An Answer*, Ankerberg & Weldon, Harvest House, 1997, p. 246
120 II, 18-20, T. E. Page [ed.] Harvard University Press, 1954

from six of the nations and cities he had conquered. With these ships guarding the causeway construction by repelling the Tyrian naval attacks, his army was finally able to complete its giant engineering project, a 3.5 mile long sea bridge from the mainland out to the fortress island. He then led his multinational army and naval force in a direct assault on Tyre.

"As Ezekiel predicted, many nations made Tyre their plunder," continue Ankerberg and Weldon. "Thus, it was only after seven full months of immense toil, in which literally the very dust of the old city was scraped from the shore and cast into the sea, that Tyre was conquered – and Alexander's army finally marched across a *200-foot wide* causeway into the island city. This occurred in 332 BC."

Say what you like about Old Testament prophets, but the book of Ezekiel has been dated to 571 BC. What are the odds of describing a series of military sieges against a named city 240 years in the future (unlike the vague names used by Nostradamus) and describing, "They will ... throw your stones, timber and rubble into the sea."? How many armies waste time deconstructing conquered cities and throwing them into the sea? None. Except for this one. The tide literally washed over what was left of the main settlement of Tyre, in its new form as a causeway and, in almost certainty, peasant fishermen would have used the new feature as a way to get their nets further out into the bay.

"I will make you a bare rock, and you will become a place to spread fishnets. You will never be rebuilt, for I the LORD have spoken."[121]

Tyre, as it was, could not be rebuilt,[122] as most of the original architecture is underwater, forming the foundations of the causeway. Successive cultures swinging through, including the Romans, have built their own towns on the ground scoured clean by Alexander, and today the area features housing scattered around the edges of the old (Roman era) ruins, and more importantly the entire causeway has been thoroughly reclaimed and built on top of. The area, incidentally, has reportedly been hit by no fewer than 11 tsunami since Alexander's time, so the waves have washed it on a number of occasions.

Certainly, the detail in many biblical prophecies dwarfs anything

---

121 From *Palestine and Syria: Handbook for Travellers* by Karl Baedeker, 5th Edition, 1912
122 For further information on the Tyre prophecy, J P Holding's analysis at Tektonics is worth perusing: http://www.tektonics.org/uz/zeketyre.html. For the sake of balance, the Infidels objections to Tyrian prophecy can be found at this site http://www.infidels.org/library/magazines/tsr/1999/2/992tyre.html , although having studied it I found it a semantic rather than substantial series of objections. For example, Farrell Till (again) complains that the mainland city was named Ushu, not Tyre. This is little more than obfuscation: as historian Katzenstein notes, Tyre was a kingdom and Ushu was its mainland supply town ("Besides the city itself, well-protected by its location on an island, the kingdom of Tyre included a strip of mainland, whose center was the town of Ushu." (Katzenstein, H.J., "The History of Tyre", 1973, p29). The reference to Tyre in the Bible, then, can refer to the city as well as the kingdom land

offered in modern psychic shows. To many, this proves another strand of the divinity code has been woven into the Bible.

One of the world's leading atheist websites, Infidels.org, naturally denies this possibility. But as you're about to see, its own back-up explanation is nonetheless an admission of the existence of God:

"They claim that the Bible is filled with recorded events that prophets foretold years and even centuries before they happened," writes Infidels' Farrell Till. "They argue that there is no way to explain how these predictions could have been so accurately made except to conclude that the Holy Spirit enabled the prophets who uttered them to see into the future. In prophecy fulfillment, then, they see evidence of God's direct involvement in the writing of the Bible.

"A very simple flaw in the prophecy-fulfillment argument is that foreseeing the future doesn't necessarily prove divine guidance. Psychics have existed in every generation, and some of them have demonstrated amazing abilities to predict future events. Their "powers," although mystifying to those who witness them, are not usually considered divine in origin. If, then, Old Testament prophets did on occasions foresee the future (a questionable premise at best), perhaps they were merely the Nostradamuses and Edgar Cayces of their day. Why would it necessarily follow that they were divinely inspired?" asks Till.

Hello?? Once you let one supernatural pixie into the room (psychic ability) you let them all in. You can't *admit* the possibility of clairvoyance (seeing the future) on the one hand, whilst *denying* the possibility that other supernatural things exist. And has he even *read* Nostradamus? I mean, most of the ancient Frenchman's quatrains read as if he'd been enjoying a long session smoking hooch before putting pen to paper:

"In the third month, at sunrise,
the Boar and the Leopard meet on the battlefield.
The fatigued Leopard looks up to heaven
and sees an eagle playing around the sun.

To see where the atheist website has hit the rocks, you first have to understand the central question: Is it possible to foresee the future? Under natural laws the answer is no.

Whilst Time is a dimension created within our universe, it appears to be a one way street. Einstein calculated that Time slows down relative to the speed you travel. Even a cyclist biking along at 30 km/h for an hour has slowed down their own reality (albeit by a nanosecond over a lifetime) compared with somebody standing still for the same hour. A person driving a car around town might have gained two nanoseconds compared to the one standing still. The faster you go, the more Time slows down for you. Thus the occupants of a spaceship traveling at the speed of light will theoretically not age at all no matter where they travel in the universe, because Time stands still at the speed of light. To observers watching the spacecraft through a giant telescope on earth, however, time will continue to pass. It will take four earth years for the craft to reach Alpha Centauri, the nearest star system. To the crew of the spaceship, it is a mere blink. They have not aged a day, let alone four years.

If the ship were to then leap to a star system 25,000 light years away, again it would be a mere blink in terms of time for those onboard. But the observers on earth would be long dead, some 25,000 years in the past.

It is for this reason that interstellar travel is considered unlikely. It too would be a one way journey – there'd be nothing left to come home to. One could set out to colonise another planet (presuming you could find one capable of sustaining life), but you could not radio back to earth for extra supplies, nor could you probably return.

But the bigger point is this: It is one thing to slow down time (by traveling on a fast-moving object). It is a totally different thing to travel backwards in time or forward in time. According to science, the future does not yet exist. It is dependent entirely on the choices and actions of every single living entity on the planet. If I choose to turn right instead of left, will I embark on a journey that changes world history? For many people throughout history the answer has been "yes".

In other words, the future is contingent on what we do in the present. There is no natural or scientific fix for this, which is one reason scientists are incredibly skeptical of claims that anyone can see into the future.

How, then, do we explain the phenomenon?

If seeing into the future is indeed possible for some people, it would be positive proof of the divinity code. And not just any god will suffice. A pantheistic deity, who essentially is the universe, is as much trapped by Time as we are, and could hardly "see into the future". The task could only fall to a deity that dwelt outside our universe, and therefore outside Time. Let me draw you an analogy as to how it might work.

Imagine the universe is a giant globe, like a planet. Imagine a spot marked X on this Time-globe, representing the moment you were born. A timeline stretches from X across to another point on the globe's surface, until it reaches a point Y, where you will die at some moment in the future. Your timeline, if you look closely at it, is intersected tens or hundreds of thousands of times by the timelines of other people in your life, even those of people you merely walk past in the street or sit next to on a train. A being outside Time looks at this globe and has the capability of spinning it around (Google Earth-style) to focus on a particular point, or a particular timeline. At whim, this being can zero in on your timeline, pick up any portion and throw it up on a giant TV screen replaying that portion of your life, even if that portion has not yet played in your life.

Only a God who dwells outside Time (and therefore outside of and not reliant on the universe) can achieve this. In real terms, only a Theistic or Deistic God could fit this particular bill. And by definition, only a Theistic God *would* do it (because a Deistic one, by definition, is not interested in humanity and certainly doesn't go around giving them visions of the future).

Farrell Till at Infidels has shot himself in both feet with his argument that successful prophecy in the Bible may be mere "psychic ability" to see the future instead. As I've just pointed out, scientifically the future has not happened yet and there can be no natural explanation for someone who sees future events successfully. A *supernatural* explanation, yes. But a natural one, no. Invoking "psychic ability" as an argument against the existence of God is fatally-flawed.

Nevertheless, Till makes an interesting point as his argument continues:

"Even the Bible recognizes the possibility that uninspired prophets can sometimes accurately predict the future:

'If there arises among you a prophet or a dreamer of dreams, and he gives you a sign or a wonder, and the sign or wonder comes to pass, of which he spoke to you, saying, 'Let us go after other gods' – which you have not known – 'and let us serve them,' you shall not listen to the words of that prophet or that dreamer of dreams, for Yahweh your God is testing you to know whether you love Yahweh your God with all your heart and with all your soul' (Deut. 13:1-3, NKJV with Yahweh substituted for "the LORD").

"By the Bible's own testimony, then, natural psychic ability could offer a perfectly sensible explanation for any example of prophecy."

Ah, no. If you read the passage Till quoted more carefully, God is issuing a warning. If a prophet's prediction of the future comes true, and that prophet doesn't give credit to God and in fact uses it as an opportunity to lead you away from God, then God help you if you take that prophet's advice. What God is really saying is that the ability to see the future is a direct gift from God, and anyone who uses it for a contrary religious purpose or for their own glory is in serious trouble.

The Old Testament was big on prophecy, but with a couple of provisos:

prophecy from God was always accurate. Prophecy from imposters was not. Prophecy from God that was misused by the prophet for their own glory would still be accurate, but the fate of the person who misused it and those who went along with him would involve slow-roasting over an eternal flame.

So the Old Testament predicts the coming of a Messiah. Unsurprisingly, people who don't believe God exists are turning over every stone they can to try and disprove the Messianic prophecies.

On the "Debunking Christianity" blogsite, a former Christian pastor turned "committed atheist" named Joe Holman, claims to have nailed Jesus Christ firmly back in his coffin by debunking what he says are key prophecies about him.

His doubts, he said, arose after reading John 19:36, "These things happened so that the scripture would be fulfilled: 'Not one of his bones will be broken'."

According to Holman, who was teaching a bible class at the time, his own Bible helpfully referenced the original prophecy back to Psalm 34:20.

"Ah, here I would be able to show the class one of the 'astounding' prophecies of Scripture that 'proves beyond a doubt' that Jesus was the Christ. What I discovered was, shall we say, underwhelming:

19 A righteous man may have many troubles,
but the LORD delivers him from them all;
20 he protects all his bones,
not one of them will be broken.

"This is certainly an inspiring verse of Scripture, but you would have to be a fool to take it as a prophecy of the Messiah. I was left in the truly awkward position of explaining to the class why John took a verse like this and wrenched it so violently from its original context."

Perhaps. But the danger for many people is that a *little* knowledge is a dangerous thing. In ex-Pastor Holman's case, he simply didn't know his Bible well enough, or alternatively he needs a Bible with better margin references. In actual fact, I would argue Ps 34:20 is not out of context at all. However, I don't need to go anywhere near it to successfully re-establish the credibility of the passage in John.

The answer he sought is actually in the Book of Numbers, 9:12. This is a passage about the Passover Lamb, the sacrifice offered at Passover each year by Jews as thanks for God delivering them from Egypt. Passover was the festival that Christ was crucified on the eve of, and in Christian terms he himself became "the Lamb of sacrifice" in place of the Passover Lamb. Anyway, the verse itself says of the Lamb:

"They must not leave any of it till morning, or break any of its bones."

The context of the verse provides a slam-dunk parallel to the crucified Christ. Just like the sacrificial lamb used at Passover, not only were Christ's bones intact, but unusually the Romans gave permission for his body to be removed from the cross before nightfall. So this particular verse speaks directly to the crucifixion events hundreds of years later.

Another of Holman's challenges is the passage in Matthew 2:23.

"And he came and dwelt in the city called Nazareth, that it might be fulfilled which was spoken by the prophets, 'He shall be called a Nazarene'." "I'm sad to say that in my 20 years as a Christian," writes 33 year old Holman, "I never realized that Matthew makes reference to a prophecy that doesn't even exist! Try as you may, you will nowhere find a place in the Old Testament where it unambiguously declares the Messiah would be a Nazarene."

At one level he is entirely right. There is no direct reference to the future Messiah doing a stint in Nazareth. But again, Holman needed to drink more deeply at the well of knowledge. Nazareth was an insignificant village in the northern province of Galilee. Quite often in the Bible, provinces and towns are used interchangeably to show nationality or residence.

So we come to a prophecy in the Book of Isaiah, 9:1.

Helpfully, this chapter actually carries the title "To Us a Child Is Born". Happy with the context? You should be. The verse reads:

"Nevertheless, there will be no more gloom for those who were in distress. In the past he humbled the land of Zebulun and the land of Naphtali, but in the future he will honour Galilee of the Gentiles, by the way of the sea, along the Jordan – The people walking in darkness have seen a great light; on those living in the land of the shadow of death a light has dawned…"

The Isaiah chapter continues, with one of the most evocative prophecies in the Old Testament:

"For to us a child is born, to us a son is given, and the government will be on his shoulders. And he will be called Wonderful Counselor, Mighty God, Everlasting Father, Prince of Peace.

"Of the increase of his government and peace there will be no end. He will reign on David's throne and over his kingdom, establishing and upholding it with justice and righteousness from that time on and forever."

Few university-accredited biblical scholars doubt that this is a Messianic prophecy. No ordinary child in Israel could ever be called "Mighty God" without invoking claims of blasphemy. Nor is it just about his name. No ordinary child would "reign on David's throne...forever". The mission given to this child, as well as the names, are thoroughly Messianic.

Nor was this prophecy tampered with after the fact by a bunch of happy-clappy Pentecostal Christians trying to re-write the Bible to suit their belief. Chapters 1-39 of the Book of Isaiah are acknowledged, even by the harshest of scholars, to date to around 700BC. The earliest physical copy we have dates from 100BC, and was found amid the Dead Sea Scrolls at Qumran.

There is no escape from the implications of Isaiah chapter 9. The Messiah would be born as a child, he would eventually rule forever, and he would spend time in Galilee, where Nazareth is. It doesn't say he will be born in Nazareth, merely that he will "honour" the region – in the same way that a famous athlete brings honour to the country they represent.

Isaiah is a fascinating prophet. He is also the source of the much debated "virgin birth" prophecy at Isa. 7:14.

"The Lord himself will give you a sign: The virgin shall be with child and will give birth to a son and [they] will call him Immanuel."[123]

Christopher Hitchens claims Isaiah's verse is taken out of context.

"Saint Matthew [bases] everything on a verse or two from the prophet Isaiah which told King Ahaz, almost eight centuries before the still unfixed date of the birth of Jesus, that 'the Lord shall give you a sign; a virgin will conceive and bear a son'[124]. This encouraged Ahaz to believe that he would be given victory over his enemies ... The picture is even further altered when we know that the word translated as 'virgin', namely *almah*, means only 'a young woman'.

"In any case," continues Hitchens, "parthenogenesis [the fertilization of a woman's egg without sperm] is not possible for human mammals, and even if this law were to be relaxed in just one case, it would not prove that the resulting infant had any divine power."

John Spong climbs in here as well. His main arguments (unsourced) are that "First, the word 'virgin' is not in the original Hebrew text of Isaiah 7:14. Second, the Isaiah text in Hebrew implies not that a woman will 'conceive', as Matthew quotes it, but that a woman '*is with* child'. Where I come from, that means she is not a virgin!"

Both Spong and Hitchens appear persuasive at first glance, but both get a number of crucial facts wrong. The word *almah*, which Isaiah used in his prophecy, is used interchangeably in the Hebrew Old Testament to

---

123   The Dead Sea Scrolls manuscripts suggest the word 'they' was inserted in this verse to describe how the people would see the child. "Immanuel" means, literally, "God with us".
124   Hitchens is quoting the King James Version translation

describe both virgins specifically, and unmarried 'maidens' – which to the old fire and brimstone Hebrews meant the same thing anyway. A maiden was expected to be a virgin or God help her!

Although modern critics translate *almah* as 'young woman', with everything that connotes in our modern promiscuous society, this would be a 180 degree shift from ancient Hebrew understanding. As the authoritative *Vines Dictionary* of ancient Hebrew and Greek words notes:

"That *almah* can mean virgin is quite clear in Song of Solomon 6:8: 'There are threescore queens, and fourscore concubines, and virgins without number'. Thus all the women in the court are described. The word *almah* represents those who are eligible for marriage but are neither wives (queens) nor concubines [lovers]…

"In Gen. 24:43 the word describes Rebekah, of whom it is said in Gen 24:16 that she was a 'maiden' with whom no man had had relations.

"Thus, *almah* appears to be used more of the concept 'virgin' than that of 'maiden', *yet always of a woman who had not borne a child.*" [my emphasis]

Hitchens believes Matthew was merely gilding the lily by using the word 'virgin' when he referred back to the Isaiah prophecy. However, Matthew was using another version of the Old Testament known as the Septuagint, which had been progressively translated from Hebrew to Greek from 250 BC onward. The Septuagint translators believed the Isaiah verse to be messianic, and they used the Greek word *parthenos*, which again means a sexual virgin, in their translation.

It is true that the ancient Hebrews had another word sometimes used to describe a virgin, *betulah*, but this was more often used to describe virility and fertility as part of the expected package. In the Isaiah 7:14 verse, the use of *almah* makes more sense bearing in mind Mary's unmarried, virginal state at the time she became pregnant via the Holy Spirit.

For the record, nowhere in the Old Testament, *not once*, is *almah* used to describe a married woman, which would be conclusive proof that the word could mean a non-virgin. Attempts by some atheist sites to link the prophecy to other women in the Bible fail, because the other women they put forward are all married and had previously borne children (and none had sons that the people referred to as "God with us"). *Betulah*, incidentally, the alleged real Hebrew word for 'virgin' if you believe the critics, *is* used in Joel 1:8 to refer to a married woman.[125]

So Hitchens' attempt to rubbish the virgin birth prophecy on the basis of the meaning of *almah* fails. You'll recall he tried appealing to the science

---

125 The Infidels website wrongly records that *betulah* is *only* used to describe 'virgins', and uses this error on their part to try and negate the intent of the prophecy on the matter, saying "parthenogenesis is not possible" for human females. In other words, he argues that God could not have made Mary pregnant because, well, that would violate a biological law which shows only a sperm can fertilise an egg. For a God who can materialize the entire universe out of nothing in a nano-second, the task of re-wiring Mary to make her pregnant would be a mere Sunday afternoon distraction. Arguments from people like Hitchens and Dawkins, that deny the possibility of God doing because it would violate a law, amuse me, evoking images of mice that roared.[126] We have laws against traffic offences as well, which are violated every day, even by the politicians who make them.

Turning to Spong's remaining point, an alleged mistranslation of the ancient Hebrew where the virgin is not apparently about to 'conceive' but is already "with child", we find the good Bishop out of his depth again.

There are two very small variations in the ancient Hebrew word *harah*, centering on the letter 'r'.

The future tense, 'will conceive' (which appears in the Hebrew Old Testament) has a vowel symbol like this underneath:

ד

The present tense, of the word, hareh, "is pregnant" is illustrated with three dots underneath instead:

∵

Sadly for Spong, that's not the version in the book. The problem, on all sides of the debate, is that the ancient Hebrews had no written vowels. The root word for 'have a baby' was written *hrh* in Hebrew, and the context supplies the meaning. When Spong makes assertions that the word definitely meant "is with child" he's either ignorant or deceiving his readers. The shade of meaning he looks for can only be proven if we know whether the vowel should have been an 'e' instead of 'a'. And we don't know that. The context suggests a virgin *will* conceive because, as Spong correctly deduces, a virgin who is now pregnant is technically no longer a virgin. Thus, his own logic shoots him in the foot.

Don't just take my word for it. The Isaiah Scroll found at Qumran as part of the Dead Sea Scrolls, and dated to at least 100 years before Christ,[127] is translated by scholar Fred Miller: "[{Behold}] the *virgin shall conceive* and bring forth a son and he shall call his name Immanuel."[128]

---

126 There is an argument from critics that Christianity 'borrowed' its myth of a virgin birth deity from older religions. I tackle that in a later chapter.

127 http://www.allaboutarchaeology.org/dead-sea-scrolls-2.htm

128 http://www.ao.net/~fmoeller/qa-tran.htm

So here we have two major messianic prophecies from Isaiah. The task of naming the Messiah's birthplace, however, falls to the prophet Micah, a generation before Isaiah, around 720BC or slightly earlier.

In Micah 5:2, God speaks through the prophet to his people and says:

"But you, Bethlehem Ephrathah, though you are small among the clans of Judah, out of you will come for me one who will be ruler over Israel, whose origins are from of old, from ancient times....

"He will stand and shepherd his flock in the strength of the LORD, in the majesty of the name of the LORD his God. And they will live securely, for then his greatness will reach to the ends of the earth. And he will be their peace."

The first and last of these three major prophecies about the Messiah, written and published 700 years before the birth of Christ, are too tough for Hitchens to tackle, so he doesn't. Richard Dawkins – ignoring the virgin birth prophecy – nonetheless tries to give the born-in-Bethlehem prophecy a crack.

"When the gospels were written, many years after Jesus' death, nobody knew where he was born. But an Old Testament prophecy (Micah 5:2) had led Jews to expect that the long awaited Messiah would be born in Bethlehem," says Dawkins.

"In the light of this prophecy, John's gospel specifically remarks that his followers were surprised that he was *not* born in Bethlehem: 'Others said, This is the Christ. But some said, Shall Christ come out of Galilee? Hath not the scripture said, That Christ cometh of the seed of David, out of the town of Bethlehem, where David was?' "

First things first. I've just shown you the Isaiah 9:1 verse that predicted the Messiah would bring honour to Galilee. The fact that some of Jesus' critics (and Dawkins) were unaware of the specific verse doesn't change the reality that it was in there, and that we have a physical copy of the prophecy pre-dating Christ's birth by 100 years.

Second point. The author of John (believed to be the apostle himself) is not going to draw attention to something if it is actually a problem for him. Clearly John was comfortable with the Bethlehem prophecy, and reporting the debate that surrounded Christ at this particular time. In many respects, the mention of Bethlehem suggests John is supporting Matthew and Luke's Gospels on the Bethlehem birth.

Thirdly, Dawkins' interpretation is misleading. The people who raised the objections were not "followers" of Jesus but those of a mind to stone him.

To be fair to the atheist websites however, there is an ongoing debate about whether the prophet Micah intended referring to Bethlehem the village, or a particular individual named "Bethlehem", who is mentioned in the book of 1 Chronicles. Let's deal with that.

The "Debunking Christianity" site claims that:

"Reading the Micah passage carefully, it refers not to a town (Bethlehem as a town didn't exist in Micah's day, as far as I know) but to a particular clan that this messiah figure would be related to (see 1 Chron. 4:1-9 for a genealogical listing of Ephrathah, the father of Bethlehem)."

Allegation 1: the town of Bethlehem did not exist in Micah's day (720BC).

This passage from the Palestinian municipality governing Bethlehem today should lay that claim to rest:[129]

"Three thousand years before the birth of Christ, Bethlehem was already known as a Canaanite settlement. Canaanite tribes who settled in Palestine, built small cities surrounded by walls for protection against the attacks of raiders. One of these cities was Beit Lahama known today as Bethlehem. So, the word Bethlehem is derived from Lahmo the Chaldean god of fertility,[130] which was adopted by the Canaanites as Lahama. In accordance with the Canaanite practice of building temples to their gods, they built a temple for Lahama on the present mount of the Nativity which overlooks the fertile valleys of the region. Walls, ramparts and other structures in different sites in Bethlehem clearly establish its Canaanite origin 3000 years before the birth of Jesus.

"Bethlehem was mentioned around 1350 BC in the Tell al-Amarna letters, from the Egyptian governor of Palestine to the Pharaoh Amenhotep III. It was depicted as an important staging and rest stop for travelers from Syria and Palestine going to Egypt. The letters also signify that it was a border city of mid-Palestine and an outpost looking out towards the desert. The Philistines had a garrison stationed in Bethlehem because it was a strong strategic point. They entered the land of the Canaanites, mingled with its people and settled in the southern coasts between Jaffa and Gaza. The Philistines had achieved military supremacy over the greater part of the country around 1200 BC, and called it Palestine.

"The narrative of the Old Testament mentions Bethlehem in the first book of the Bible when Jacob , son of Abraham , and his family were journeying to the city of Hebron passing by Bethlehem (Ephrata) (Genesis 35: 16-19). There, his wife Rachel died giving birth to Benjamin, and he buried her by the side of the Bethlehem Road where her tomb has been a

---

129   http://www.bethlehem-city.org/English/City/index.php
130   Hence the more recent association of the word *lehem* with bread, or food and produce. The word *Ephratha* means 'bountiful' or 'fruitful'

shrine to this day: "And Rachel died, and was buried in the way to Ephrath, which is Bethlehem." In that time, Bethlehem was a small, walled town erected on a hill in the northern part of the present town of Bethlehem. The name of Bethlehem (Ephrata) "the fruitful" itself suggests a pastoral and agricultural life. The tale of Ruth, the Moabite, and Boaz suggests an atmosphere of idyllic rusticity that is still obvious today (Ruth 2-4). Ruth's grandson was King David of whose lineage Christ was born."

Thank you, Palestine, I think we get the message of Bethlehem's existence loud and clear. What about the rest of the atheist websites' allegations?

Farrell Till, over at Infidels, writes:

"What many people who stand in awe of this alleged prophecy fulfillment don't know is that a person named Bethlehem was an Old Testament character descended from Caleb through Hur, the firstborn son of Caleb's second wife, Ephrathah (I Chron. 2:18; 2:50-52; 4:4)."

Important, Till argues, is the use of the Hebrew word '*lp*, which the King James Bible translates as "thousands" and the NIV translates as "clans". The Micah passage in question, just to refresh your memory, reads:

"But you, Bethlehem Ephrathah, though you are small among the clans [thousands] of Judah, out of you will come for me one who will be ruler over Israel, whose origins are from of old, from ancient times…"

This, says Till, is strong evidence that Micah was not referring to the town of Bethlehem at all, but to a clan of that name.

"The fact that the Bethlehem in this verse was described as "little among the thousands of Judah" casts serious doubt on Matthew's application of the statement. In a region as small as Judah, one could hardly speak of a town as one of "thousands," yet in terms of a Judean clan descended from Bethlehem of Ephrathah, it would have been an appropriate description for an obscure family group that hadn't particularly distinguished itself in the nation's history."

Allegation 2: Bethlehem refers to the clan, not the place.

Farrell Till overlooks a fundamental point here. If you read the Book of 1 Chronicles carefully, you'll see Till's assertion "that a person named Bethlehem was an Old Testament character descended from Caleb" probably does not stack up. It hinges on the Hebrew word *ab*, translated as "father". But whilst it did mean biological father, the word also meant "chief" or "leader" and is repeatedly used in that context in the Bible.[131]

Of the 53 references to Bethlehem in the Bible, 51 refer to the village and only two appear to refer to an individual, prefixed in both cases as "father

---

131 *Strong's Exhaustive Concordance of the Bible*, definition of *ab*

[ab] of Bethlehem". But in each case, the supposed "father" of this individual named Bethlehem is a different person. In one case it is a man named Salma, in the other it is a man named Hur. Did the alleged man named Bethlehem have two fathers? Far more likely that the proper translation of "father" in this context is "leader", which implies that Salma and Hur were both leaders of the town of Bethlehem in their respective generations.

Often, disputes over the accuracy of the Bible swing on the meanings of obscure words, and the Micah prophecy is a perfect example. You'll recall in the paragraphs above the significance of the word *'lp*, translated as "thousands" or "clans". Adding to the problem of translating ancient Hebrew is the fact that the Jews did not have any written vowels or commas before 700AD. Ths vryn vn schlrs hv t gss th mssng vwl nfrmtn s th mnng s vbl.

Kenneth Kitchen, a Professor Emeritus of Egyptology and expert on the ancient Near East, sets out a clear example of how this small Hebrew word can confuse:[132]

"In Hebrew, as in English, words that look alike can be confused when found without a clear context. On its own, 'bark' in English can mean the skin of a tree, the sound of a dog, and an early ship or ancient ceremonial boat. Only the context tells us which meaning is intended.

"The same applies to the word(s) *'lp* in Hebrew. 1) we have *'eleph*, 'thousand', which has clear contexts like Gen. 20:16 (price) or Num. 3:50 (amount). But 2) there is *'eleph* for a group – be it a clan/family, a (military) squad, a rota of Levites or priests etc...And 3) there is *'lp*, a leader, chief, or officer."[133]

Kitchen then spells out the obvious kinds of problems, many of which are cited as "errors" in the Bible:

"The question has been asked by many: Are not the 'six hundred three thousand five hundred fifty people' in such passages as Num. 2:32 actually 603 families/squads/clans, or leaders with 550 members or squads commanded? Or some such analogous interpretation of the text?

"It is plain that in other passages in the Hebrew Bible there are clear examples where *'eleph* makes no sense if translated 'thousand' but good sense if rendered otherwise, e.g., as 'leader' or the like. So in 1 Kings 20:30, in Ahab's time a wall falling in Aphek could hardly have killed 27,000 men; but 27 officers might well have perished that way. In the previous verse (29) we may equally have record of the Aramean loss of 100 infantry

---

132 *On The Reliability Of The Old Testament*, K A Kitchen, Eerdmans, 2003, p. 264
133 It is this last translation that may be why Matthew's version of the Micah prophecy differs slightly from Micah's, substituting "small among the clans" with "least among the rulers [chiefs] of Judah".

officers in one day (with concomitant other losses?), rather than the loss of 100,000 troops overall."[134]

Makes sense, really. And it illustrates the dangers of shouting "Eureka! I have found an error!" prematurely, when in fact you may be relying on the vagueness of a very ancient language written for a culture now dead.

On the weight of the evidence and the fact that Micah was making a prophetic verse, and the later claims of Christ to be that Messiah hailing from Bethlehem, the prophecy appears to have been filled.

So far then, we have seen three major prophecies regarding the future Messiah, written 700 years before Jesus was born. All of which withstand the best efforts of critics to find a hole.

Let's have a look at some others.

In 2 Sam. 7:14, God is recorded speaking to King David about a future descendant of his.

"When your days are over and you rest with your fathers, I will raise up your offspring to succeed you, who will come from your own body, and I will establish his kingdom. He is the one who will build a house for my Name, and I will establish the throne of his kingdom forever. I will be his father, and he shall be my son."

The prophet Isaiah had much to say on signs of the Messiah's arrival. In Isa. 40:3, he writes that the Messiah would be heralded in advance by a messenger, "A voice of one calling: 'In the desert prepare the way for the LORD; make straight in the wilderness a highway for our God'."

John the Baptist is the character most have in mind here, the wild man in the desert warning people to repent and turn to God. Like Jesus, there is corroborating evidence outside the Bible for his existence and the events of his life. For those unfamiliar with the story, John baptized Christ in the river Jordan and at that moment "the Holy Spirit descended on him in bodily form like a dove. And a voice came from heaven: 'You are my Son, whom I love; with you I am well pleased'."

This event, it is said, fulfilled another Messianic prophecy from Isaiah 700 years earlier, where he foretold in this brief extract from a much longer passage, "The Spirit of the Lord will rest on him".

Another Isaian prophecy, 61:1, picks up on this theme further:

"The Spirit of the sovereign LORD is on me, because the LORD has anointed me to preach good news to the poor. He has sent me to bind up the brokenhearted, to proclaim freedom for the captives and release from

---

134 Whoops, there go 50% of the postings on skeptic websites, where critics understandably have rubbished some of the seemingly ridiculous numbers in the Old Testament. I think we can consign that problem to history and move on

darkness for the prisoners, to proclaim the year of the LORD's favour."

These were the words, incidentally, that Christ used the very first time that he preached in the synagogue at Nazareth,[135] effectively declaring to his audience that he himself was the fulfillment of the prophecy.

But it was not just the arrival of the Messiah that was prophesied. Isaiah (again) wrote an epic verse that eerily foretells his final days:

3 He was despised and rejected by men,
a man of sorrows, and familiar with suffering.
Like one from whom men hide their faces,
he was despised, and we esteemed him not.

4 Surely he took up our infirmities
and carried our sorrows,
yet we considered him stricken by God,
smitten by him, and afflicted.

5 But he was pierced for our transgressions,
he was crushed for our iniquities;
the punishment that brought us peace was upon him,
and by his wounds we are healed.

6 We all, like sheep, have gone astray,
each of us has turned to his own way;
and the LORD has laid on him
the iniquity of us all.

7 He was oppressed and afflicted,
yet he did not open his mouth;
he was led like a lamb to the slaughter,
and as a sheep before her shearers is silent,
so he did not open his mouth.

8 By oppression and judgment he was taken away.
And who can speak of his descendants?
For he was cut off from the land of the living;
for the transgression of my people he was stricken.

---

135 Luke 4:17-20

9 He was assigned a grave with the wicked,
and with the rich in his death,
though he had done no violence,
nor was any deceit in his mouth.

10 Yet it was the LORD's will to crush him,
and cause him to suffer,
and though the LORD makes his life a guilt offering,
he will see his offspring and prolong his days,
and the will of the LORD will prosper in his hand.

11 After the suffering of his soul,
he will see the light of life and be satisfied;
by his knowledge my righteous servant will justify many,
and he will bear their iniquities.

12 Therefore I will give him a portion among the great,
and he will divide the spoils with the strong,
because he poured out his life unto death,
and was numbered with the transgressors.
For he bore the sin of many,
and made intercession for the transgressors.[136]

Anyone remotely familiar with the passion of the Christ will recognize the main points: Jesus was rejected by the crowd when Pilate asked them to show mercy. He suffered and was despised. He carried the sorrow of the people, and God allowed him to be tortured as part of the burden he carried. As the gospels record, Christ's body was pierced by nails on the cross, and by a Roman spear at the very end. He was crucified at Passover, like a lamb to the slaughter. He was crucified alongside two thieves (the wicked), yet laid to rest in the tomb of wealthy Joseph of Arimathea.

Remember, this passage was written hundreds of years before Christ was even born. It exists in physical copies of the Dead Sea Scrolls that pre-date Christ by a century.[136]

Another prophecy in the same vein is found in Psalm 22. At verse 1 are

---

136 Judaism now teaches that the verse is meant to refer to the State of Israel and the Jewish people's collective suffering. It cannot be, of course, because verse 53:9 states that the suffering servant has never deceived or used violence – offences the Israelites were repeatedly guilty of throughout the Old Testament. It is very significant that – prior to Christians using this verse in favour of Christ – Jewish rabbis once taught that this verse referred specifically to the Messiah. See: http://www.iclnet.org/pub/resources/text/m.sion/jmiisa53.htm

the words Jesus cried out to God from the cross:

"My God, my God, why have you forsaken me?"

Have we not all cried that ourselves at some point in our lives? And in case you are wondering, the reason Christ called it out was because he had to die on the cross as a man, not God. To achieve that, all supernatural links with Heaven were severed short time before his death. In a sense, the lights of divinity went out, and Christ found himself alone in the universe, hanging on a cross, in pain, dying as a human would die.

But the Psalm continues:

7 All who see me mock me;
they hurl insults, shaking their heads:

8 "He trusts in the LORD;
let the LORD rescue him.
Let him deliver him,
since he delights in him."

To put this prophecy in perspective, fast forward a thousand years to the moment of crucifixion, and the Gospel of Matthew, 27:41:

41 In the same way the chief priests, the teachers of the law and the elders mocked him. 42 "He saved others," they said, "but he can't save himself! He's the King of Israel! Let him come down now from the cross, and we will believe in him.

43 "He trusts in God. Let God rescue him now if he wants him, for he said, 'I am the Son of God.' " 44 In the same way the robbers who were crucified with him also heaped insults on him.

Now cut back to Psalm 22:16, dating from around 1000 BC:

16 Dogs have surrounded me;
a band of evil men has encircled me,
they have pierced my hands and my feet.

It is worth noting that crucifixion had not been invented when the Psalm was written, and wouldn't be for a good 800 years. Why would a Psalmist refer to the bizarre case of someone's hands and feet being pierced? I don't think I need to re-visit the nailing issue. Another verse in this psalm that is very intriguing is verse 14:

14 I am poured out like water,
and all my bones are out of joint.
My heart has turned to wax;
it has melted away within me.

It is intriguing for this reason. John's Gospel records that because the crucifixions had taken place on the eve of the Passover festival, the bodies of the two thieves and Christ could not be left on the cross overnight.

"Because the Jews did not want the bodies left on the crosses during the Sabbath, they asked Pilate to have the legs broken and the bodies taken down. The soldiers therefore came and broke the legs of the first man who had been crucified with Jesus, and then those of the other. But when they came to Jesus and found that he was already dead, they did not break his legs."[137]

I probably need to explain something here. Crucifixion was normally a lengthy and agonizing death, but because of the time constraints this particular series had to be shortened. The Roman way of achieving this was to break the legs of victims nailed to the crosses (and by break I mean seriously break). The aim was to ensure that the victim could no longer support his weight and would slump down (presuming the agony did not kill him), thereby suffocating him relatively swiftly as he hung there like a dead weight. It was only because Christ was already dead that the soldiers saw no need to break his legs. But just to make doubly sure he was dead, they ran him through:

"Instead, one of the soldiers pierced Jesus' side with a spear, bringing a sudden flow of blood and water."

The significance of this goes back to Verse 14 above, and is probably lost on many readers: your heart is surrounded by a sac called the pericardium. This sac contains up to half a cup of clear fluid which, to observers, would appear like water. When the soldier pierced Christ's heart he allowed the water to pour out, and being a narrow wound on a corpse hanging above the ground it would be reasonably spectacular.

Jesus, if an ordinary human, could do many things. But he could not control the manner in which he died, nor the stunning resemblance to prophecies written up to a thousand years earlier.

Dawkins, and others, don't deal with flaws in their arguments like this. Instead, Dawkins moves on to focus on Luke's account of the circumstances surrounding Christ's birth.[138]

"Luke says that, in the time when Cyrenius (Quirinius) was governor

---

137 John 19:31-35
138 *The God Delusion*, Richard Dawkins, Bantam 2006, p. 93

of Syria, Caesar Augustus decreed a census for taxation purposes, and everybody had to go 'to his own city'. Joseph was 'of the house and lineage of David' and therefore he had to go to 'the city of David, which is called Bethlehem'.

"That must have seemed like a good solution," writes Dawkins, "except that, historically, it is a complete nonsense, as A. N. Wilson in *Jesus* and Robin Lane Fox in *The Unauthorised Version* (among others) have pointed out.

"Why on earth would the Romans have required Joseph to go to the city where a remote ancestor had lived a millennium earlier?"

With the right snort of derision, Dawkins gets away with his question. But not for long. A British Museum exhibit, a papyrus dated 104 AD, describes a similar Roman census requiring citizens to return to the cities of their birth, regardless of where they were now living:

"Gaius Vibius Mazimus, Prefect of Egypt: Seeing that the time has come for the house to house census, it is necessary to compel all those who for any cause whatsoever are residing out of their provinces to return to their own homes, that they may both carry out the regular order of the census and may also attend diligently to the cultivation of their allotments".[139]

The idea in those times, particularly when people lacked surnames as we know them (you didn't really think Jesus' last name was 'Christ' did you?), was to identify a person with the location they grew up in, where their family hailed from. Thus, you have Saul of Tarsus, Jesus of Nazareth, Joseph of Arimathea or – if you were a wanderer – you'd be linked back to your father, hence John the Baptist living in the desert was initially called John, son of Zechariah.

The Romans may have been great soldiers, but they were also great bureaucrats. Administering most of the known world required the kind of public servant who took pleasure in inflicting pain and inconvenience – like modern bureaucrats, in other words. Rome could not have cared less whether they were making you go 70 miles by foot through country infested by robbers and lions: the piece of papyrus they were holding said you had to be there or you didn't pass 'Go' and went directly to jail instead.

Dawkins then has a go at what appears to be a glaring error in Luke's Gospel, the reference to a census under Quirinius as governor.

"Luke screws up his dating by tactlessly mentioning events that historians are capable of independently checking. There was indeed a census under Governor Quirinius – a local census, not one decreed by Caesar Augustus for the Empire as a whole – but it happened too late: in

---

139 Frederick G. Kenyon, Greek Papyri in the British Museum, 1907, plate 30

AD 6, long after Herod's death. Lane Fox concludes that 'Luke's story is historically impossible and internally incoherent'.

"In the December 2004 issue of *Free Inquiry*, Tom Flynn, the Editor of that excellent magazine, assembled a collection of articles documenting the contradictions and gaping holes in the well-loved Christmas story..."

Just to see the quality of Dawkins' source, we checked out *Free Inquiry's* article online, and found this:

"Roman records mention no such census; in fact, Roman history records no census ever in which each man was required to return to the city where his ancestral line originated. That's not how the Romans did things."

Wake up and smell the papyrus in the British Museum, boys.[140]

What we do know of Roman censii is this: we have papyrus records of censii taking place in 20 AD, 34 AD, 48 AD, 62 AD and of course 6 AD and 104 AD. The clue here is that they took place roughly every 14 years. Allowing for the fact that there was of course no Year 0, go back 14 years from 6 AD and you land around 8 BC, which fell during the time of Herod (he died in 4 BC). We don't have the paper records for 8 BC, but nor do we have them for a host of other years.

Luke talked of the census being an empire one, rather than just local, and there are records of Rome issuing instructions for a census in Gaul around 9 BC, and a similar one in Egypt at the same time. There were no computers, email or telephones back then, so censii usually took a long time to complete; from the time of issuing orders to finalizing counts could be years.

So a census decreed in 8 BC appears to fit the evidence nicely. It probably took months to organize and took place during 7 or 6 BC. Although technically Judea was not fully Roman, in practice the kingdom was already paying tribute to Rome by this stage, and was a Roman vassal state.[141] Herod may have had his own reasons for going along with the plan, including declining health.

But what of the Quirinius problem? Both Dawkins and Hitchens make

---

140   This same issue is raised by Spong in *JFTNR*, p. 22. But we do have evidence of Romans requiring people to return to their towns of origin. Indeed, the Gospel of Luke records that "everyone went to his own town to register". This is in the paragraph, Luke 2:1-3, that sets out the Roman decree. In the following paragraph we are told that Joseph decided to return to Bethlehem because he belonged to the line of David. It is not suggested in the brief biblical reference that the Romans were ordering Joseph to go to Bethlehem for Davidic reasons – in fact the suggestion is ludicrous because the Romans wouldn't have known Joseph's background nor cared. It appears to have been a choice Joseph made because he wished to be counted of that line. It may even be that this was the town of Joseph's birth, and the fact that Bethlehem and Nazareth were in separate Roman administrative provinces may also have been a factor. We simply are not told, so to argue the point endlessly is pointless, so to speak

141   The Roman historian Tacitus, writing in *Annals*, records that Augustus carried out a census of "the number of citizens and allies under arms, of the fleets, of subject kingdoms, provinces, taxes" etc. Key phrase in there is "subject kingdoms" – of which Judea clearly was.

much in their books of the fact that Quirinius was not made Governor of Syria until 6 AD – ten years after the death of Herod – according to the Jewish historian Josephus, therefore Luke must be wrong.

Let's deal with the Quirinius problem head on. A number of scholars now believe that problem may be solvable, and that Quirinius may have been an acting governor of the region in place of the incompetent Varus – funnily enough – between 10 and 7 BC, and that his appointment in 6 AD was his second crack at the job, albeit his first in full title, as Glenn Miller points out.

"The possibility that Quirinius may have been governor of Syria on an earlier occasion (*Chronology of the NT) has found confirmation in the eyes of a number of scholars (especially W. M. Ramsay) from the testimony of the *Lapis Tiburtinus* (CIL, 14. 3613)," records one overview of the problem. "This inscription, recording the career of a distinguished Roman officer, is unfortunately mutilated, so that the officer's name is missing, but from the details that survive he could very well be Quirinius. It contains a statement that when he became imperial legate of Syria he entered upon that office 'for the second time' (Lat. *iterum*). The question is: did he become imperial legate of Syria for the second time, or did he simply receive an imperial legateship for the second time, having governed another province in that capacity on the earlier occasion?...The wording is ambiguous. Ramsay held that he was appointed an additional legate of Syria between 10 and 7 BC, for the purpose of conducting the Homanadensian war, while the civil administration of the province was in the hands of other governors, including Sentius Saturninus (8-6 BC), under whom, according to Tertullian (Adv. Marc. 4. 19), the census of Lk. 2:1ff. was held."[142]

There are a couple more aspects to this census business. Firstly, as scholars on all sides have been forced to concede, Luke has proved extremely reliable in noting down correct historical facts throughout the two books he wrote, Luke and Acts. Much of the information, particularly in Acts, has only recently been corroborated by archaeologists. In other words, he went to the trouble of recording detail, and got those details right wherever experts have been able to cross-check. Given his attention to detail, then, we should not automatically assume he got it wrong about an early census. Secondly, there is always the possibility that a later scribe copying one of the first copies of Luke's Gospel added the piece about Quirinius in an assumptive error of their own.

However, I've saved the best till last: a very telling document is referred

---

142 http://www.christian-thinktank.com/quirinius.html

to by the Roman historian Tacitus in his Annals, and it is The Acts of Augustus[143]. This document records that the Emperor *did indeed* order a census in 8 BC.[144]

"When I was consul the fifth time (29 BC), I increased the number of patricians by order of the people and senate. I read the roll of the senate three times, and in my sixth consulate (28 BC) I made a census of the people with Marcus Agrippa as my colleague. I conducted a lustrum, after a forty-one year gap, in which lustrum were counted 4,063,000 heads of Roman citizens. Then again, with consular imperium I conducted a lustrum alone when Gaius Censorinus and Gaius Asinius were consuls (8 BC), in which lustrum were counted 4,233,000 heads of Roman citizens."

The case against Luke on the census, then, appears to be closed. A Roman imperial record, carved in stone around 15 AD, undeniably shows an Empire-wide census ordered in 8 BC which, by the time it reached the subject kingdoms of Israel was probably taking place in 6 BC. The only question left hanging is the exact status of Quirinius, but given Roman reports that he may have been an acting governor at one point we no longer have hard evidence that Luke got it wrong, especially as Luke pointedly used the word *hegemoneuontos* – "in charge of", rather than the official word for Governor, *legatus*.

Finally, after 2000 years, we are quibbling about an alleged historical mistake made in one paragraph of Luke. We assume we know more from this far away than he did. Perhaps, if it could be shown that Luke was sloppy with his facts we would be right to be skeptical. Sir William Ramsay, however, who spent 15 years trying to debunk Luke as a historian and discredit the New Testament,[145] came away singing his praises.

"Luke is a historian of the first rank . . . This author should be placed along with the very greatest of historians."

The reason for this about-turn? Luke mentions 32 countries, 54 cities and nine islands and makes no mistakes. In Ramsay's eyes, that's pretty impressive.

If you wish to read a more detailed destruction of the Robin Lane Fox book that Richard Dawkins relied on, the website is listed below.[146]

There is more evidence in favour of a 6 or 7 BC birth of Christ. Although there has been much debate about "the star of Bethlehem", one of the best

---

143 http://en.wikipedia.org/wiki/Res_Gestae_Divi_Augusti

144 http://classics.mit.edu/Augustus/deeds.html (see clause 8)

145 http://www.leaderu.com/everystudent/easter/articles/josh2.html

146 Glenn Miller, http://www.christian-thinktank.com/quirinius.html Richard Carrier at Infidels has waded in from the atheist perspective http://www.infidels.org/library/modern/richard_carrier/quirinius.html, and James Holding at Tektonics runs a comparison of both arguments at http://www.tektonics.org/af/censuscheck.html

candidates is a major conjunction of Saturn and Jupiter that began in 7 BC and occurs only once every 900 years according to astronomers.[147] Being a planetary conjunction, it moves over time, and thus could have been what guided the Magi from Persia in the first place. Secondly, being a planetary conjunction, it is the sort of sign the Magi would have been looking for. A clue to precisely this is found in Matt 2:2, where the Magi visit Jerusalem to see King Herod and ask:

"Where is the one who has been born King of the Jews? We saw his star *when it rose* and have come to worship him."[148]

This sequence of events also explains another reference that Dawkins has problems with in Matthew's Gospel – the slaughter of the innocents.

According to the Matthean account, around 18 months to two years after Christ was born, King Herod realized he'd been tricked by the Magi, and ordered the deaths of all the boy children under the age of two in Bethlehem and nearby. Joseph and Mary were warned by an angel to flee to Egypt with young Jesus in advance of this slaughter.

A birth in 7 or 6 BC not only fits the timeframe of the expected census, but it also allows time for Herod to be still alive nearly two years later and angry enough to slaughter the under-twos in Bethlehem. Herod died in 4 BC, which also fits the timing in that Joseph and Mary would not have had to spend too long hiding in Egypt.

There is no other historic mention, outside of Matthew's Gospel, of the slaughter of the innocents, but there is probably good reason for this. Firstly, Bethlehem was not a large town, and the number of children killed may have been few in number. Secondly, Herod was known for frequent acts of random cruelty, murdering members of his own family when it suited him, so an additional series of murders for no apparent reason would not necessarily merit special mention by historians.

Thirdly, given that these events happened two thousand years ago, we don't have very good archaeological records, and certainly not enough to categorically declare that just because we don't have them, this somehow proves it never happened. Only a fool would be so brazen.

Christian researcher James Patrick Holding takes a similar line:[149]

"Although much has been made of the Slaughter of the Innocents – and indeed, any such event would be tragic – there is no reason to assume that it could be considered high on the list of Herod's atrocities in terms

---

147 David A. Pardo: *A Statistical Solution to the Star of Bethlehem Problem*
http://cura.free.fr/xx/20pardo.html
148 The verse is usually translated, "saw his star in the east" but some manuscripts have "when it rose". A planetary conjunction would indeed rise.
149 http://www.tektonics.org/qt/slaughtinn.html

of scope or magnitude. How many boys aged two and under could there have been in and around the tiny city of Bethlehem? Five? Ten? Matthew does not give a number.

"Josephus says that Herod murdered a vast number of people, and was so cruel to those he didn't kill that the living considered the dead to be fortunate. Thus, indirectly, Josephus tells us that there were many atrocities that Herod committed that he does not mention in his histories – and it is probable that authorizing the killing of the presumably few male infants in the vicinity of Bethlehem was a minuscule blot of the blackness that was the reign of Herod.

"Being that the events of the reign of Herod involved practically one atrocity after another – it is observed by one writer, with a minimum of hyperbole, that hardly a day in his 36-year reign passed when someone wasn't sentenced to death – why should any one event in particular have touched off a rebellion, when others in particular, including those recorded by Josephus, did not? Herod probably died in March or April of 4 BC; the Slaughter would therefore have occurred during one of his last two years on earth, and it is ridiculous to say that the things he did in the previous 34 years – equally, if not more so, a time of political unrest among the Jews – was insufficient to incite rebellion, whereas killing a few male infants in a backwater suburb would be sufficient in comparison. (Also…it is doubtful that Josephus recorded EVERY atrocity performed by Herod; if he had, his works would be rather significantly larger!)

"The Slaughter of the Innocents, though, is something that fits in perfectly with the character of Herod. (Also, is it perhaps not too far a reach to wonder whether Herod – who had his own son assassinated – hired vigilantes of some sort to perpetrate the Slaughter, and that it was not connected to him until his death which was shortly thereafter, when it was too late for anyone to vent their anger on him?)"

But those prophecies are not the only ones dealing with Christ.

Farrell Till, at Infidels, cites what he claims is an error by Christ:

"Jesus claimed another fulfillment of nonprophecy in Luke 24:46. Speaking to his disciples on the night of his alleged resurrection, he said, 'Thus it is written and thus it was necessary for the Christ to suffer and to rise from the dead the third day'.

"That the resurrection of Christ on the third day was prophesied in the scriptures was claimed also by the Apostle Paul in 1 Corinthians 15:3-4: 'For I delivered to you first of all that which I also received: that Christ died for our sins according to the Scriptures, and that He was buried, and that He rose again the third day according to the scriptures.' In two different places, then, New Testament writers claimed that the resurrection of the Messiah on the third day had been predicted in the scriptures. Try as they may, however, bibliolaters cannot produce an Old Testament passage that made this alleged third-day prediction. It simply doesn't exist," exclaims Till.

Unless, of course, Christ was referring to Hosea 6:1-2:

"He has injured us, but he will bind up our wounds. After two days he will revive us; on the third day he will restore us, that we may live in his presence."

Another favourite on atheist websites is Jesus' parable of the mustard seed, where he says, "The kingdom of heaven is like a mustard seed, which a man took and planted in his field. Though it is the smallest of all your seeds, yet when it grows it is the largest of garden plants and becomes a tree, so that the birds of the air come and perch in its branches."[150]

The atheist sites claim this is clear proof of a mistake by Jesus, proving he could not be God, because a mustard seed is not the smallest seed in the world.

The clear qualifier in the sentence however is "which a man took and planted in his field". Christ wasn't talking about all possible seeds in the world, because again tales of the rare Brazilian tree orchid[151] would be a little esoteric to a Hebrew farmer 2000 years ago and might have led to a whole bunch of questions beginning with, "Where's Brazil?" and "What's an orchid?". Instead, he was limiting his discussion to the seeds that a farmer would ordinarily use.

These are examples of some of the objections raised by critics like Dawkins and Hitchens. They can sound dramatic when taken out of context, but don't stack up when scrutinized more closely. Of course, as the old saying goes, a lie can be halfway around the world before truth even makes it out the front door.[152]

---

150   http://dqhall59.com/parable_of_the_mustard_seed.htm (This site contains photos and descriptions of mustard plants growing wild in Israel)

151   Just as an interesting aside to this, Mark 4:31 writes the verse this way: "It is like a mustard seed, which is the smallest seed you plant in the ground". This still carries the focus of seeds normally planted in Palestine, but the distinction "in the ground" is useful because the rare Brazilian tree orchid, *Gomesa crispa*, does not grow in the ground but in the canopies of rainforests, high above the ground

152   For readers who are interested in further exploring the alleged "errors" in the Bible, see this article for some examples of the mistakes many critics make: http://www.tektonics.org/af/ebestart.html

CHAPTER 10

DID CHRIST REALLY EXIST?

"Lewis assumes on no firm evidence whatever that Jesus actually was a character in history"

Christopher Hitchens, *God Is Not Great*

I N MY TIME I'VE HEARD many conspiracy theories, but this one is the granddaddy of them all. Is it possible that Jesus Christ never actually existed? Of the more than 10,000 university-accredited New Testament scholars around the world, fewer than six would venture that Jesus Christ was a mythical character. Yet, far away from cloistered academic halls of learning, and their vast libraries of ancient texts, out on the street today there are many people who believe Christ never existed.

Much of that is down to one man, not a qualified New Testament scholar, but a qualified atheist named Earl Doherty whose 1999 book *The Jesus Puzzle* set off a buzz among the less-educated internet atheists, but generated little more than hoots of laughter from academic atheists.

Eight years later, a 2007 debate over whether Doherty's work is "notable" saw the man himself post this message on Wikipedia:

"This is ridiculous. I am generally considered to currently be the world's leading Jesus mythicist. My books and website have had a huge impact on this controversial issue and are known around the globe. And this is not "notable"?"[153]

Not only is he the "leading Jesus mythicist", he's very close to being the only one. Collectively the group could have its AGM in a phone booth and still have room for a third member.

Doherty, a historian, draws his inspiration from a Professor of the German language, George Wells, whose articles and a couple of books

---

153 For now, the quote can be found at http://en.wikipedia.org/wiki/Talk:Earl_Doherty

in the late 90s argued that Christ was not a real historical figure in the early first century but a legendary one, even in the Apostle Paul's day, who might have lived a century or two earlier.

"Wells postulates," writes Earl Doherty, "that Paul and other Christians of his day believed that "Jesus" had lived in obscurity at some unknown point in the past, perhaps two or three centuries before their time. The problem is, there seems to me to be no more evidence in the epistles that Paul has such a figure in mind than there is for his knowledge of a Jesus of Nazareth who had lived and died during the reign of Herod Antipas. Rather, everything in Paul points to a belief in an entirely divine Son who "lived" and acted in the spiritual realm, in the same mythical setting in which all the other savior deities of the day were seen to operate."

According to Doherty, Christ was nothing more than an amalgamation of a bunch of pre-Christian deity myths rolled into one.

The historian Michael Grant, an expert in Roman and Greek history and publisher of dozens of academic books and papers on the point, is scathing about the "Jesus Myth" theory:

"To sum up, modern critical methods fail to support the Christ myth theory. It has 'again and again been answered and annihilated by first rank scholars.' In recent years, 'no serious scholar has ventured to postulate the non historicity of Jesus' or at any rate very few, and they have not succeeded in disposing of the much stronger, indeed very abundant, evidence to the contrary."[154]

Regardless of the fact that few if any experts in the field believe the theories put forward by Wells and Doherty, they or their variants have taken hold in popular culture, so let's examine some of the ideas in detail.

Firstly, did Christ exist as a real, historical person?

THE EXISTENCE OF CHRIST:

The argument raised by armchair atheists is that you can't trust the Bible in anything, because it is biased. If we were to apply the same logic to all ancient historical works we'd be left with nothing to read, because most of the publishing back in ancient times was done to please people higher up the political food chain. The trick is to discern what is fact and what is padding added to flatter somebody, and that usually is not too difficult given that the same practices continue today.

So to investigate the historical reality of Christ, the New Testament documents are extremely useful. However, they are not the first piece of evidence we'll turn to. Instead, we can turn to the libraries of the Empire

---

154 *Jesus: An Historian's Review of the Gospels* , Michael Grant, Scribner, 1995

of Rome itself for proof of Christ.

Cornelius Tacitus was a Roman historian, born somewhere around 55 AD, who was commissioned to write extensive histories of the Empire. Only two of these giant works, the Annals and the Histories, survive in any form to this day. There are believed to have been 18 volumes in Annals and 12 in Histories, all of which were written by hand, which should give you some idea of the work involved. It is in Annals, which covers the period 14 AD through to the death of Nero in 68, that the first exhibit of evidence comes.[155] Here, Tacitus is discussing the infamous great fire of Rome, where Nero supposedly fiddled as his city burned and was widely suspected of having ordered the blaze in the first place. According to Tacitus, Nero was none too happy at taking the rap:

"Consequently, to get rid of the report, Nero fastened the guilt and inflicted the most exquisite tortures on a class hated for their abominations, called Christians by the populace. Christus, from whom the name had its origin, suffered the extreme penalty during the reign of Tiberius at the hands of one of our procurators, Pontius Pilate."

From the passage, it is clear there has been no Christian tampering. The tortures devised for Christian prisoners are described as "exquisite", and the group practices "abominations" in the eyes of Tacitus. The key point however is the confirmation that Christ was crucified during the reign of Tiberius by Pontius Pilate.

But as Tacitus records, Nero's tortures were designed also to shut down the early Christian religion, which appeared to be spreading like wildfire after the crucifixion:

"A most mischievous superstition, thus checked for the moment, again broke out[156] not only in Judea, the first source of the evil, but even in Rome, where all things hideous and shameful from every part of the world find their centre and become popular.

"Accordingly, an arrest was first made of all who pleaded guilty; then, upon their information, an immense multitude was convicted, not so much of the crime of firing the city, as of hatred against mankind.

"Mockery of every sort was added to their deaths. Covered with the skins of beasts, they were torn by dogs and perished, or were nailed to

---

155 http://www.earlychristianwritings.com/tacitus.html
156 Many scholars, like J.N.D Anderson in his book, *Christianity: The Witness of History*, suspect Tacitus may actually be making a glancing reference here to the reports of Christ's resurrection from the grave. The Romans had presumed that the crucifixion would be the end of it, and the gospels themselves reveal Jesus' followers scattered after he failed to prove he was God by saving himself from the Cross. However, as news began to spread of the Resurrection, thousands reportedly converted to Christ in those first few months and the religion "again broke out"

crosses, or were doomed to the flames and burnt, to serve as a nightly illumination when daylight had expired."

In case you are wondering how this was done, the Christians were dipped in pitch, tied to stakes, and set alight as "candles".

"Nero offered his gardens for the spectacle," says Tacitus, "and was exhibiting a show in the circus [Coliseum], while he mingled with the people in the dress of a charioteer or stood aloft on a car."

The gruesome displays appear to have backfired on the Roman emperor, however, based on Tacitus' evidence.

"Hence, even for criminals who deserved extreme and exemplary punishment, there arose a feeling of compassion; for it was not, as it seemed, for the public good, but to glut one man's cruelty, that they were being destroyed."

Tacitus would have been aged nine or ten when Rome caught fire. In all likelihood, he would have been a witness to the purge of the Christians after the event; certainly he would have been aware of it in a city with no newspapers but where news spread rapidly via word of mouth.

There is considerable speculation amongst academics about where he found the information on Pontius Pilate, and whether the latter may in fact have sent a report of the crucifixion to Rome as part of the routine reporting process. Others believe Tacitus, who wrote Annals around 115 AD, was probably already aware of the wider stories concerning Christ because of the growing problems the religion was causing for the Roman Empire by that time.

Whilst it is not a direct, "I myself saw Christ", eyewitness account, it is nonetheless regarded as strong evidence that Christianity was making an impact in Rome only 30 years after Christ's crucifixion, and that a man named Christ was indeed executed by Pilate during the reign of Tiberius.

Another Roman historian from the same period who refers to Christianity is Suetonius, the chief secretary to Emperor Hadrian (AD 117-138) and who therefore also had access to imperial records. In a section on Emperor Claudius, who reigned from AD 41-54, Suetonius notes:

"Because the Jews at Rome caused continuous disturbances at the instigation of Chrestus, he [the Emperor] expelled them from the city."

Critics have argued that Chrestus may not mean Christ, and of course that's an argument no one will ever get to the bottom of. But as scholar Gary Habermas notes:

"Suetonius refers to a wave of riots which broke out in a large Jewish community in Rome during the year 49 AD. As a result, the Jews were banished from the city. Incidentally, this statement has an interesting corroboration in Acts 18:2, which relates that Paul met a Jewish couple from Pontus named Aquila and his wife Priscilla, who had recently left Italy because Claudius had demanded that all Jews leave Rome."

If indeed the riots had in fact been caused by Christians, the Book of Acts would not record it as a Jewish problem in the way it has. It is reasonable therefore to suspect that Suetonius was assuming, or the source documents he was working from were assuming, that the problem was somehow connected to those troublesome Christians.

That Suetonius didn't like Christians, and was aware of the divine claims they made, is evident from another passage:

"After the great fire at Rome…punishments were also inflicted on the Christians, a sect professing a new and mischievous religious belief."

The words "new and mischievous" strongly suggest Suetonius was briefed on what Christians believed, and didn't like it.

The Jewish historian Josephus, writing as court historian for Rome's Emperor Vespasian, around 90AD, refers to Jesus Christ twice in his *Antiquities*. The first is a reference to Christ's younger sibling, James, and how Jewish priests used the death of Roman Governor Festus in 62 AD to have James executed.

"But the younger Ananus who, as we said, received the high priesthood, was of a bold disposition and exceptionally daring; he followed the party of the Sadducees, who are severe in judgment above all the Jews, as we have already shown. As therefore Ananus was of such a disposition, he thought he had now a good opportunity, as Festus was now dead, and Albinus was still on the road; so he assembled a council of judges, and brought it before the brother of Jesus the so-called Christ, whose name was James, together with some others, and having accused them as law-breakers, he delivered them over to be stoned."

Jospehus knew that the word "Christ" meant "Messiah", and his inclusion of it here was specifically to identify which Jesus (it was not an uncommon name in its day) and more to the point which James he was referring to.

Thus we have an even stronger historical record that not only did Jesus the "Christ" exist, but he had a brother named James who continued to have a profile in Jerusalem – a profile sufficient to have angered conservative Jews to stone him to death.

These days, of course, you'd have to be a member of the Exclusive Brethren distributing an election pamphlet in New Zealand or Australia to warrant such a fate.

However, whilst that is an excellent passage for illustrating the extreme likelihood that Christ did indeed walk the paths of Galilee, it is not the only reference from Josephus. The second reference is much more hotly contested:

"Now there was about this time Jesus, a wise man, *if it be lawful to call him a man,* for he was *a doer of wonderful works,* a teacher *of such men as receive the truth with pleasure.* He drew over to him both many of the Jews, and many of the Gentiles. *He was the Christ,* and when Pilate, at the suggestion of the principal men among us, had condemned him to the cross, those that loved him at the first did not forsake him; *for he appeared to them alive again the third day; as the divine prophets had foretold these and ten thousand other wonderful things concerning him.* And the tribe of Christians so named from him are not extinct at this day."

Does all of that sound like the writing of a Jewish Roman who didn't have much time for Christ? No, it doesn't to me either. This passage, known as the Testimonium Flavium, appears to have been tinkered with by Christians over the years in much the same way political parties today are caught tinkering with their Wikipedia entries.

The key phrases that academics believe have been added after the fact (interpolated) are in italics. If you take them out, you are left with:

"Now there was about this time Jesus, a wise man, for he was a teacher. He drew over to him both many of the Jews, and many of the Gentiles. And when Pilate, at the suggestion of the principal men among us, had condemned him to the cross, those that loved him at the first did not forsake him. And the tribe of Christians so named from him are not extinct at this day."

Stripped of its excesses, the passage still refers to a man named Jesus, crucified by Pilate, whose followers continue long after his death.

So was Christ a mythical figure? Christopher Hitchens seems to think so, but apart from Earl Doherty and a couple of others, he's pretty much alone.

"Some writers may toy with the fancy of a 'Christ-myth', but they do not do so on the ground of historical evidence," writes the late F.F. Bruce, the Rylands Professor of biblical criticism at the University of Manchester.

"The historicity of Christ is as axiomatic for an unbiased historian as the historicity of Julius Caesar. It is not historians who propagate the Christ-myth theories."[157]

Even George Wells, whose theories kicked off the current 'Christ-myth' resurgence, thinks it is getting out of hand:

"Doherty tells that he was launched on the path of skepticism by my own critical work, but finds that my skepticism does not go far enough. This is certainly a novel criticism for me to face."[158]

157 *The New Testament Documents: Are They Reliable?*, F F Bruce, IVP, 1964
158 http://www.infidels.org/library/modern/g_a_wells/earliest.html

Ironically, even the atheist website Infidels is distancing itself from this embarrassing theory:

"I think there is ample evidence to conclude there was a historical Jesus," writes Jeffrey Jay Lowder. "To my mind, the New Testament alone provides sufficient evidence for the historicity of Jesus, but the writings of Josephus also provide two independent, authentic references to Jesus."

Arch-liberal John Shelby Spong is another who stops well short of suggesting a mythical Christ, and in fact puts up a spirited defence of his reality:

"Jesus was, first of all, a human being who actually lived at a particular time in a particular place. The man Jesus was not a myth, but a figure of history from whom enormous energy flowed – energy that still in our day cries out to be adequately explained.

"There will always be those who, following a special agenda, begin to assert that Jesus himself was a legendary creation. I find their arguments unconvincing for a number of reasons.

"First, a person setting out to create a mythical character would never suggest that he hailed from the village of Nazareth. Yet he was known as Jesus of Nazareth and, because that village was in Galilee, he was called a Galilean. Neither label claims the sort of dignity that might commend itself to mythology. Nazareth was a small, dirty insignificant town of no notable distinction. Even people in the rest of Galilee looked down upon it…Yet despite the negative image attached to Nazareth, there is no effort in the gospels to hide Jesus' humble origins.

"If Jesus were only a mythological character, why would the mythmakers create a myth that would embarrass them? This minor detail would have been changed, I submit, if it could have been changed. It was not changed, however, because it was too indelibly a part of the Jesus memory. Nazareth was the place from which Jesus emerged. Jesus was a Galilean. Both facts vibrate with counterintuitive historicity."[159]

Spong gives other reasons as well, but you get the picture.

So the next time anyone suggests to you there's no proof that Christ even existed, you know the answer.

IS THE CENTRAL JESUS CHRIST STORY BASED ON OLDER MYTHS?

Many newspaper headlines have been captured by stories proclaiming that scholars have found Christianity is really based on much older myths. We all know that Christmas, for example, was once the pagan Winter Solstice feast, and that Easter borrows much of its rebirth symbolism from

159 *Jesus For The Non Religious*, Spong, p. 208

Eostre, an Anglo-Saxon/Germanic goddess of spring. The Catholic monk Bede, writing around 700AD, noted that the Anglo-Saxon inhabitants of England named the month of April, "Eostre". It doesn't take a rocket scientist to figure out that a Christian feast celebrating Christ's resurrection (which is always tied to the Jewish Passover and is usually in April) will be called "Easter" by illiterate peasants because that is the month it falls in. Additionally, the Church found the theme of death and resurrection easy to overlay across the top of the ancient spring goddess festival.

Does that mean that Christianity is based on older myths, or simply that it overtook them?

The evidence will show it overtook them. There's a "documentary" doing the rounds on YouTube at the moment called *Zeitgeist*, which purports to show how essential parts of the Christian story are borrowed from more ancient beliefs. How factual is it? Not very. It claims, for example, that a Roman god named Attis was crucified, lay dead for three days, and then resurrected. It claims that the deity Mithras, originally a Persian god, died for three days and was then resurrected. It claims Christianity borrowed its resurrection story from these and other pagan gods like Osiris of Egypt.

Well, first of all, let's test the historical evidence. What is the earliest physical documentation we have describing a resurrected pagan god?

"The first real parallel of a dying and rising god does not appear until AD 150, more than 100 years *after* the origin of Christianity," writes New Testament scholar Norman Geisler. In other words, standing on the sidelines watching Christianity spread like wildfire, pagan priests figured they needed a "me too!" story to match it and maintain their market share.

"If there was any influence of one over the other," continues Geisler, "it was the influence of the historical event of the New Testament on mythology, not the reverse.

"The only known account of a god surviving death that predates Christianity is the Egyptian cult god Osiris. In this myth, Osiris is cut into fourteen pieces, scattered around Egypt, then reassembled and brought back to life by the goddess Isis. However, Osiris does not actually come back to physical life but becomes a member of a shadowy underworld."

And of course, no one claims to have seen the wispy ghost of Osiris, whereas there were up to 500 sightings of the resurrected Christ, some of whom had a meal and prayed with him.

As British professor C. S. Lewis – who specialised in Greek and Roman mythology – has pointed out, the Greek and Roman accounts are clearly mythical, storytelling literature. By contrast, the writings in regard to Christ pin the details to an actual historical figure and are not written in mythic form but in a journalistic style. So essentially, no parallel to the Christian story prior to Christ. What about Attis and Mithras, then?

"*Zeitgeist* states that Attis (a Roman deity) was crucified, dead for three days and then resurrected," says Charlie Campbell, a theologian at Calvary Chapel Vista in Southern California. "This is absolutely not true to the mythological account. In the mythological story, Attis was unfaithful to his goddess lover, and in a jealous rage she made him insane. In that insanity, Attis castrated himself and fled into the forest, where he bled to death. As J. Gresham Machen points out, 'The myth contains no account of a resurrection; all that Cybele [the Great Mother goddess] is able to obtain is that the body of Attis should be preserved, that his hair should continue to grow, and that his little finger should move.' *Zeitgeist's* claims that Attis was crucified and resurrected are not only inaccurate but very misleading. And that is just the tip of the iceberg. The alleged resurrection of Attis isn't even mentioned until after 150 A.D., long after the time of Jesus."

We're left essentially with Mithras, then, as the great hope of those trying to claim that the Christ story was borrowed from more ancient religions.

"*Zeitgeist* claims that Mithras, a mythological Persian deity, was dead for three days and then resurrected. I am no scholar on ancient Mithraism," concedes Campbell, "but nowhere in any of the reading I've done on the topic has Mithras' death even been discussed, let alone *Zeitgeist's* story about three days in a grave and a resurrection. Edwin Yamauchi, a historian and author of the 578 page *Persia and the Bible* concurs. He says, 'We don't know anything about the death of Mithras'."[160]

Nor is there any reference in the Persian Mithraism to sacrificing a bull and being 'baptised' in its shed blood – the one common feature to all of Roman Mithraism. This has led to growing speculation that the two religions are totally separate, and that the Romans merely borrowed the name of Mithras to lend their new religion an air of Eastern intrigue. No archaeological artifact of Roman Mithraism has been dated earlier than around 150 AD.[161]

In other words, it is almost a certainty that Mithraism pirated key doctrines from Christianity, like this one:

"*Et nos servasti eternali* (sic) *sanguine fuso*, 'And us thou has saved by shedding the eternal blood'."[162]

Remember: Mithraism in the Roman Empire came long after Christianity, but they don't tell you that on the internet websites or books by some atheist fundamentalists.

160 *The Case for the Real Jesus*, Lee Strobel, Zondervan, p 172
161 http://www.frontline-apologetics.com/mithras.htm
162 *The Cults of the Roman Empire*, Robert Turcan, p. 226

Biblical scholar Dr Ronald Nash sums it all up:[163]

"Which mystery gods actually experienced a resurrection from the dead? Certainly no early texts refer to any resurrection of Attis. Attempts to link the worship of Adonis to a resurrection are equally weak. Nor is the case for a resurrection of Osiris any stronger. After Isis gathered together the pieces of Osiris's dismembered body, he became "Lord of the Underworld."....And of course no claim can be made that Mithras was a dying and rising god. French scholar Andre Boulanger concludes: 'The conception that the god dies and is resurrected in order to lead his faithful to eternal life is represented in *no* Hellenistic mystery religion'."

What about the virgin birth? John Shelby Spong authoritatively states (but without sourcing it) that "Virgin births were a familiar tool in the ancient world to explain the extraordinary qualities of a leader".

Zeitgeist suggests the Greek god Dionysus had a virgin birth, and Christianity stole the motif. But University of Miami history professor Edwin Yamauchi disagrees:

"There's no evidence of a virgin birth for Dionysus. As the story goes, Zeus, disguised as a human, fell in love with the princess Semele, the daughter of Cadmus, and she became pregnant. Hera, who was Zeus's queen, arranged to have her burned to a crisp, but Zeus rescued the fetus and sewed him into his own thigh until Dionysus was born. So this is not a virgin birth in any sense."[164]

Author Lee Strobel discounts the Mithras virgin birth[165] accounts as well, given that Mithras is recorded as leaping fully formed out of a rock.

"Unless the rock is considered a virgin, this parallel with Jesus evaporates."

There is a fascinating side-debate flaming all over the internet in regard to a claim by author Acharya S that an Iranian temple at Kangavar carries an inscription, allegedly from 200 BC, dedicating the temple to "Anahita, Immaculate Virgin Mother of Lord Mithras", which seems a little too convenient. No-one has so far stumped up with photos of this alleged inscription, and online Wikipedia notes "there is no historical evidence". This is probably because every other reference has Anahita and Mithras as colleagues, rather than mother and son. Cybersleuths have tracked the phrase to a 1993 essay by a student without sources. Thanks to Acharya's books the phrase is now widely quoted on atheist sites as "proof" of a virgin birth for Mithras.

---

163 *The Gospel and the Greeks: Did the New Testament Borrow from Pagan Thought?*, Ron Nash, p. 161-162
164 *The Case for the Real Jesus*, Lee Strobel, Zondervan, p. 180
165 http://www.tektonics.org/copycat/mithra.html

A check of archaeological references has so far failed to locate anything remotely like this inscription however,[166] and a Zoroastrian archaeological site offers pictures online of what is left of the Temple of Anahita, saying the inscription dedicates it to the goddess as "guardian angel of the waters".[167]

Extensive research by an Ancient Iranian Studies centre on the Anahita cult fails to make the link that Acharya S does, either.[168]

Even if it were true, however, several problems emerge. Firstly, the Isaian prophecies that the Saviour of the World would be born of a virgin through the Jewish line *pre-date* the Anahita temple by between 200 and 500 years. In other words, the concept of a Jewish Messiah to save the planet came hundreds of years before the Persian temple. Secondly, the Jews were captives in Babylon and heavily involved with the Medo-Persian conquerors of Babylon. Given the existing biblical references, it is highly conceivable that highly popular aspects of the Jewish religion such as the coming Messiah struck a chord with the Zoroastrians who adapted the Isaian and Danielic prophecies to the local scene. Thirdly, this would explain why any suggestion of Mithras being virgin-born, if indeed it genuinely exists, arose very late in the Persian myths. We know Mithras had been worshipped from around 1400 BC, but traditionally he was rock-born and we have no evidence of any virgin claims for him until this alleged temple reference that Acharya S dates to around 200 BC. Having reviewed the evidence, I think we can safely confine the Mithras "virgin birth" myth to the dustbin of history.

Zeitgeist offers up the Hindu deity Krishna[169] as "born of a virgin". Yamauchi, again, shoots it down:

"That's not accurate. Krishna was born to a mother who already had seven previous sons, as even his followers concede."

In an online essay,[170] Ronald Nash sums up the main reasons why the public can safely ignore claims that Christianity was just another mystery religion. On the death of Christ compared with other alleged saviour gods, he writes:

"The best way to evaluate the alleged dependence of early Christian beliefs about Christ's death and resurrection on the pagan myths of a dying and rising savior-god is to examine carefully the supposed parallels. The death of Jesus differs from the deaths of the pagan gods in at least six ways:

(1) None of the so-called saviour-gods died for someone else. The

---

166 http://www.derafsh-kaviyani.com/english/anahita.html
167 http://www.vohuman.org/SlideShow/Anahita%20Kangavar/Anahita-00.htm
168 http://www.cais-soas.com/CAIS/Religions/iranian/anahita.htm
169 Even more embarrassing for those who make these claims, the Hindu scriptures are written so recently that stories of Jesus Christ's crucifixion are embedded in them
170 http://www.iclnet.org/pub/resources/text/cri/cri-jrnl/web/crj0169a.html

notion of the Son of God dying in place of His creatures is unique to Christianity.[171]

(2) Only Jesus died for sin. As Gunter Wagner observes,[172] to none of the pagan gods "has the intention of helping men been attributed. The sort of death that they died is quite different (hunting accident, self-emasculation, etc.)."

(3) Jesus died once and for all (Heb. 7:27; 9:25-28; 10:10-14). In contrast, the mystery gods were vegetation deities whose repeated deaths and resuscitations depict the annual cycle of nature.

(4) Jesus' death was an actual event in history. The death of the mystery god appears in a mythical drama with no historical ties; its continued rehearsal celebrates the recurring death and rebirth of nature. The incontestable fact that the early church believed that its proclamation of Jesus' death and resurrection was grounded in an actual historical event makes absurd any attempt to derive this belief from the mythical, nonhistorical stories of the pagan cults.[173]

(5) Unlike the mystery gods, Jesus died voluntarily. Nothing like this appears even implicitly in the mysteries.

(6) And finally, Jesus' death was not a defeat but a triumph. Christianity stands entirely apart from the pagan mysteries in that its report of Jesus' death is a message of triumph. Even as Jesus was experiencing the pain and humiliation of the cross, He was the victor. The New Testament's mood of exultation contrasts sharply with that of the mystery religions, whose followers wept and mourned for the terrible fate that overtook their gods.[174]"

On the question of rebirth, he says:

"Liberal writings on the subject are full of sweeping generalizations to the effect that early Christianity borrowed its notion of rebirth from the pagan mysteries.[175] But the evidence makes it clear that there was no pre-Christian doctrine of rebirth for the Christians to borrow. There are actually very few references to the notion of rebirth in the evidence that has survived, and even these are either very late or very ambiguous."

Wrapping it up, Nash takes a pot-shot at the dodgy scholarship abounding on the internet and in popular bestselling books:

"Liberal efforts to undermine the uniqueness of the Christian revelation

---

171 *The Son of God*, Martin Hengel, Fortress Press, 1976, p. 26
172 *Pauline Baptism and the Pagan Mysteries*, Gunter Wagner, Edinburgh: Oliver and Boyd, 1967, 260ff
173 *Ortheus and Greek Religion*, W. K. C. Guthrie, 2d ed. (London: Methuen, 1952), 268
174 A. D. Nock, "Early Gentile Christianity and Its Hellenistic Background," in *Essays on the Trinity and the Incarnation*, ed. A. E. J. Rawlinson (London: Longmans, Green, 1928), 106
175 *The Gospel and the Greeks*, Ronald Nash (Richardson, TX: Probe Books, 1992, pp. 173-178

via claims of a pagan religious influence collapse quickly once a full account of the information is available. It is clear that the liberal arguments exhibit astoundingly bad scholarship. Indeed, this conclusion may be too generous. According to one writer, a more accurate account of these bad arguments would describe them as 'prejudiced irresponsibility'."

One of the biggest ironies however, is that sacred Hindu scriptures supposedly originating 5,100 years ago mention Christian Bible stories. In his book, *Divine Harmony, Christ in the Holy Books of the East,* Arvindaksha Menon translates the various stories that pop up in an ancient Hindu veda:

"Adaman [Adam] and his wife Havyavathy [Eve] are born with all the virtues, complete control of the senses and the spiritual forbearance of the mind. God creates a captivating paradise and gifts it to Adaman to live happily. Adaman reaches beneath the tree of sin in the garden, eats its forbidden fruit, tempted by Kali disguised as a snake, resulting his carnal desires come alive, which culminates in his involving in sexual intercourse with Havyavathy," says Menon. "The Bible narrates the same episode word by word in the book of Genesis."[176]

A little later, Menon paraphrases another portion of the veda:

"Then it was predicted that a master (Patriarch) will come by the name of Moosa (Moses) and his faith will spread all over the world. When the era of Kali has reached three thousand years (This is the 5095th year of that era. So it is two thousand years ago) Jesus Christ appears with the name "Easa Maseeha" [Jesus Messiah] in the land of Huna [Judah]. Here we should remember that Jesus Christ is 'Easa Maseeha' in Hebrews. At that time it was King 'Shakapathi' who ruled that land. In the mountainous terrain of Hunadesha the King's meeting with a white clad male is described thus: King Shaka asked 'May I know, who you are!'. With apparent joy that male replied, 'Know that I am the Son of God. I am born in the womb of a virgin. 'Easa Maseeha' is my well known name'."[177]

On the basis of the ancient and venerated Hindu scrolls, are we to assume that Hinduism knew 3000 years BC about Jesus Christ? Or is it more likely that because the surviving Hindu scriptures date from hundreds of years *after* Christianity, that even mighty Hinduism was borrowing the Christian story and making it its own?

But it's not just pagan gods that Christianity was falsely accused of borrowing its religion from. So too in regard to alleged pagan miracle workers.

One of these was reportedly Apollonius of Tyana, who died about 98

176 http://www.answering-islam.org/Mna/hindu.html
177 Bhavashya purana- Prathisarga parva, IIIrd part- 2nd chapter- 23rd verse. http://www.geocities.com/Athens/Olympus/6265/chap4.html

AD in Ephesus, Greece. Very little is known of Apollonius, mostly from a "biography" in the style of a modern romantic fiction novel, written by Philostratus. The author recounts how Apollonius wandered the face of the earth during the first century, working miracles and raising people from the dead. Sounds like a familiar story, and again there's a catch: the story of Apollonius was not written until 200 AD, a hundred years *after* his death and 170 years after the death of Jesus. It seems Empress Julia, wife of Rome's Emperor Septimius Severus, was researching in preparation for her own ordination as a High Priestess in Roman polytheism, and wanted to use the Apollonius stories against the increasing strength of Christianity. Scholar Jane Lightfoot speculates Philostratus may have woven a double-edged sword into the story, aimed at Rome itself as well as the Christians:

"At one point, Apollonius is brought to trial before the Emperor Domitian [note: 81-96 AD], suspicious of a man who claims to be a god. Apollonius takes an option apparently unavailable to Christ in a similar position before Pontius Pilate: confounding his captors he simply vanishes into thin air. Pagan biography has here become fantastic wish-fulfillment – an assertion of unanswerable superiority before tyrannical Rome on the one hand, and the galloping blight of Christianity on the other."[178]

Given that the story was written two centuries after Christ, it is useless to suggest that Christianity borrowed its themes from Apollonius.

Interestingly, the Wikipedia entry on Apollonius notes a reference to him as "a wandering ascetic/philosopher/wonderworker of a type *common* [my emphasis] to the eastern part of the early empire."

This is another frequent misconception raised about Christ – that he was just one of hordes of itinerant miracle workers stalking the highways and ditches of the Middle East. In actual fact, it is not true.[179]

"It is in this light that we must judge the accounts we possess of other miracle-workers in Jesus' period and culture," writes theologian A E Harvey. "We have already observed that the list of such occurrences is very much shorter than is often supposed. If we take the period of four hundred years stretching from two hundred years before to two hundred years after the birth of Christ, the number of miracles recorded which are remotely comparable with those of Jesus is astonishingly small.

"On the pagan side, there is little to report apart from the records of cures at healing shrines, which were certainly quite frequent, but are a rather different phenomenon from cures performed by an individual

---

178 *Literature in the Greek and Roman Worlds: A New Perspective.* Oliver Taplin (ed). Oxford:2000
179 http://www.christian-thinktank.com/mqfx.html

healer. Indeed it is significant that later Christian fathers, when seeking miracle workers with whom to compare or contrast Jesus, had to have recourse to remote and by now almost legendary figures of the past such as Pythagoras or Empedocles."[180]

The Christian miracles – divine, instant healings, raising people from the dead – these were things that the public had *never* seen before, not even in sophisticated Greece. Proof of this can be found in the Book of Acts, 14:8-18, where the Greeks react to the instant healing of a crippled local identity by presuming the Christians to be incarnations of no less a god than Zeus:

"In Lystra there was a man sitting who could not use his feet and had never walked, for he had been crippled from birth. 9 He listened to Paul as he was speaking. And Paul, looking at him intently and seeing that he had faith to be healed, 10 said in a loud voice, "Stand upright on your feet." And the man sprang up and began to walk.

"11 When the crowds saw what Paul had done, they shouted in the Lycaonian language, "The gods have come down to us in human form!" 12 Barnabas they called Zeus, and Paul they called Hermes, because he was the chief speaker. 13 The priest of Zeus, whose temple was just outside the city, brought oxen and garlands to the gates; he and the crowds wanted to offer sacrifice.

"14 When the apostles Barnabas and Paul heard of it, they tore their clothes and rushed out into the crowd, shouting, 15 "Friends, why are you doing this? We are mortals just like you, and we bring you good news, that you should turn from these worthless things to the living God, who made the heaven and the earth and the sea and all that is in them. 16 In past generations he allowed all the nations to follow their own ways; 17 yet he has not left himself without a witness in doing good—giving you rains from heaven and fruitful seasons, and filling you with food and your hearts with joy." 18 Even with these words, they scarcely restrained the crowds from offering sacrifice to them."

If the world had been full of genuine miracle workers, the Greeks would not have been so stunned by what they saw. It was a natural reaction to assume the power came from God.

Glenn Miller of Christian Think-Tank – the counterbalance to Infidels on the web, makes the point[181] that archaeologists and historians know of *no* miracle-working itinerants in Palestine leading up to the time of Christ:

---

180 *Jesus and the Constraints of History*: Bampton Lectures 1980, A. E. Harvey, Duckworth:1982, p 103
181 http://www.christian-thinktank.com/mqfx.html

"When we discussed several of the alleged parallels to Jesus, we noted that the period immediately before Jesus was devoid of any major or patterned miracle claims. None of the Messianic claimants of the pre-Jesus period made claims to miracles. There are no literary 'heroes' of the immediate period doing wonderful works. All the supernatural events of the period are basically oracular/prophetic. We noted that Theissen had called this one of the most skeptical periods in Ancient History.

"However, as soon as the gospel stories of Jesus get circulated – then miracles by others start popping up all over! Apollonius gets 'rehabilitated' as a wonderworker (although it doesn't actually look like it was intended to be a factual account). And these Jewish messianic claimants all start offering 'a sign' as proof of their messianic status…

"These post-Jesus messianic claimants are pre-Destruction (70 AD) and therefore are of the generation that witnessed Jesus' many miracles. Why wouldn't they be open to the miraculous after that Larger-than-Life Love? As we noted earlier, there is a high probability (argued by Theissen and others) that the miracle stories of Jesus – widely and early circulated and argued by Christians with pagans – created a 'miraculous expectation' that led to an increase in 'actual credulity' of Late Antiquity.

"Exorcism, as a category, is not represented *at all* in the pre-Christian accounts (note: seven exorcisms are ascribed to Jesus in the gospels)," says Miller.[182]

Scholar John Meier, in his book *A Marginal Jew – Rethinking The Historical Jesus*, makes the telling point that it's still very hard to find any *performed* miracles, post-Christ, either:

"It cannot be stressed too much that when Josephus polemicizes against 'false prophets' and 'charlatans' like Theudas (*Antiquities* 20.5.1 §97-98) or the unnamed Egyptian (*Ant.* 20.8.6 § 160-70; cf. *Jewish Wars* 2.13.5 §261-62), he presents them as *promising* the people signs of deliverance. Shortly before the final storming of Jerusalem a 'false prophet' promises 'signs of deliverance' and persuades many desperate Jews to flee to the temple (*J. W.* 6.5.2 §285). Josephus likewise speaks in more general terms of 'deceivers', who enticed people into rebellion by promising them that if they followed them into the wilderness, there God would show them 'the signs of deliverance' (*J W.* 2.13.4 §259; cf. *Ant.* 20.8.6 §167-68). In A.D. 73 a weaver called Jonathan persuaded the Jews of Cyrene to follow him into the wilderness, so that there he could show them 'signs and apparitions' (*J.W.* 7.9.1 §437-42). All of these popular leaders, whatever their precise agenda, are sometimes referred to by scholars as 'sign prophets'. In one sense that

---

182 http://www.christian-thinktank.com/mq6.html

is correct, since they all promise 'signs' or the equivalent thereof. But the phrase 'sign prophets' can easily lead the unwary reader astray. *Josephus never says that any of these 'deceivers' actually performed miracles.* Strictly speaking, they do not belong under the rubric of 'miracle-worker'...Thus, Jesus of Nazareth stands out as a relative exception in *The Antiquities* in that he is a named figure in 1st-century Jewish Palestine to whom Josephus is willing to attribute a number of miraculous deeds (*Ant.* 18.3.3 §63)."[183]

In his Christian Think-Tank essay,[184] Glenn Miller cites this appraisal from Werner Kahl:

"In fact, the two characteristics (being an *immanent bearer* of numinous power and having *more than one* healing miracle story attributed to it) are shared only by Jesus in the gospels and Apollonius in Philostratus' *Vita*. Since Philostratus' *Vita* dates from around 220 C.E., it is evident that the description of Jesus in the gospels is distinct from the other extant contemporary traditions of the first century C.E. insofar as the BNP's [Bearers of Numinous Power] of those stores are *transcendent* [already in heaven, saint-like] figures. Indeed, we know of *only one other case in the entire miracle story tradition of antiquity* before Philostratus' *Vita Apollonii* of an immanent bearer of numinous power, and then only in a singular version of his miracle, Melampous according to Diodorus of Sicily."[185]

So, in other words, when Richard Carrier at the atheist website Infidels says "Miracles were…a dime a dozen in this era," you know he's either got his facts wrong or he simply can't count. Especially when you consider that not one charismatic miracle-worker – *not one* – appears anywhere in recorded history in the 250 years leading up to Christ.[186] Sure, after Christ, they are indeed "a dime a dozen" (or at least they claim to be, albeit no miracles were actually performed). But not *before*. And *that* is the important bit.

Christ was making a unique claim: that he alone was God incarnate, God made flesh, who came to earth to warn all humans of an approaching Armageddon and a choice of faith they would have to make, each of them, before they died. As proof of his claim to be God, Christ performed miracles. As you've seen, no other alleged "miracle worker" in history comes close to what Christ did.

Even John Dominic Crossan, a liberal scholar of Jesus Seminar fame, admits that Christ performed "plurally attested miracles":

---

183 *A Marginal Jew – Rethinking the Historical Jesus*, John P. Meier, Doubleday: 1991, 592
184 http://www.christian-thinktank.com/mq6.html
185 *Wehner Kahl, New Testament Miracle Stories in the Religious-Historical Setting*: A Religionsgeschichliche Comparison from a Structural Perspective, Gottingen: Vandenhoeck & Ruprecht, 1994
186 http://www.christian-thinktank.com/mq6.html

"Jesus was both an exorcist and a healer...I take...A Leper Cured... and...Blind Man Healed as not only typically but *actually historical*."[187]

The significance of Christ's actions in healing people like this may be lost on us today, but British New Testament scholar Tom Wright says it wasn't lost on the Jewish authorities of Christ's time:[188]

"The evidence from Qumran suggests that, in some Jewish circles at least, a maimed Jew could not be a full member of the community.[189] In addition to the physical burden of being blind, or lame, or deaf, or dumb, such a Jew was blemished, and unable to be a full Israelite. How far this was taken in Jesus' day it is difficult to assess. But we know that at least in Qumran it was a very serious matter.

"This means that Jesus' healing miracles must be seen clearly as bestowing the gift of *shalom*, wholeness, to those who lacked it, bringing not only physical health but renewed membership in the people of YHWH.

"The effect of these cures, therefore, was not merely to bring physical healing; not merely to give humans, within a far less individualistic society than our modern western one, a renewed sense of community membership; but to reconstitute those healed as members of the people of Israel's God. In other words, these healings, at the deepest level of understanding on the part of Jesus and his contemporaries, would be seen as part of his total ministry, specifically, part of that open welcome that went with the inauguration of the kingdom – and consequently part of his subversive work, which was likely to get him into trouble."

And if it was trouble Christ was looking for, it was coming in spades.

---

187 *The Historical Jesus*, John Dominic Crossan, Harper Collins, 1992, p. 332
188 *Jesus and the Victory of God*, N T Wright, Fortress Press, 1996, p. 192
189 1QSa 2.3-11 (Vermes 1995 [1962], 121)

CHAPTER II

THE GOSPEL TRUTH

"It is sobering, too, to discover how little basis there is for many of the dates confidently assigned by modern experts to the New Testament documents"

John Robinson, *Redating The New Testament*

ALL OF THIS, THEN, IS the prelude to the main feature, the New Testament gospels. As indicated earlier, Richard Dawkins, Christopher Hitchens and John Shelby Spong all hinge their bestselling books on the claim that the gospels were written decades, perhaps 40 to 90 years, after the death of Christ.

This, argue the critics, would be sufficient time for myths and legends to build up around Jesus Christ. I lost count in the Spong book how many times he tried to emphasise that "the ablest scholars" had conclusively dated Mark, the earliest of the gospels, to no earlier than 70 AD. As was a constant problem with Spong's shocking scholarship, his claims were unsourced.[190] Matthew probably wasn't written until 90 AD according to Spong, with Luke around 100 AD and John later still. By placing the gospels this late, Spong makes a case that the virgin Mary and Bethlehem stories were fabrications made up by the gospel writers – people incidentally who probably could never have directly known Christ themselves because

---

190 In sharp rebuke, a recognized New Testament scholar, Yale graduate Luke Timothy Johnson, has this to say of Spong in his book *The Real Jesus*: "I was asked over the past few years to review a series of Historical Jesus books, and finally the volume that culminated the Jesus Seminar's first efforts...My reviews of these works were as dismissive as I could make them, since I regarded the books as representing a kind of second-rate scholarship. It was only when my review of Bishop Spong's *Born of a Woman*...stimulated a flood of outraged letters from readers who considered Spong to be an intellectual hero of the faith...that I was forced to recognize that something serious was going on culturally. I realized for the first time that this sort of ersatz scholarship was being taken for the real thing and that, more startling, the sort of stuff being purveyed by Spong was actually being accepted as the purest gospel by those who called themselves Christian

of the time separation and who were simply making up the story as they went along.

The problem with this theory is that it is wrong. Yes, it was the dominant theory a hundred years ago, but it is not the most credible any more.

The dating of the gospels falls into two camps. There are those who will not and do not believe in the possibility of prophecy. These people, when faced with verses where Christ appears to refer to the Romans trashing the Jewish temple in 70 AD, presume because of their existing bias that the relevant gospel must have been written *after* the trashing, and the words put into Jesus' mouth. It is widely agreed, by both liberals and conservatives, that the Gospel of Mark was the first one written. Liberals therefore date it to 70 AD or later because of passages like this:

"As he was leaving the temple, one of his disciples said to him, 'Look, Teacher! What massive stones! What magnificent buildings!'

" 'Do you see all these great buildings?' replied Jesus. 'Not one stone will be left on another; every one will be thrown down'."[191]

When the Romans attacked Jerusalem some forty years later, they burned the temple. The heat melted the gold inside, which ran through the cracks of the foundation stones. To get at the gold, the Romans had to tear the temple apart, literally rock by rock.

If you do not and cannot believe in the supernatural, under any circumstances, then naturally you must take the position that Mark's Gospel had to have been written after the event.

Those who are not biased in advance against possible supernaturalism have a different view. Based not so much on Mark, but on the historical and chronological detail in Luke/Acts, the second group of scholars believes Acts was written no later than 62 AD. The evidence that points to this includes:

• The last piece of chronological evidence in the Book of Acts is the reference in Acts 24:27 to the appointment of Festus, the new Roman Procurator in Judea, which we know from other sources happened somewhere between 55 and 59 AD.
• After a hearing before Festus, Paul decides to appeal to Caesar in Rome, and is shipped there under guard in the final chapters of Acts. Acts ends with Paul under house arrest in Rome for two years, but still alive.
• There is no mention in the Book of Acts of the executions of James, the brother of Jesus in 62 AD, Paul in 64 AD or the apostle Peter in 65.

191 Mark 13:1-2

Nor is there any mention of the massive crackdown on Christians by the Emperor Nero in 64 AD.

All of these things would be highly relevant to a gospel writer sensitive to prophecies of a coming apocalypse, the return of Jesus Christ and the end of the age. After all, you recall from earlier in the book that Christians were rounded up like animals, and thrown to the lions, or burnt alive covered in tar at imperial garden parties. The ensuing Roman crackdown on rebellious Jews from 66 onwards culminating in the destruction of the Temple in Jerusalem in 70 AD, and the last stand at Masada in 72 AD, would again have been an absolute must-have for the gospel writers looking to prove to their Jewish colleagues that Christ's prophecy about the destruction of the temple had come true, and that Christ was truly the Jewish Messiah. Further, the early Christians would have seen this as the start of Armageddon.

But these things are not in there, even though the gospels are full of ancient prophecies that the gospel writers have hauled in to back up what Christ said or did; so many in fact that atheist critics accuse the gospel writers of being desperate in their search of fulfilled prophecies.

So why would the dramatic events of 62 AD onwards not appear? The most logical reason is that the events had not happened when Acts was written.

Yet Acts was written *after* Luke. We know this because both books are dedicated to a patron named Theophilus, and Acts begins, "In my *former* book, Theophilus..." before briefly describing the Gospel of Luke.

So if Acts was written before 62 AD, the Gospel of Luke had to have been written even earlier, possibly in the mid to late 50s. And because, as I've already pointed out, the critics generally all agree that Mark's Gospel was published first, that means Mark may have been out in the late 40s, and certainly by the early 50s.

Lending definitive weight to this are Paul's epistles. Now this poses a problem for Spong because he is adamant in his own book that we can trust the dating on the Pauline letters – "the entire Pauline corpus, written no earlier than 50 and no later than 64".[192] Having established this, let's now turn to 1 Corinthians, which contains a number of quotations sourced directly from the gospels of Mark and Matthew. At 1 Cor. 7:10-11, for example, Paul explicitly repeats a teaching which he acknowledges is Christ's directly:[193]

"To the married I give this command (not I, but the Lord): a wife

---

192   *JFTNR*, Spong, p. 26
193   Given that, apart from his road to Damascus experience, Paul never met Christ during Jesus' earthly ministry, his insistence that this is a teaching of "the Lord" means it can only have been sourced to gospel traditions

must not separate from her husband. But if she does, she must remain unmarried or else be reconciled to her husband. And a husband must not divorce his wife."

Compare that to Christ's words in the Gospel of Mark, 10:11-12:

"Anyone who divorces his wife and marries another woman commits adultery against her. And if she divorces her husband and marries another man, she commits adultery."

Additionally, Paul cites Jesus' instructions to the disciples in Matthew 10:9 about a preacher being "worth his keep",[194] and Luke 10:8 on the requirement for disciples to eat what is given to them when offered hospitality.[195]

The Lukan reference is not sourced from Mark or Matthew, but we know that Luke accompanied Paul for parts of his journeys so could have passed on some of his own collected quotes of Jesus Christ, which would account for the unique Luke reference.

Either way, to claim as John Shelby Spong does, that the Gospel of Mark was not written until 70 AD, 15 years after Paul wrote 1 Corinthians, and six years after Paul was executed, is ludicrous. To go further and suggest that Matthew didn't get written until the mid 80s and Luke/Acts as late as 100 AD – a staggering 45 years after 1 Corinthians, beggars belief.

Spong needs to spin this yarn in order for you to believe the rest of his book. But if he is wrong about the dating of the gospels (and he is), then Spong's whole analysis collapses (and remember it has already suffered a death blow from the latest scientific data on the Big Bang and the uniqueness of Earth).

But it gets worse for Spong. In 1 Thessalonians 5:2-3, Paul writes:

"...for you know very well that the day of the Lord will come like a thief in the night. While people are saying, 'Peace and safety', destruction will come on them suddenly, as labour pains on a pregnant woman, and they will not escape."

Now compare Christ's words in the Gospel of Matthew, 24:8:

"...These are the beginning of birth pains..."

And at 24:19:

"Let no one in the field go back to get his cloak. How dreadful it will be in those days for pregnant women..."

Then, at Matt 24:42-43:

"Therefore, keep watch, because you do not know on what day your Lord

---

194 1 Cor. 9:14 "In the same way, the Lord has commanded that those who preach the gospel should receive their living from the gospel"
195 1 Cor 10:27 "If some unbeliever invites you to a meal and you want to go, eat whatever is put before you without raising questions of conscience"

will come. But understand this: if the owner of the house had known at what time of night the thief was coming, he would have kept watch…"

The 'thief in the night' line does not appear in the earliest gospel, Mark, but instead in Matthew.[196]

Crushing for Spong and his late-gospels theory, Paul's first letter to the Thessalonians is one of the earliest New Testament documents, dating to as early as 49 AD. Clearly and unequivocally, Paul had access to gospel documents or pre-gospel documents of some kind.[197] Not only that, they were documents that showed Christ as God and avenging Messiah at the Second Coming. This, incidentally, is part of the proof that the Catholic Church did not magically "invent" the divinity of Jesus in 325 AD. The divinity card was already in play virtually the moment Christ was crucified.

For pretty much the same reasons I've outlined here, the late arch-liberal New Testament scholar John A. T. Robinson (regarded as the modern inspiration for the "Death of God" movement of the sixties), and cited as an icon by Spong,[198] has come to the conclusion that all of the epistles and the gospels, even John's, must have been written prior to the fall of Jerusalem in 70 AD.[199] Which also shoots down Spong.

How much weight can be given to Bishop Spong's opinions (mostly unsourced)? Denver Seminary's Craig Blomberg, an accredited New Testament scholar with a string of academic textbooks, rather than mass market paperbacks, to his name, is dismissive.[200]

"Bishop Spong is neither trained as a New Testament scholar, nor do his writings ever read as if he's giving a representative take, even on more liberal criticism. He's just trying to debunk the whole thing, relegating virtually everything to 'myth'."

But, says Blomberg, the 'myth' idea being pushed by elderly theologians trained in the 50s and 60s is itself outdated.

---

196 Notwithstanding my own acceptance of the majority critical belief that Mark was the first gospel, I should note for the record that it was the common belief of first century Christian bishops that Matthew's Gospel was published first, in Aramaic, for Palestinian Jews, and was then furiously copied into Greek for use by the wider church. Some even claimed to have seen a copy in the original language (no fragments of an Aramaic version now exist). The Matthean gospel could in fact have been out by 40 AD, because a savage crackdown on Israel's Christians from 42 AD by King Herod Agrippa scattered many disciples who, according to the ancient sources, took Matthew's Gospel with them to preach elsewhere around the Mediterranean.
197 In a discussion on TheologyWeb (http://www.theologyweb.com/forum/showpost.php?p=684814&postcount=1), it is pointed out that Paul's mission to the gentiles began in the city of Antioch – the same city where Matthew's Gospel is believed to have originated. Thus, it makes sense to find Paul quoting Matthew, then picking up themes from the later Luke's Gospel in later letters like 1 Corinthians
198 *JFTNR*, Spong, p. 135
199 *Redating The New Testament*, John A. T. Robinson, Westminster, 1976
200 Interview with the author, Feb 2004

"In many ways they are the ones appealing to an outmoded worldview, going back to [theologian] Rudolf Bultmann nearly 100 years ago when in some of his earliest writings he talked about how modern man in an Age of Science could no longer believe in the supernatural. That's certainly not what philosophers of science are saying in the 21st century. They're leaving the question of God very much open."

One final thing here – the idea that Jesus was "voted" God by the Roman Catholic Church in 325 AD. If that was true, how then do we explain the following ancient writings?

This first is a letter to Emperor Trajan from a Roman official, Pliny the Younger, probably written around 104 AD whilst he was Magistrate of Bithynia, regarding his torturing of local Christians in an order to stamp out the religion:[201]

"They were accustomed to meet on a fixed day before dawn and sing responsively a hymn to Christ as to a god, and to bind themselves by oath, not to some crime, but not to commit fraud, theft, or adultery, not falsify their trust, nor to refuse to return a trust when called upon to do so. When this was over, it was their custom to depart and to assemble again to partake of food--but ordinary and innocent food. Even this, they affirmed, they had ceased to do after my edict by which, in accordance with your instructions, I had forbidden political associations. Accordingly, I judged it all the more necessary to find out what the truth was by torturing two female slaves who were called deaconesses. But I discovered nothing else but depraved, excessive superstition.

"I therefore postponed the investigation and hastened to consult you. For the matter seemed to me to warrant consulting you, especially because of the number involved. For many persons of every age, every rank, and also of both sexes are and will be endangered. For the contagion of this superstition has spread not only to the cities but also to the villages and farms. But it seems possible to check and cure it."

History shows Pliny was wrong in his last sentence, but nonetheless the letter provides clear proof that people were already (and another portion of his letter records these practices had been going on in his area for *at least 25 years*) worshipping Christ "as to a god".

The Emperor's response shows he knew exactly that Christ was seen as God, because the solution involved getting people to re-swear allegiance to Roman gods:[202]

"If they are denounced and proved guilty, they are to be punished, with

201 http://www.mc.maricopa.edu/~tomshoemaker/handouts/pliny.html
202 http://www.mc.maricopa.edu/~tomshoemaker/handouts/pliny.html

this reservation, that whoever denies that he is a Christian and really proves it," said Trajan, knowingly, " – that is, by worshiping our gods – even though he was under suspicion in the past, shall obtain pardon through repentance."

Then there's the evidence from mid second century Greek satirist Lucian:[203]

"The Christians, you know, worship a man to this day – the distinguished personage who introduced their novel rites, and was crucified on that account...You see, these misguided creatures start with the general conviction that they are immortal for all time, which explains the contempt of death and voluntary self-devotion which are so common among them; and it was impressed on them by their original lawgiver that they are all brothers, from the moment that they are converted, and deny the gods of Greece, and worship the crucified sage, and live after his laws. All this they take quite on faith, with the result that they despise all worldly goods alike, regarding them merely as common property."

It would be fair to say Lucian had contempt for Christians, but his description clearly shows the crucified Christ was seen as a resurrected God.

All the Council of Nicaea did in 325 AD, nearly 200 years later, was rubber-stamp what hundreds of thousands of Christians around the Mediterranean already believed. Christ was God, an expression of the Holy Trinity which, of course, Paul had been preaching on from the get-go – around 34 AD.

Bang. There goes another of Hitchens' and Dawkins' arguments

203 http://www.sacred-texts.com/cla/luc/wl4/wl420.htm

CHAPTER 12

ARE MIRACLES EVEN POSSIBLE?

"Proving a miracle requires competent diagnosis of a pre-existing organic disease. Since the faith-healing business attracts many quacks, verifying alleged miraculous healing requires more than a smiling patient"
David Clark, *In Defense of Miracles*

A FLOW-ON COROLLARY OF THE WONDER-WORKING Christ is the vexing issue of miracles. John Shelby Spong lays his cards pretty much on the table:

"Let me begin by stating my conclusion both up front and clearly," he says in a paragraph buried halfway down page 54 of his book. "I do not believe that miracles...ever happen. I also do not believe that the miracles described in the New Testament literally occurred in the life of Jesus of Nazareth or that of his disciples."

Spong grounds his disbelief in "the insights of our post-modern scientific world". Except, as you've seen in the earlier chapters of this book, the post-modern scientific world is in chaos trying to explain the miracle of the Big Bang and ultimately snarling from their corner that perhaps "a" god created the Universe but, like Elvis, he has now left the building.

Straight away you can see that Spong's appeal to science to rescue him from both God and the miraculous is now well and truly doomed. He should have written *Jesus For The Non-Religious* about thirty years ago, because it is now thoroughly out of date.

We can argue about the divinity of Jesus Christ, and the particular merits of Christianity over other religions, yes. But arguing over the existence of a God who created the Universe in a miraculous act of divine fiat is now pretty much pointless. As we've seen, when even the world's top atheist debaters are retreating on this front, lesser-equipped beings like Spong or Lloyd Geering have no hope of holding their fort.

Faced with the hard scientific evidence of a creation event, Spong's 'I don't believe that miracles ever happen' speech crumbles. He apparently knows it, because he does not address the Big Bang or the creation of the Universe in his argument against the miraculous.

What, then, is his motivation? It appears to be that old human frailty, pride.

"I do not *want* [my emphasis] to worship a God that I cannot challenge," he writes on the opening page of Chapter 1. Christian cynics would undoubtedly point out that Satan allegedly made pretty much the same comment shortly before being evicted from the heavenly realm, according to the traditional stories. Spong then continues on page 54: "I do not wish to be told that…I have to remain a child or at least childlike before a parental supernatural deity."

In other words, the whole "God is a *supreme* being" argument *offends* Spong. Examine his logic for a moment in reverse, however. Is Spong seriously suggesting that anyone on this planet, even the brightest scientific minds, come anywhere close to the intelligence and power needed to create a Universe? Is Spong really trying to compare himself favourably to a god, any god? It seems that way. He sees himself as an equal, a grown-up alongside God.

"I do not…believe in a deity who does miracles – nor do I even want such a God," he almost shouts from the page. "I do not wish to live in a world in which an intervening deity acts capriciously to accomplish the divine will by overriding the laws of nature."

It is pretty obvious from those passages that Spong's refusal to believe in miracles is not based on a lack of evidence. Even if the evidence could be proven to him, he would "not want such a God".

Spong is joined by Thomas Nagel, a philosophy professor at New York University:

"I want atheism to be true and am made uneasy by the fact that some of the most intelligent and well-informed people I know are religious believers. It isn't just that I don't believe in God and naturally, hope there is no God! I don't want there to be a God; I don't want the universe to be like that."[204]

Christopher Hitchens doesn't want that particular God to exist either, and Richard Dawkins – as we've already seen – believes only the God "Multiverse" can perform creation miracles.

This is where I have a real problem with the rise in New Atheism – the fundamentalist variety. It is not actually rational. I could not actually make the same statements in *favour* of God's existence that Nagel and Spong make against it. To me, an idea or belief is worth following only

---

204 *The Last Word*, Thomas Nagel, Oxford University Press, 1997, p. 130

if it is true. The universe is what it is. If that includes the Christian deity, then so be it. If it turns out to have no deity, then so be it. I believe in the evidence for Christianity because, rationally, I find it to be overwhelming. I did not become a Christian because I "wanted" God to exist. Nor would I embrace atheism merely because "I don't want God to exist". What I "want" appears irrelevant, even childish, as an aspiration.

Forget what any of us – you, me, Spong, whoever – *want* to believe about miracles, then. The only real, objective questions are, can they happen and do they happen?

Dawkins, for all his faults, makes an interesting point. Unlike some who believe there can be no crossover between religion and science, Dawkins clearly believes that when religions make historical truth claims, they can indeed become testable by science.

"Did Jesus have a human father, or was his mother a virgin at the time of his birth? Whether or not there is enough surviving evidence to decide it, this is still a strictly scientific question with a definite answer in principle: yes or no."

Do miracles happen, yes or no?

In December 2006, *Investigate* magazine published a "miracles" issue for the Christmas season. We chose a series of events that had been medically verified at top shelf hospitals around the world, involving named individuals. These are not 'friend-of-a-friend' stories, they are first-hand accounts from the doctors, nurses and patients involved. The following are the miracles featured in that issue:[205]

MIRACLE 1
Documented by Mayo Clinic, USA, 1981
MARLENE KLEPEES: Cured of Cerebral Palsy

Do a search on Google. Punch in the words, "cured of cerebral palsy". Of the more than four billion pages now indexed by the world's largest search engine, only 26 carry the phrase "cured of cerebral palsy", and only in the negative. One famous international author once traveled to Lourdes in France, hoping the waters would deliver him from his own cerebral palsy. They didn't, and he wrote a book about it. It is a medical condition, as the expert websites will tell you, that has no cure. Which makes the first of these miracles even more stunning:

From the moment of her birth in the early 1960s, Marlene Klepees' life was hard. Real hard. Weighing little more than a kilo at birth, this

---

205 *Investigate*, Dec 06. Additional reporting by Ken Hulme, Rick Settoon, Gorman Woodfin of the CBN Network, USA tiny child developed cerebral palsy as a result of the birth trauma. It's a condition that afflicts millions of people worldwide, to varying degrees, and is often caused by oxygen deprivation at birth or some kind of similar medical misadventure. As those affected grow older their conditions often worsen – their bodies simply refusing to obey motor commands and becoming disfigured and twisted. Muscular spasms can set in, and although the sufferer's mental capacity and IQ are unaffected they are increasingly trapped in a flesh and blood jail cell from which they can no longer even communicate.

So right from the get-go, Marlene had been dealt what many would call a dud hand. It was, however, about to get worse.

When she was just one year old, Marlene's parents were killed in a motorbike crash. Alone, afflicted and barely conscious of the world around her, the little girl was sent to live with her great-grandparents and – when they became too old to care for her – foster parents.

She remembers her school years, and that she didn't have many playmates. Children, especially in the sixties and seventies, didn't understand as much about disabilities as they do now.

But she did have some friends who cared, and when a Christian youth rally came to her Missouri hometown in the early seventies those friends took 12 year old Marlene with them. Crippled and unable to walk, the message of a Father in Heaven nonetheless resonated with the girl who'd never had the chance to know her own father. She made a decision, at the age of 12, to pray the prayer of salvation and commit her life to Jesus Christ.

"I was his, and he was my Dad," Marlene told the US Christian TV network CBN earlier this year, "and that was it, forever. I just thought that if I was born with cerebral palsy, I must be born with it because God created me that way. I didn't realize he wanted people healed. I didn't realize he wanted good things for everyone, so, at first, I just thought 'Well, there's got to be a reason for it. He's smarter than I am'."

Despite becoming a Christian, however, Marlene's condition worsened. Some of her muscular spasms during her teenage years were severe enough to leave her caregivers with broken bones themselves. Marlene became almost totally paralysed from the neck down with 'contractures' – where elastic ligaments between joints and muscles turn fibrous and rigid, resulting in permanent, claw-like deformity, and she could no longer see without the aid of very heavy corrective lenses.

In an interview with *Investigate*, she spells it out.

"I was a quadriplegic. Gosh, there wasn't much I *could* do. I could communicate some, I could see some, I could hear totally fine."

That was the frustrating part: trapped in a body where she could hear and understand everything, but communicate very little.

With what was left of her endowment money following the deaths of her family, Marlene's caregivers turned to the world's leading research hospital, the Mayo Clinic in Rochester, Minnesota, as their final hope for Marlene. Perhaps there was some new experimental drug, therapy or surgery that could give the teenager a better quality of life.

In December 1980, Marlene Klepees was wheeled into St Mary's Hospital – part of the Mayo Clinic facility, where a barrage of tests and treatments began.

But nothing worked. There was no improvement and, after four months, the money was running out. The decision was made to discharge Marlene into the care of a Missouri nursing home for the rest of her natural life – she was not yet aged 20.

In despair, Marlene remembers crying out to God in tears, thumping the arm of her wheelchair with her clawed hand. And that's when she received a vision.

"The vision," she says softly to herself as she talks to *Investigate* down a phone line from Missouri. "I first saw a young lady out riding her bike on beautiful green grass, then I saw myself inside a church. I didn't recognize the church, but I was still in my wheelchair. I had on rust-coloured corduroy pants, a striped velour shirt, there's a few people gathered around praying for me and there's one man in particular that God showed me in more detail – he was tall, blond-haired, had on a grey pin-striped suit, and then at the end of the vision in great big bold black letters it gave a date of March 29th, three weeks hence.

"I knew it was from God. There was no question I knew it was from the Lord. They were getting ready to send me back to Missouri to a nursing home, so I thought that's what was going to happen. But it didn't. And I thought I was seeing the inside of a church in Missouri, and obviously I hadn't because on the 28th of March I was still laying there in Three Mary Brigh (a ward in the Mayo Clinic's St Mary's Hospital), and nothing had changed during that period of time."

By this time, the three weeks had almost passed with no visible change in Marlene's circumstances, and the church in her vision may as well have been a million miles away. The following day, March 29, was supposed to be the day she would be healed.

"I thought that God really wanted to heal me, but there wasn't any way he was going to do it, because I really truly thought that I'd sinned or something. Because I thought, how was he going to get me to that church? I knew he could heal me but I didn't understand how he was going to get me somewhere when there wasn't anybody to get me there."

Again, she cried out in her heart to God, asking him to deliver the miracle.

"[God] spoke to me, and he said to have the nurse get the Yellow Pages and he would give the name of the church and the person who'd be praying for me. And when morning came and the nurse looked through the Yellow Pages, there was two lines that glowed off the page: Open Bible, Scott Emerson, and a phone number. And the nurse called the number and the pastor came down.

"That was probably the neatest part: the pastor went looking for several hours before he found us. The nurse had given the room number and he didn't get the room number down right and he went looking from room to room until he found us."

When the nurse opened the door, standing there was a blond-haired man wearing the grey pinstripe suit Marlene had seen in her vision.

"And then he came in, and agreed that the vision was the inside of his church. But he didn't seem anxious to take us there at all. Finally they start asking questions and he says 'Yes, our church believes in healing but we've never had any, and you plan on me starting on this one?!' "

Little wonder that Emerson was skeptical. As he looked at the racked and paralysed body facing him, he found it hard to believe that his prayer and his church could truly change Marlene's life. Especially as no one has ever been cured of cerebral palsy. But Marlene knew she would be.

"The nurse had already got a pass from the doctor and they loaded me in his car and took me to the church. It wasn't anything all that different. They pushed me up to the front, they anointed me with oil and they started to pray. I really didn't feel anything.

"They asked if I wanted to stand up on faith and I didn't know what that really meant. But when they stood me up the contractures fell out of my body, my feet hit the floor and I felt the floor for the first time in my life. Now I didn't walk pretty, it was ugly. But every lap we made the better it got.

"I don't know there was anything going through my mind except 'God is so good!' The thing that I realized, and the thing that I know, is that God didn't pick me or choose me for anything. Yes, he picked or chose me for a purpose, but my healing didn't have anything to do with the purpose of my life, it's for everyone. And I knew that. I knew it wasn't a reward for anything.

"Everything worked. There wasn't anything that didn't move. I started off pigeon-toed, but we just kept on making laps. The people praying for me understood more than I did, they were screaming and yelling and jumping. It was non-stop."

Scott Emerson, the pastor who prayed for her that day, in a little church with only seven worshippers, remembers the event as if it were yesterday.

"Her knees and her toes pointed together, and everything was pointed in," he told the CBN network. "But with each step that she took, they started to straighten out. And as her toes and her knees straightened out she got stronger and stronger. She took a few steps on her own, and then was literally running around the church."

And in case anyone is still muttering coincidence, or the power of suggestion, there's still the issue of Marlene's near blindness:

"My eyesight was healed, totally. Instant. Prior to that I wore glasses, they were thick, they were prisms. My eyes got really warm, and I took off the glasses, and instantaneously I could see. There wasn't anything I even had to do to get that to work.

"That was Sunday night. On Monday [Mayo] ran all kinds of tests on me, and on Tuesday I spoke in front of a whole bunch of doctors in this conference room. And they actually applauded when I walked in. They asked me questions and I started answering them, and I went home that afternoon.

"All of them admitted it was something greater than them. I mean, they knew it had been some form of miracle. People talk all the time about doctors not being receptive and that's just hard for me to relate to. Because I don't think there's many doctors who haven't seen a miracle."

Today, 25 years later, Marlene Klepees bears no signs of the disease that kidnapped her childhood. She rides her bike through green fields, she runs a floral business, and she tells little churches throughout America about the day God healed a cripple and let the blind see.

But it is the records from the Mayo Clinic, arguably the world's most prestigious medical research facility, that perhaps offer the last compelling word on this particular miracle:

"You returned to the rehabilitation unit that evening walking, something you'd never done since your admission to the unit. And when I saw you back at the clinic some weeks later, you'd improved even more. All signs of previous abnormality were gone. You were able to walk perfectly normal, and your eyesight had improved so much that you did not need to wear spectacles. We were all very thrilled and happy with the outcome of your condition."

MIRACLE 2
Documented by Starship Hospital, Auckland, 2001
ETHAN FALETAOGO: Cured of Leukaemia
When six year old Auckland boy, Ethan Faletaogo, went to his doctor, feeling unwell, his mother wasn't ready for the diagnosis that followed a barrage of medical tests a few hours later. Ethan, explained medics

at Auckland's Starship Children's Hospital, had acute lymphoblastic leukaemia, a particularly aggressive form of the bone marrow cancer.

"I was just a wreck, a wreck, just knowing that I had this healthy boy and then a week later finding out he wasn't healthy at all and he was going to die," remembers Ethan's mum Ripene today.

"My whole world came down. Not knowing God at that time, my sister came – who was saved – so it was a whole change."

Starship placed Ethan on chemotherapy in an effort to control the leukaemia, but the child developed complications: an opportunistic, parasitic fungal infection called rhizopus set in to his lungs. As the medical journals note, rhizopus is "usually fatal" in its own right, and in pediatric cases nearly always. It is not a common infection: in more than 15 years of operation, New Zealand's premier children's hospital had never had a case until Ethan's.

The doctors, led by pediatric oncologist Dr Lochie Teague, warned Ethan's family that survival was now touch and go. They suggested it might be time to contact a priest. To a mostly non-Christian family, the turn of events was shocking. But Ethan's auntie was a Christian, and she rang a Christian friend and asked her to come in and pray for the stricken boy.

It was the night of September 11, 2001, in New Zealand and across the world a group of Islamic terrorists claiming to represent their god were just boarding four airliners as early morning broke on America's east coast. But in Auckland, just after midnight, it was life, not death, being preached. Josephine Martin stood beside a small boy's bedside while relatives looked on, and began to pray for a real miracle. She told *Investigate* she had a vision of a large black mass in the child's lungs, and Jesus Christ showed her the mass shrinking away to nothing.

For the relatives gathered, it was a bittersweet moment. Wasn't this whole Christ business a myth? Was all this hocus-pocus just giving them false hope? Ethan's auntie turned to her sister to reassure her, remembers Ripene Faletaogo.

"She said to me, 'There is a God who knows, and who can take away your pain.'

"I just thought, 'Yeah, whatever'. I had nothing to lean on, and all I had was what the doctors were telling me, but I did turn to God and said, 'If you're real, and you really know our situation, then show me'."

But as is so often the way, Ripene's wavering faith was about to be sorely tested.

"Straight after I'd prayed, we walked into a meeting with the doctors and they told me Ethan only had between a day and three weeks left to live. Josephine [the woman who'd prayed over Ethan] was with us and she looked at me and said, 'No matter what happens, God is in control'."

Six year old Ethan, weak and close to death, then told his mother what had happened during the prayer.

"When she prayed over me, I just felt like I was walking through a long hallway, and that I was free, like I was leaving the hospital."

He then told his mother, "Don't worry Mum, God's going to heal me".

"That's when it hit me," admits Ripene now. "That was the first time I cried. I'd never cried in front of Ethan even though I saw the pain he went through and his hair falling out, his eyelashes and everything, his whole body swelling up. I saw his pain, but I never cried in front of him. That was the only time I cried – hearing Ethan say that God was going to heal him. I knew then that God was there for us.

"Three days later they went for a scan, but they had to test it so many times because the nurse had warned us the growth was likely to have swollen, but when we went into the scan it was actually gone. They kept on looking at the scans, because they couldn't understand why.

"Then they said, 'We've got good news, there's nothing there anymore'.

"They were stunned, they just didn't know what had happened. They were really unsure because they kept going back in and looking at Ethan, doing little tests and all that, but what really hit us was the nurse sitting in the room with us. She said to us, 'If you believe in miracles, you're looking at one right now'.

"But the medical staff, the excitement in their eyes. They had no idea how, and they knew at that time about our faith. I continued to share with them that we had faith in God, and it wasn't my faith but more Ethan's faith."

Not only had the rhizopus infection almost totally disappeared. So too had the leukaemia.

"The leukaemia, he'd been off treatment by then for several weeks, and when they operated on him [to confirm the disappearance of the rhizopus] they found the leukaemia had gone too."

Today, five years later, at the insistence of medics, Ethan and his mother still make six monthly visits to Starship just to check his health. Each time, it's been perfect. The same nurses are still on the ward, says Ripene.

"They just say, 'Here comes our miracle boy'."

MIRACLE 3
Documented by Aurora Medical Centre, Wisconsin, 2001
CINDY ASMUS: Cured of Parkinson's Disease
It's another one of those phrases worth Googling just for the sheer fun of seeing next to nothing turn up. Only a handful of references on the entire internet to "cured of Parkinson's", mostly referring to the future possibility

of someone like Michael J. Fox being "cured of Parkinson's" if stem cell treatment is permitted. There is currently no known cure for Parkinson's and no medically recorded case of it disappearing. Except this one.

At the age of 44, Wisconsin-based Cindy Asmus knew something was wrong.

"It would take me a really long time to try and make my fingers work. I had to think, 'I'm going to do this'. Even tying my shoe, brushing and flossing my teeth, holding onto a pen and writing were hard to do," she told CBN's miracle special.

Initially the symptoms were merely annoying. Then, after a couple of years, they degenerated into the uncontrollable tremors typical of Parkinson's. Doctors broke the bad news, and it didn't go down well with a woman who'd been a devout Christian.

"You pray all the time that God wasn't going to let this happen. It actually does get diagnosed. There's a part that thinks, 'I've been before the elders. Like his word says, I've been anointed, we've prayed and we've claimed'. Yet I was still diagnosed with it. That was hard."

For a woman who'd once been active, simple things became epic voyages of frustration.

"I was trying to put the cap back on the pen, and my brother in law was watching me trying to get it. I finally had to line my hands against the table to put the cap on the pen because it was really hard even to do that."

Like many Christians who suffer, her overarching prayer was always, 'Why me?'

Finally, after deciding she could take it no more, Cindy responded to one more offer of prayer.

"I came to church on Sunday, and the pastor had done an altar call – if anybody needed prayer, if anybody needed anything, come up. I went up to the altar and just knelt there. I said, 'God, you have got to help me because I can't deal with this anymore'. A peace started coming over me. At that time, that wonderful small voice of God came and said, 'I'm going to heal you, but it is not time yet'."

They say the Lord moves in mysterious ways, and his timing is equally so. Nothing further happened for months, until a midweek Bible study night in June 2001.

"It wasn't this big, special night that anything particular happened. We always have a prayer request at the end and we pray for needs. At the very end of that, the pastor walked over – which he had done so many times before – and prayed for this illness to leave.

"As he started praying, it was like I began to shake a little bit more. I don't even know how long we prayed. All of a sudden, everything stopped, every bit of shaking stopped. All I kept thinking was, 'I'm not shaking. I'm not shaking anymore'. That's all I kept thinking because I hadn't been able to still my hands in months.

"It was so unreal to just sit there and be still and not have any part of my body move."

Today, Cindy Asmus' life has returned to normal: shoelaces, stairs, writing, eating – none of those mundane tasks pose a challenge anymore.

Investigate spoke to Dr Eric Duwell, Cindy's physician in Wisconsin, who confirmed the CBN report on her case was accurate.

MIRACLE 4
Documented by Vanderbilt Children's Hospital, Tennessee, 2004
ETHAN STACY: Cured of Leukaemia

Another Ethan, another documented medical miracle. In this case, newborn Ethan Stacy developed acute myelogenous leukaemia, a particularly nasty strain of the bone marrow cancer similar to the one that hit New Zealand's Ethan Faletaogo. Barely three weeks old, Ethan's parents Mandy and Chad had to do what no parent should have to – find a burial plot for their baby son in a Nashville cemetery. As they walked between the gravestones on their grim task, back at Vanderbilt Children's Hospital their tiny son was already in the care of a hospice nurse, his body in the final stages of shutting down.

Speaking to *Investigate* at the end of a late shift, Dr Melissa Rhodes, one of the lead pediatric oncologists on his case, again confirms the CBN network story we're chasing was accurate.

As she explained to CBN: "Children who are actually born with leukaemia don't usually do very well. The best that we could offer was to put Ethan through difficult chemotherapy and still not know that he would make it through."

For Ethan's parents, it was an agonizing choice. Doctors confirmed the chemotherapy was so toxic to newborns it could actually make his survival chances harder.

"We came home and I remember lying in bed and praying," Mandy told CBN. "We said 'God, give us an answer'. We both woke up the next morning and both said, 'Nope, we're not going to put him through it'.

And so, with the agreement of the medical team, Chad and Mandy took their critically ill son home to whatever fate awaited him. But again, things were about to go from bad to worse.

A case of baby spots – common in newborns – flared up because of the leukaemia and the spots themselves turned into skin tumours.

"Leukaemia itself means cancer of the blood," Dr Rhodes told CBN. "But in this particular kind of leukaemia it can also go out into the tissues. That's what we believe was happening with Ethan. He actually had leukaemia in his skin, in his hands, his feet and his legs, as well as in his liver and spleen which is more common. So he was showing that he had a very advanced disease at that point."

There was little that could be done, the hospital advised, and his parents continued to nurse him at home. Ethan stopped eating as his life force began to ebb away before his parents' eyes.

"[The nurse] told me that he might develop what's called sepsis, which would be a total body infection, and that he would go peacefully or he might haemorrhage," his mother told the network. "I would see blood in his diaper or maybe coming out of his ears. I was so scared to open up his diaper to even change it."

The hospice team arrived at the house to take over Ethan's care – a sure sign the end was nigh for Mandy and Chad's darling baby boy, but through a mother's tears the words of a Christian song came to mind.

"I remember rocking him and singing, 'Open the eyes of my heart, Lord. I want to see you'. I knew that if I just focused my mind on Christ that's the only way I could make it through."

It wasn't so much a prayer as a final, desperate cry from the heart as Mandy struggled to hold on to what was slipping away. And looking back, she's convinced that's when God heard her and stepped in.

Later that evening, Ethan's appetite returned. Just little sips, but it was enough to give his parents hope.

"I remember sitting at the kitchen table and saying, 'I believe God's healing him. I can see God working'. Then he just gradually started getting better. And over the next week, we were back up to six ounces of formula every three hours," says Mandy.

The hospital called Ethan back in to double check what was happening with his leukaemia. When the test results came through at Vanderbilt Children's Hospital, the medics were staggered. Despite having terminal blood cancer, Ethan's platelets count had recovered to 415,000 – normal range – from a low of 39,000 when he'd been sent home to die.

Dr Rhodes admits it was a surprise.

"Ethan had gotten about as sick as a baby could possibly get and then spontaneously got better. So we wanted to look. We did the bone marrow test, which showed no evidence of leukaemia. The tumours gradually went down over a period of probably a week or so. It was just remarkable to witness it."

Speaking to *Investigate* about those events, Dr Rhodes says Ethan's recovery was indeed miraculous, and while in his case there is a possible scientific explanation – even that would defy current medical knowledge.

We asked about the possible scientific explanation.

"When babies with Down Syndrome are born," says Rhodes, "they sometimes have a condition called Transient MyeloDysplasia (TMD). TMD looks just like acute leukemia- high white blood cell count with "blasts", low red blood cell count, low platelet count, and the babies can get quite sick. If you do a bone marrow biopsy, it looks and tests like leukemia.

"With TMD, doctors watch and wait and many times it goes away. If the baby gets too sick, you have to treat it with chemo like regular leukemia. Babies who have TMD with spontaneous remission have a 25-35% chance of developing true leukemia, usually within the first few years of life. The remainder do fine.

"TMD is known *only* to occur in children with Down's Syndrome. Ethan does not have Down Syndrome, so he was diagnosed with acute leukemia, not with TMD. His leukemia acted like TMD, except most babies with Down's Syndrome we would have given a bit of chemo when they got as sick as Ethan got (they have an ok prognosis if you get them through the rough spell). The prognosis of congenital leukemia is very poor, so we did not push Ethan's family to treat. When he got better spontaneously, we wondered if his true diagnosis was TMD, but as I said, he does not have any evidence of Down's Syndrome."

Given that Ethan received no chemotherapy at all, and didn't have Down's, Dr Rhodes concedes that the only possible medical explanation isn't very convincing, even to doctors.

"You can see why it is a bit complicated and why it is not such a great scientific explanation that it diminishes the miracle of his recovery."

Today, Ethan Stacy is nearly three years old, and in perfect health.

MIRACLE 5
Documented by Children's Hospital of Pittsburgh, USA, 1999
LOGAN KNUPP: Cured of Multiple Cancers

At eight months of age, Logan Knupp was just like any other baby boy: the apple of his parents' eyes. When Alan and Lisa Knupp noticed their son starting to get cross-eyed from time to time, they initially didn't realize it was serious. But a series of tests at Pittsburgh's Children's Hospital soon put paid to that.

"When they told us, 'Don't plan his first birthday', they were being honest," Lisa Knupp told the CBN network in the States.

"When you're first told that it's a cancerous tumour, your mind automatically says…he's going to die," says father Alan.

Surgeons explained that tiny Logan had a golf-ball sized tumour on his brain, and that they would try to operate to save the infant's life the next day. That evening, beside Logan's hospital bed, Lisa Knupp believes an angel came to the doorway in the soft twilight of a darkened children's ward.

"I didn't see a face. It was just an outline. All I heard was, 'You're going to see a miracle.' I know it was an angel. It was all this bright light, and you couldn't see a face."

As Logan emerged from the theatre the next day, there was good news and bad. He'd survived the operation and the brain tumour had been removed. But the cancer was malignant and had already spread. In medical terms it was a metastatic tumour called a glioma, nearly always fatal.

Pediatric oncologist Regina Jakacki, one of America's leading doctors in her field chosen to head National Institutes of Health medical studies, took the Knupps through the diagnosis, showing them the MRI scans.

"This large mass is the tumour," she explained. "You can see it best coating the brain stem here where this thick white is coating the front part of the brain stem."

Another MRI scan followed, and Dr Jakacki confirmed the worst: the tumour had spread the entire length of baby Logan's spinal cord.

"Normally there is dark around the entire outside of the cord. You see this white, lumpy stuff in front surrounding the cord going all the way down – that's all tumour."

For Lisa and Alan Knupp, the angel's reassuring promise suddenly seemed a long, long way away.

"I can remember, I have three older brothers, and they were in the hallway," Alan told CBN. "They just held me up and cried with me. I thought it was the end. I mean, I thought it was just a matter of days until he died."

"I felt like the walls had just caved in," says Lisa. "I hit rock bottom, like the whole world just stopped. Everything stopped."

Doctors warned the family to prepare for the inevitable.

"The prognosis for cure was slim to none," says Dr Jakacki. "The prognosis is very bad when you have a child whose tumour has spread and you can't use radiation without damaging the brain to the point it's not worth doing it."

After a crisis meeting, they opted to give Logan a low dose of chemotherapy, the first of what would be many at the rate of one a month.

Because Logan's tumour was "very aggressive", there was a danger it would actually grow bigger by feeding on the chemotherapy itself.

"We don't want to give a lot of chemotherapy if it's not going to work," says Dr Jakacki.

Then, in echoes of Starship Hospital's Ethan Faletaogo, the family turned to their church and a Christian woman named Marty who prayed for baby Logan.

"There was an overwhelming awareness that God was healing him right then," Marty told CBN. "As I prayed, I actually was aware that God was literally severing this cancer. I saw him lay an ax to the base of the cancer, and the tumour was being totally severed, totally destroyed."

The next morning, Logan was due for another MRI scan, but the results astounded the MRI technician – the tumour on the spine had vanished.

"I even called the attending radiologist that was on that day," says the MRI tech. "We reloaded his previous scan and compared them, and there was absolutely nothing there. It was incredible, nothing short of a miracle."

Doubting the MRI, doctors took a spinal tap to check the physical evidence at the cellular level. It too came back blank. Logan was cancer free.

Reviewing the MRI's for the TV network, Jakacki took viewers through the changes:

"There is no longer any tumour coating the spinal cord at all. Now you can see the normal spinal fluid around the outside of the spinal cord, which is no longer swollen. There are no white areas at all where there used to be. There is a complete disappearance of all visible tumours. That is miraculous."

Logan Knupp is about to turn eight years old, and fighting fit. The oncologist who treated him, Dr Regina Jakacki, told *Investigate* from Pittsburgh Children's Hospital:

"I consider his recovery miraculous and I have not seen anything as dramatic since then."

Investigate also published a sidebar-story, examining possible reasons for the miraculous:

Although the word "miracle" is bandied about by many religions, it means different things to each. In pure Buddhism, the world is an illusion and therefore any miracle in the world is equally illusory. Because Buddhism, like other Eastern religions, does not recognize a personal God interacting with Creation, the idea of "miracle" in the Christian sense is an alien concept.

Instead, BuddhaNet records Buddhist "miracles" as "being able to multiply oneself, fly through the air, hear things over a long distance, read other people's minds, remember one's former lives and know how to destroy the defilements of the mind. Only the last three of these is considered to be important. There is little doubt that the Buddha had a cautious attitude to these and other miraculous powers. He pointed out that they could simply be due to "magic" or "fraud" rather than genuine spiritual accomplishments."

In sharp contrast to the self-focused "miracles" of Buddhism, Christianity's miracles in the New Testament concentrate primarily on relieving the suffering of others, and demonstrating God's power to intervene directly in the affairs of men.

"As you go," Christ told his disciples at Matt. 10:7-8, "preach this message: 'The kingdom of heaven is near'. Heal the sick, raise the dead, cleanse those who have leprosy, drive out demons. Freely you have received, freely give."

Theologian Norman Geisler, at Southern Evangelical Seminary in the US, says miracles serve three functions: to glorify the nature of God, to underline the truth and power of Christ so that the public may recognize Christian leaders are preaching with the authority of God, and lastly to provide evidence and a rational basis for belief in God.

Miracles provide extraordinary evidence to validate extraordinary claims.

Genuine miracles come from God, not from the person doing the praying.

Yet ask many church pastors and they'll tell you healing miracles can be a double-edged sword. Why are some healed and not others?

Marlene Klepees, the woman cured of cerebral palsy, tells *Investigate* she has a theory.

"I truly believe it's God's will for everyone to be healed. Let me explain just a little bit: just like I believe it's God's will that everyone be born again and have Jesus in their heart. A lot of people won't, but it doesn't mean [God's] hand was too short or his blood didn't work. But, the other thing to think about is: the apostle Peter's shadow healed them all. But they weren't all saved in his shadow, but they were all healed.

"So I believe this with all of me – the greatest evangelistic tool on Earth today is healing and restoration. Matthew 9:6 says 'The reason God heals is so that all men may know he has power on Earth to forgive sin". And I believe that's why Jesus went around healing everyone – so the crowds could understand the authority that Christ had on the Earth to forgive sin."

She also thinks miracle healings don't rely so much on faith as on a genuine compassion and an obedient heart.

"You know what, I don't think it takes much faith. Galatians 5:6 says faith works through love. Jesus said about the centurion, 'I've not seen so great a faith in all of Israel', and the centurion was not even serving the Lord. Here was a man who had servants but he chose to go and walk on the behalf of one of those servants – to put effort out – and God saw it."

As to skeptics who deny miracles, or suggest that prayer is simply false hope, Marlene points to her Mayo Clinic records and the reality that no one has ever been cured of cerebral palsy, but only by the hand of God.

"[Miracles] obviously do happen! I'm very blessed. I literally see miracles on a daily to weekly basis – I mean, I see them all the time. Regularly. I hardly ever have a week without a miracle – major ones. God's just *good*."

And then there are those, even Christians, who don't see them at all. For some, it is because their church no longer believes in miracles, or because they mistakenly believe miracles were only given to Jesus' first disciples, and not to all Christians since.

But again, as Norman Geisler notes, not even those who witness miracles are guaranteed to accept them.

"Not all witnesses to a miracle believe. In this event, the miracle is a witness against those who reject this evidence. John grieved: 'Even after Jesus had done all these miraculous signs in their presence, they still would not believe in him'. (Jn 12:37)

"Jesus himself said of some, 'They will not be convinced even if someone rises from the dead' (Lk 16:31)."

One of Christ's own disciples, doubting Thomas, fell into this category until he touched the resurrected Messiah. "How much more blessed are those who have not seen, and yet believe?" Jesus challenged him.

There is also an aspect of cultural conditioning. In parts of the world where spirituality is high, such as Africa and South America, people are not clouded by Western post-modern skepticism. If you're a tribal African villager who's seen a voodoo witchdoctor performing spells and summoning demons into the village, then you expect the Christian God to be even more powerful.

The sheer size of the Christian faith in that part of Africa[206] dwarfs anything New Zealand, Australia or even America could offer. Evangelical rallies in Nigeria are on record as attracting up to *two million people*. To the Africans, all this is normal. The huge crowds, the miracles – this is what they expect from the God who created the Universe: action, power, supernatural signs and wonders.[207]

---

206 http://www.christianitytoday.com.au/ct/2000/novemberweb-only/34.0.html
207 *Charisma* magazine has done a fascinating feature report on the pro's and con's of the Nigerian church, and its impact on Western society. Many churches in Europe are now being led by Nigerians, an ironic reversal of the original missionary activity. http://www.charismamag.com/display.php?id=5792

And on a continent where Christianity is locked in a power struggle with both miracle-less Islam and tribal shamanism, Christianity's rapid growth is directly linked to the healing miracles on display.

In the West however, where great cathedrals lie almost empty or populated by New Age Anglicans who don't believe in God, there are no lightning bolts or witchdoctors paralysed by the power of the Holy Spirit. Instead, it's considered a miracle that people bother turning up to those churches at all.

Much of the West's thinking on miracles comes from an eighteenth century Scottish philosopher named David Hume, whose writings established what we now know as the religion of 'secular humanism'.

Hume's basic argument was that the laws of nature suggested natural causes for everything. Miracles violated the laws of nature, yet human experience has shown natural laws are inviolable, ergo, miracles cannot occur. As some might have spotted, it is a circular argument because it begs the question: how do we know the laws of nature can never be violated? Just because humans can't do it does not mean that a higher being is similarly restricted.

In the 20th century, one of Hume's leading supporters was British philosopher and prominent atheist Antony Flew. However, in 2004, Flew publicly renounced his atheism on scientific grounds: after a lifetime of arguing against the existence of either God or miracles, he was presented with the scientific evidence in favour of Intelligent Design and found it compelling.

Atheism lost arguably its strongest voice – a bit like Darth Vader choosing the light. And that, many Christians would contend, was indeed a miracle.

Now, let's examine the implications of these reported and documented alleged miracles, by looking at how Hitchens and Spong would like us to interpret them. Citing skeptic David Hume, Hitchens suggests two alternatives:

"If you seem to witness such a thing, there are two possibilities. The first is that the laws of nature have been suspended (in your favour). The second is that you are under a misapprehension, or suffering from a delusion. Thus the likelihood of the second must be weighed against the likelihood of the first."

Based on that definition, it is patently obvious from the accounts above that delusion and misapprehension have to be ruled out. There were clear documented medical conditions/terminal illnesses pre-existing, which then vanished. Whilst a doctor could conceivably be "deluded" about the existence of a disease in the first place, I don't think we can rationally extend that excuse to cover MRI scans and blood test results. So using the gauntlet that Hitchens throws down, it is more rational to believe that the events detailed above were examples of divine suspension of the natural order in the victims' favour.

Like it or lump it, that's what the scientific evidence itself is suggesting. John Spong can call it "capricious" until the cows come home; he can rant about not wanting to worship a God who does such things because the whole idea offends him. But he cannot realistically say that these events never happened.

Convinced by his own anti-supernatural bias, Spong admits that he has no choice but to assume that the Christ miracles never happened, simply because miracles – to him – are impossible. Instead, he approaches biblical miracles purely as a metaphor, a story told to inspire rather than to be believed.

Spong suffers from errors in his baseline assumptions, however, that skew his logic and make his conclusions dodgy. He portrays miracles as "capricious" acts where God actively chooses to reward one and not the other in order to control behaviour. Like most of his book, Spong provides no sources for many of his assertions, which appear mainly to be a stream of consciousness emanating from the Spong household.

As other theologians have pointed out, the primary purpose for miracles in the ancient texts appears to have been one of proof of authority. By calming storms, raising people from the dead and healing thousands, Christ was demonstrating his authority over creation in a way no other religious leader on the planet ever has. Buddha performed no miracles. The Qu'ran does not record any miracles by Muhammed (although the much later-written hadiths do, probably in response to Christian miracle claims) and Muhammed certainly never claimed to be divine in any way, shape or form.

Miracles, then, were not and are not "rewards" for good behaviour, where a worthy follower is saved and an unworthy "heathen" is left to rot. Even in the New Testament, strangers were healed of whom there is no record of a conversion to Christ. Whether you chose to become a Christian was a matter of your own free will; whether or not God chose to perform a miracle was a matter of his free will.

If Spong could somehow disengage his mind from its biases, and simply see miracles as objective evidence of the existence of a supernatural god, rather than the pattern of reward and punishment he proposes in his book, he would come to realize his error. By performing miracles Christ was saying, "You can take me or leave me, but you cannot deny my authority".

This is not an imposition of divine will on humankind, it is merely putting a stake in the ground to declare, "I am who I say I am". Spong is free to reject that Christ (as indeed he vehemently and scathingly does), just as others are free to accept him, and Spong would reject him even if the evidence was crystal clear, because he's on record saying he wants nothing to do with that kind of deity.

"A miracle-working deity improvises as life unfolds," complains Spong. "A miracle-infested[208] world is an unpredictable, sometimes chaotic place. If the laws that govern our lives can be set aside for divine intervention, nothing is stable or trustworthy."

How then would Spong, Hitchens or Dawkins rationalize the following extract from left-wing preacher, Tony Campolo's book[209]:

> When it comes to being led by the Spirit, sometimes there's a lot of fun to be had.
>
> Several years ago I was invited to speak at a small Pentecostal college located near Eastern college where I teach, I love going to this little school because the people there seem to be so much in touch with the power of the Holy Spirit.
>
> Before the chapel service, several of the faculty members took me into a side room to pray with me, I got down on my knees and the six of them put their hands on my head and prayed for me asking the Holy Spirit to fill me up and use me effectively as I spoke to the students. Pentecostals seem to pray longer and with more dynamism than we Baptists do. These men prayed long, and the longer they prayed, the more they leaned on my head. They prayed on and on and leaned harder and harder. One of them said "do you feel the Spirit, do you feel the Spirit"? To tell the truth I felt something right at the base of my neck, but I wasn't sure it was the Spirit.
>
> One of the faculty members prayed at length about a particular man named Charlie Stoltzfus. That kind of ticked me off and I thought to myself, – if you're going to lean on my head, the least that you can do is pray for me! He prayed on and on for this guy who was about to abandon his wife and three children. I can still hear him calling out "Lord! Lord! Don't let that man leave his

---

208 JFTNR, John Shelby Spong, Harper Collins 2007, p. 56. Very loaded phrasing here, don't you think? To me it borders on a hatred of the entire concept of Christ as traditionally understood.
209 Let Me Tell You A Story, Tony Campolo, Thos. Nelson Publishing, 2000, p. 61

wife and children! Send an angel to bring that man back to his family. Don't let that family be destroyed! You know who I am talking about ... Charlie Stoltzfus. He lives down the road about half a mile on the right-hand side in a silver house trailer!"

I thought to myself with some degree of exasperation, *God knows where he lives... What do you think God's doing, sitting up there in heaven saying, 'give me that address again'?*

Following the chapel talk I got in my car and headed home. I was getting on the Pennsylvania turnpike when I saw a young man hitchhiking on the side of the road. I picked him up. (I know you are not supposed to, but I'm a Baptist preacher and whenever I can get someone locked in to where I can preach to him, I do it) As we pulled back onto the highway I introduced myself. I said, "Hi my name's Tony Campolo. What's your name?"

He said, "My name's Charlie Stoltzfus...."!

I didn't say a word. I drove down the turnpike, got off at the next exit and turned around and headed back. When I did that he looked at me and said, "Hey, mister! Where are you taking me?!"

I said, "I'm taking you HOME!"

He said, "why?"

And I said, "Because you just left your wife and three children RIGHT?"

He said "RIGHT! RIGHT!"

He leaned against the passenger door the rest of the way staring at me. I drove off the turnpike and onto a side road – Straight to his silver house trailer. When I pulled into the drive he looked at me with astonishment and said "How'd you know I lived here?"

I said "God told me!"

Well. I believe that God did tell me. I think that God may set up things like that, just for fun. I mean if you're God, you're probably having a pretty sad time of it looking down on all the things that are going on in the world. I can just imagine God nudging Peter and saying, "Hey Pete, Watch this".

I told Charlie. "You get into that house trailer because I want to talk to you and your wife."

He ran into that mobile home ahead of me. I don't know what he said to his wife, but when I got in the house trailer her eyes were as wide as saucers. I sat them down and said, "I'm going to talk, and you're going to listen."

Man did they listen! And during that next hour I led both of them into a personal relationship with Jesus. Today that guy is a Pentecostal preacher down South.

When the Spirit leads, there are all sorts of surprises in store for us.

Is Spong going to call Campolo, a Democrat-voting liberal with a degree in sociology, a liar? Does he suggest that things like this are just made up? In fact, Spong ignores modern miracles for the same reasons he rejects the gospel miracles – he doesn't want them to be true because it offends his worldview.

But as Richard Dawkins reminds us, being offended by something does not make it untrue, and the scientific test, 'did it happen, yes or no?' is the only valid test to apply.

Christopher Hitchens appeals to Ockham's Razor, the law devised by a Franciscan monk in the Middle Ages which says that the simplest explanation for something is usually the best, and the more cartwheels you have to perform to prove your story, the less rational it is.

So, which is more rational and easier to believe? That God spoke to Tony Campolo through a prayer session? Or that a bunch of men praying coincidentally recited the name, circumstances and address of a man they knew, and that the same man coincidentally just happened to be hitchhiking and that coincidentally Campolo later just happened to pick him up? It wasn't a set-up because the man given the pseudonym "Stoltzfus" had not yet become a Christian, and the "coincidences" were what encouraged him and his wife to convert – this after he had just left her – and Campolo attests that the man went on to become a preacher.[210]

If the above events happened, and they did, then Spong, Dawkins and Hitchens have some explaining to do, because according to their theories things like this don't happen.

The Stoltzfus case backs up the claim that miracles are proof of God's sovereignty. In this particular case, the event achieved two goals. One, the subject of the tale was so stunned at the supernatural event that he converted to Christianity and became a preacher, thus falling in the category of "extending God's kingdom". On the other hand, the story is cited here and elsewhere as a proof of the existence of God. Does Islam have a similar equivalent it can point to? No. Buddhism? No. Only Christianity has these kinds of proofs. Stoltzfus was not being "rewarded"

---

210   "You are quite right that my story about Charlie Stoltzfus is a story about a real person, but I changed his name. When I first started telling this story, he wrote to me and let me know that he wanted me to keep his name anonymous. I have honored that request." – Tony Campolo, email to author 2 Nov 07

for leaving his wife – the purpose of the miracle was to recruit him and others to work for this "capricious" God.

It is against this background, of the ongoing modern miraculous, that I now turn to the ancient miraculous. We have already established in this book 1) That leading scientists are openly comparing the creation of the Universe to "the Christian account in Genesis"; and 2) That leading atheist thinkers, even Dawkins himself, have been forced to concede the Universe might need a Creator (which they then argue is the god "Multiverse"); and 3) That the latest scientific evidence is showing the Universe is incredibly fine-tuned to sustain on Earth itself; and 4) That miracles consistent with a theistic interpretation of the Universe appear to be taking place in modern times.

Armed with this set of prior evidences, is it still *impossible* to believe that a Creator may have intervened in human history in the past as well?

Approached philosophically, the answer must be "No". A God capable of creating the Universe is equally capable of parting a sea, making the sun appear to stand still in the sky (or even *really* making the earth stop rotating[211]), carrying out an immaculate conception and raising people from the dead.

Because the moment you open the door to one Great Sky Fairy, you open the door to all things supernatural in principle. By this, I *don't* mean that the world is *actually* crawling with werewolves, pixies and whatever, but I do mean that once we allow on a rational basis for the supernatural to exist via a creation deity, then there is no logical basis on which to exclude other supernatural events or agents. Each has to be assessed on the evidence.

Miracles? If the scientific evidence regarding creation makes belief in God rational, then it also makes miracles possible.

What then of the Bible's most controversial miracle, the Resurrection? If you want to see Ground Zero of the culture wars, this is it.

---

211   For some reason this story in the Bible, Joshua 10:12-14, is a real problem for skeptics. "It couldn't happen," they say, "because the catastrophic effects would destroy earth and all life." Why? Any God capable of bringing the planet to a halt in its daily rotation is equally capable of protecting the creatures on the surface from ill-effects. Equally, such a God could alter the space-time continuum for the people in the affected area – effectively speeding up their own reality on those battle plains so that they achieved in five real minutes what to them appeared to take 12 hours. In this sense, time for them stood still, while in fact the planet kept spinning and no one fell off the edge. A more valid question for skeptics to ask might be, "Why would God bother?", but it could be that God wanted to allow Joshua's Army to complete their task, or it could have been a morale boosting proof of whose side God was on. Whatever the reason, to argue against it (or the virgin birth, or the Resurrection etc) on the basis that it would be *too hard* for the creator of the Universe is possibly the dumbest argument in the skeptic arsenal. Can we prove the sun stood still? Of course not. Can we prove it didn't happen? Of course not. Is it likely in the normal course of events? Never. Is it logically impossible? Not if God exists

CHAPTER 13
APOCALYPSE NOW

"A man who was merely a man and said the sort of things Jesus said would not be a great moral teacher. He would either be a lunatic – on a level with the man who says he is a poached egg – or he would be the Devil of Hell…Either this man was, and is, the Son of God: or else a madman and something worse"

C. S. Lewis, *Mere Christianity*

O F ALL THE MIRACLES IN the Bible, the biggest one of all in human terms, and most inexplicable, is the resurrection of Jesus Christ from the tomb 1,977 years ago. If Christ genuinely transcended death, and walked out of that crypt transformed, then there is no escaping the reality – not only of the supernatural – but of Christ's claim to be God. And with the 2000th anniversary of that event looming in 2030, it is receiving increasing attention.

I will elaborate further on the various theories surrounding the resurrection soon, but first some context regarding the position Christ found himself in. You'll recall we've previously examined Messianic prophecies suggesting the Messiah would be born in Bethlehem, would be tortured for the sin of the world, would triumph over death and become King of nations. When Jesus is recorded in his first synagogue speech at Nazareth, he chooses to read out one of these prophecies from the book of Isaiah.[212]

One of the questions we need to examine is whether there's any evidence Christ believed himself to be the Messiah, or indeed believed himself to be God. There is a popular misconception that the idea of "Christ as God" did not arise in the gospels themselves until the last one, the Gospel of

---

212 Luke 4:17-20

John, and did not become commonly believed until the Council of Nicaea in 325 AD where – as the conspiracy theory goes – the Catholic Church destroyed anything to the contrary and re-wrote the Bible to only include books supporting the divinity of Christ.

"It is quite clear," writes a former Baptist pastor in a letter to *Investigate* magazine on the topic,[213] "that in the first three gospels [Mark, Luke and Matthew] Jesus simply never taught that to live in right relation with God you had to 'believe that he was the son of God and that he died on the cross for our sins'. Nor indeed is there any requirement to 'believe in him…

"Our huge error has been to get our 'salvation theology' almost exclusively from John's Gospel, written as late as 20 to 30 years after the other three gospels."

Is the ex-pastor right? A glance at the early gospels (the 'synoptics') suggests not.

"I tell you, whoever acknowledges me before men, the Son of Man will also acknowledge him before the angels of God. But he who disowns me before men will be disowned before the angels of God." – Luke 12:8-9

"The Son of Man will send out his angels, and they will weed out of his kingdom everything that causes sin and all who do evil. They will throw them into the fiery furnace, where there will be weeping and gnashing of teeth. Then the righteous will shine like the sun in the kingdom of their Father. He who has ears, let him hear." – Matt 13:41-43.

What do these two verses tell us? Firstly, that Christ claims he can determine the spiritual fate of all humans, including those who reject him. Secondly, the Matthean verse tells us that Christ commands the angels. It also tells us that the "his" of "his kingdom" is "The Son of Man". We are then told that the righteous "will shine like the sun in the kingdom of their Father". Whose kingdom? The Father's, who we now can see is also the Son of Man in the context of this verse. Christ is not just saying he is equal to God: he is saying he *is* God.

"All authority in heaven and on earth has been given to me. Therefore go and make disciples of all nations, baptizing them in the name of the Father and of the Son and of the Holy Spirit, and teaching them to obey everything I have commanded you." – Matt 28:18-20.

Not only is Christ saying that he has the complete (all) authority of heaven, but in both of these passages he is also laying out the doctrine of the Holy Trinity – a doctrine that critics try to claim only emerged in 325 AD.

I would remind readers to keep this in context: no other major religious

213 *Investigate*, May 2002 edition

leader in history has *ever* claimed to *be* God. The claims that Christ made about himself were not only outrageous, they were blasphemous inside the strict Jewish culture he was born into, and his claims remain unparalleled in human history.

There is evidence in the earliest of the gospels, Mark, that Christ believed he could empower his followers to perform miracles.

"No one who does a miracle in my name can in the next moment say anything bad about me, for whoever is not against us is for us. I tell you the truth, anyone who gives you a cup of water in my name because you belong to Christ will certainly not lose his reward." – Mark 9:39-41.

But in case you still harbour nagging doubts that Christ thought he was both Messiah and deity, consider these passages from the first gospel, Mark as he discusses the signs of the end:

3As Jesus was sitting on the Mount of Olives opposite the temple, Peter, James, John and Andrew asked him privately, 4"Tell us, when will these things happen? And what will be the sign that they are all about to be fulfilled?"

5Jesus said to them: "Watch out that no one deceives you. 6Many will come in my name, claiming, 'I am he,' and will deceive many. 7When you hear of wars and rumors of wars, do not be alarmed. Such things must happen, but the end is still to come. 8Nation will rise against nation, and kingdom against kingdom. There will be earthquakes in various places, and famines. These are the beginning of birth pains.

9"You must be on your guard. You will be handed over to the local councils and flogged in the synagogues. On account of me you will stand before governors and kings as witnesses to them. 10And the gospel must first be preached to all nations. 11Whenever you are arrested and brought to trial, do not worry beforehand about what to say. Just say whatever is given you at the time, for it is not you speaking, but the Holy Spirit.

12"Brother will betray brother to death, and a father his child. Children will rebel against their parents and have them put to death. 13All men will hate you because of me, but he who stands firm to the end will be saved.

14"When you see 'the abomination that causes desolation'[214] standing where it[215] does not belong—let the reader understand—then let those who are in Judea flee to the mountains. 15Let no one on the roof of his house go down or enter the house to take anything out. 16Let no one in the field go back to get his cloak. 17How dreadful it will be in those days for pregnant women and nursing mothers! 18Pray that this will not take place in winter, 19because those will be days of distress unequaled from the beginning, when God created the world, until now—and never to be equaled again. 20If the Lord had not cut short those days, no one would survive. But for the sake of the elect, whom he has chosen, he has shortened them. 21At that time if anyone says to you, 'Look, here is the Messiah!' or, 'Look, there he is!' do not believe it. 22For false Christs and false prophets will appear and perform signs and miracles to deceive the elect—if that were possible. 23So be on your guard; I have told you everything ahead of time.

24"But in those days, following that distress,
   " 'the sun will be darkened,
      and the moon will not give its light;
25the stars will fall from the sky,
      and the heavenly bodies will be shaken.'[216]

26"At that time men will see the Son of Man coming in clouds with great power and glory. 27And he will send his angels and gather his elect from the four winds, from the ends of the earth to the ends of the heavens.

28"Now learn this lesson from the fig tree: As soon as its twigs get tender and its leaves come out, you know that summer is near. 29Even so, when you see these things happening, you know that it is near, right at the door. 30I tell you the truth, this generation[217] will certainly not pass away until all these things have happened. 31Heaven and earth will pass away, but my words will never pass away.

---

214   Daniel 9:27; 11:31; 12:11
215   Could also be 'he'
216   Isaiah 13:10.
217   The original Greek version of this word, *genea*, also (and in fact originally) meant race of people (a la 'genes'), so Christ may not be talking here about the people alive when he said it, nor the people alive when it happens, but of the Jews collectively – that their race would bear witness to the end. This makes sense given the foretelling of exactly this in the Old Testament, and the central role of Israel in the Armageddon scenario

This epic speech, taking place on the Mount of Olives, is known to scholars as "The Olivet discourse", and shows Jesus Christ not just certain of events at the end of days, but of his central role in it.

As former atheist C S Lewis points out in *Mere Christianity*, a speech like that leaves really only three options open: 1) Christ truly is God incarnate; 2) Jesus was deliberately lying to his followers for his own reasons; or 3) Christ was a fruitbat, a lunatic with insane beliefs about himself who'd be locked up in an instant if he showed up today.

The fourth possible option, that Jesus was a wise teacher, a good moral man, an avatar like Buddha, Confucius or Socrates, goes out the window with a speech like the Olivet discourse, according to Lewis.

"That is the one thing we must not say. A man who was merely a man and said the sort of things Jesus said would not be a great moral teacher. He would either be a lunatic – on a level with the man who says he is a poached egg – or else he would be the Devil of Hell. You must make your choice. Either this man was, and is, the Son of God: or else a madman and something worse.

"You can shut him up for a fool, you can spit at him and kill him as a demon; or you can fall at his feet and call him Lord and God. But let us not come with any patronizing nonsense about his being a great human teacher. He has not left that open to us. He did not intend to."[218]

When Christ talks about himself as "the Son of Man coming in clouds with great power and glory [who] will send his angels and gather his elect from the four winds, from the ends of the earth to the ends of the heavens", he is not in a month of Sundays talking "symbolically". Sure, he may be using some poetic licence, but the clear belief is of a future return in power and glory for the entire planet to see.

In making this incredible statement, Christ is evoking prophecies from the Book of Daniel. I've deliberately held off tackling these until now, because if a divinity code exists in the Bible then Daniel is one of its big strands.

For those who don't know the story, Daniel was one of the Hebrews captured in a Babylonian raid on Jerusalem by Nebuchadnezzar in 605 BC, and exiled with his countrymen to work in Babylon itself. His claim to fame in history was his ability to interpret dreams, and specifically the dreams of Babylon's king:

25 Arioch took Daniel to the king at once and said, I have found a man among the exiles from Judah who can tell the king

---

218 *Mere Christianity*, C S Lewis, Harper Collins, 2002 edition, p. 52

what his dream means. 26 The king asked Daniel (also called Belteshazzar), Are you able to tell me what I saw in my dream and interpret it?

27 Daniel replied, No wise man, enchanter, magician or diviner can explain to the king the mystery he has asked about, 28 but there is a God in heaven who reveals mysteries. He has shown King Nebuchadnezzar what will happen in days to come. Your dream and the visions that passed through your mind as you lay on your bed are these:

29 As you were lying there, O king, your mind turned to things to come, and the revealer of mysteries showed you what is going to happen.

30 As for me, this mystery has been revealed to me, not because I have greater wisdom than other living men, but so that you, O king, may know the interpretation and that you may understand what went through your mind.

31 You looked, O king, and there before you stood a large statue – an enormous, dazzling statue, awesome in appearance. 32 The head of the statue was made of pure gold, its chest and arms of silver, its belly and thighs of bronze, 33 its legs of iron, its feet partly of iron and partly of baked clay. 34 While you were watching, a rock was cut out, but not by human hands. It struck the statue on its feet of iron and clay and smashed them.

35 Then the iron, the clay, the bronze, the silver and the gold were broken to pieces at the same time and became like chaff on a threshing-floor in the summer. The wind swept them away without leaving a trace. But the rock that struck the statue became a huge mountain and filled the whole earth.

36 This was the dream, and now we will interpret it to the king.

37 You, O king, are the king of kings. The God of heaven has given you dominion and power and might and glory; 38 in your hands he has placed mankind and the beasts of the field and the birds of the air. Wherever they live, he has made you ruler over them all. You are that head of gold.

39 After you, another kingdom will rise, inferior to yours. Next, a third kingdom, one of bronze, will rule over the whole earth. 40 Finally, there will be a fourth kingdom, strong as iron – for iron breaks and smashes everything – and as iron breaks things to pieces, so it will crush and break all the others.

41 Just as you saw that the feet and toes were partly of baked clay

and partly of iron, so this will be a divided kingdom; yet it will have some of the strength of iron in it, even as you saw iron mixed with clay. 42 As the toes were partly iron and partly clay, so this kingdom will be partly strong and partly brittle. 43 And just as you saw the iron mixed with baked clay, so the people will be a mixture and will not remain united, any more than iron mixes with clay.

44 In the time of those kings, the God of heaven will set up a kingdom that will never be destroyed, nor will it be left to another people. It will crush all those kingdoms and bring them to an end, but it will itself endure for ever.

45 This is the meaning of the vision of the rock cut out of a mountain, but not by human hands— a rock that broke the iron, the bronze, the clay, the silver and the gold to pieces. The great God has shown the king what will take place in the future. The dream is true and the interpretation is trustworthy.

46 Then King Nebuchadnezzar fell prostrate before Daniel and paid him honour and ordered that an offering and incense be presented to him. 47 The king said to Daniel, Surely your God is the God of gods and the Lord of kings and a revealer of mysteries, for you were able to reveal this mystery.

Here's where the whole thing heats up. The Book of Daniel contains prophecy acknowledged, even in ancient Judaism, to be both Messianic and apocalyptic – in other words the book predicts events leading up to the end of the world. Like Isaiah, however, Daniel is so spookily accurate that liberal critics like Spong and Geering simply cannot accept for even a second that the book is genuine, and they argue that it must have been written later, with historic events copied into the book as fulfilled "prophecy". You'll recall Spong explained earlier that he really wasn't even interested in the evidence – if it turns out to be true then he doesn't want to be associated with the Christian God anyway.

The passages above are the first of the disputed portions.[219] In

---

219 Because Daniel happened to be right about four sequential kingdoms, liberals demanded his book be 're-dated' to 165 BC. Even that was not recent enough however to account for the yet to emerge world-conquering Roman empire (which didn't hit Palestine in a meaningful way until 63 BC). The critics next tried to suggest the final empire in the sequence must be Greece, but this analysis failed also. Since then, the discovery of portions of the Book of Daniel among the Dead Sea Scrolls at Qumran and dated to early second century BC have well and truly put the kybosh on the claimed 165 BC composition, because that would not explain how the Essenes ended up with a copy. Additionally, ancient linguistics expert Gleason Archer and others have compared the Aramaic in the Dead Sea Scrolls copy to the Aramaic in other writings from 165 BC (the Maccabean period) and found the language used

Nebuchadnezzar's dream, Daniel identifies four major empires, of which the Babylonians were first. The second, which happened on Daniel's watch, turns out to have been the Medo-Persian empire, who conquered Babylon soon after these events. The empire of Bronze was Alexander the Great 200 years later, and the empire of Iron was Rome, which wasn't an empire at all in Daniel's day.

The significance for us is that we are still living in the Roman empire today. The power in the Roman empire changed with the fall of Rome itself, but the barbarians sweeping in adopted the state religion of Rome – by this time Christianity – and adopted Roman law for their own separate kingdoms. Roman law is at the heart of European, US and Australasian legal systems today. The United Nations is an echo of the old 'Imperial Senate', with the Security Council as de-facto emperor, and virtually every country in the world has submitted itself to UN jurisdiction. We are "Rome" – the kingdom which has not yet been crushed, although Daniel predicts it is the *final* earth-governed kingdom.

This Roman kingdom however, has weaknesses – feet of clay:

"Just as you saw that the feet and toes were partly of baked clay and partly of iron, so this will be a divided kingdom; yet it will have some of the strength of iron in it, even as you saw iron mixed with clay. 42 As the toes were partly iron and partly clay, so this kingdom will be partly strong and partly brittle. 43 And just as you saw the iron mixed with baked clay, so the people will be a mixture and will not remain united, any more than iron mixes with clay."

Anyone who has read *Eve's Bite* will recognize the scenario here: Daniel talks of the final kingdom becoming brittle, weak and disunited – I argued in *Eve's Bite* (and many other commentators[220] are making the same point) that our Western civilization is on the brink of collapse. None of us are making our argument on biblical grounds, but simply on the evidence in front of all of us – internal divisions and the growth of political correctness have fundamentally weakened our culture, especially in the face of external threats.

Daniel warns however, of a "rock" carved by God himself that will usher

in the Qumran version is centuries older in style. Additionally, the author of Daniel knew tiny details of Babylonian culture (eg, its peculiar numbering system) that would not be known by a Palestinian Jew living 400 years after Babylon fell. All of this, and more, means Daniel probably was indeed written around 530 BC, which of course makes the prophecies explosive. For more detail on this, see the *Encyclopedia of Bible Difficulties*, by Gleason Archer, p. 282-293, and a fascinating article published in *The Skeptical Review* in 1998, available at http://www.infidels. org/library/magazines/tsr/1998/2/982dan.html. A devastating essay at Tektonics, http:// www.tektonics.org/guest/danielblast.html also lays out the latest archaeological information on the dating of Daniel to 530 BC.
220 Mark Steyn, Roger Scruton, Melanie Phillips, Theodore Dalrymple, Camille Paglia to name a few

in the final destruction of this weakening Roman empire and become the new and final earth kingdom. What is this "rock"?

"Jesus replied, 'Blessed are you, Simon son of Jonah, for this was not revealed to you by man, but by my Father in heaven. And I tell you that you are Petros[221], and on this rock I will build my church, and the gates of Hell will not overcome it'."[222]

Christ used the rock analogy for both Christianity and himself in the parable of the Builders, at Matt 7:24-27, and warned his disciples to cling to that rock when the coming storm finally strikes.

The apostle Paul, hammers the point home, telling the Corinthians, "that rock was Christ".[223]

In essence then, Daniel – writing some 550 years before Christ – told the Babylonian king that his dream had witnessed the future, right to the end of days, when a rock hewn by God himself would destroy the Roman civilization (ours) and create a new empire on earth.

Noting that many of the Jewish prophets had been executed by their own people for giving messages the public didn't want to hear, and foreshadowing his own crucifixion, and indeed the increasing retreat away from Christianity in our modern "Rome", Christ elaborated further on what would happen at the end of time in his Parable of the Tenants,[224] and again at the end alluded himself as the rock:

> 33 Listen to another parable: There was a landowner who planted a vineyard. He put a wall around it, dug a winepress in it and built a watchtower. Then he rented the vineyard to some farmers and went away on a journey.
>
> 34 When the harvest time approached, he sent his servants to the tenants to collect his fruit. 35 The tenants seized his servants; they beat one, killed another, and stoned a third. 36 Then he sent other servants to them, more than the first time, and the tenants treated them in the same way.
>
> 37 Last of all, he sent his son to them. 'They will respect my son,' he said. 38 But when the tenants saw the son, they said to each other, 'This is the heir. Come, let's kill him and take his inheritance.' 39 So they took him and threw him out of the vineyard and killed him.

---

221 The Greek word for rock is *petros*, or Peter, hence the disciple Simon became Simon-Peter, and then Peter
222 Matt 16:17-18
223 1 Cor. 10:4
224 Matt 21:33-44

40 Therefore, when the owner of the vineyard comes, what will he do to those tenants?

41 "He will bring those wretches to a wretched end," they replied, "and he will rent the vineyard to other tenants, who will give him his share of the crop at harvest time."

42 Jesus said to them, Have you never read in the Scriptures:
'The stone the builders rejected has become the cornerstone; the Lord has done this, and it is marvellous in our eyes'[225]

43Therefore I tell you that the kingdom of God will be taken away from you and given to a people who will produce its fruit. 44 *He who falls on this stone will be broken to pieces, but he on whom it falls will be crushed.* [my emphasis]

I think I've made the link between Daniel's "rock" and Christ fairly clear here, and there's little doubt Christ was making exactly the same link. Years after interpreting Nebuchadnezzar's dream, Daniel had a dream of his own that perplexed him. He saw four beasts in his dream, each corresponding to the four kingdoms of Nebuchadnezzar's dream. For example, the first beast was "like a lion...it had the wings of an eagle"; statues resembling this have been excavated from Babylonian sites. The fourth beast, representing the future Roman empire, was described thus:

"There before me was a fourth beast – terrifying and frightening and very powerful. It had large iron teeth; it crushed and devoured its victims and trampled underfoot whatever was left. It was different from all the former beasts, and it had ten horns.

"While I was thinking about the horns, there before me was another horn, a little one, which came up among them; and three of the first horns were uprooted before it. This horn had eyes like the eyes of a man and a mouth that spoke boastfully."

The scene in Daniel's dream then shifts to an apocalyptic vision of the last Judgment in heaven itself where "the Ancient of Days" – God himself – appears on a throne of fire, while millions of angels stand before him.

"Then I continued to watch," says Daniel, "because of the boastful words the horn was speaking. I kept looking until the beast was slain and its body destroyed and thrown into the blazing fire...

"In my vision at night I looked, and there before me was one like a son of man, coming with the clouds of heaven. He approached the Ancient of Days and was led into his presence. He was given authority, glory and

---

225 Psalm 118:22-23

sovereign power; all peoples, nations and men of every language worshiped him. His dominion is an everlasting dominion that will not pass away, and his kingdom is one that will never be destroyed."

Now, then, you can see the rock at the centre of Nebuchadnezzar's dream has become in Daniel's dream the Son of Man coming on the clouds, as the new king, the returning Messiah that Christ directly identified himself as.

In his vision, Daniel then turns to one of the angels watching this scene in heaven and asks the meaning of the vision of the iron beast with horns.

"I...wanted to know about the ten horns on its head and about the other horn that came up, before which three of them fell – the horn that looked more imposing than the others...As I watched, this horn was waging war against the saints and defeating them, until the Ancient of Days came and pronounced judgment in favour of the saints...and the time came when they possessed the kingdom.

"He gave me this explanation: 'The fourth beast is a fourth kingdom that will appear on earth. It will be different from all the other kingdoms and will devour the whole earth, trampling it down and crushing it. The ten horns are ten kings who will come from this kingdom. After them, another king will arise, different from the earlier ones; he will subdue[226] three kings. He will speak against the Most High and oppress his saints and try to change the set times[227] and the laws. The saints will be handed over to him for a time, times and half a time."[228]

The final chapter in this Messianic/Armageddon script comes in Daniel 9:24-27, where Daniel receives a message from the angel Gabriel:

"Seventy 'sevens' are decreed for your people and your holy city to finish transgression, to put an end to sin, to atone for wickedness, to bring in everlasting righteousness, to seal up vision and prophecy and to anoint the most holy.

"Know and understand this: From the issuing of the decree to restore and rebuild Jerusalem until the Anointed One, the ruler, comes, there will be seven 'sevens' and sixty-two 'sevens'. It will be rebuilt with streets and a trench,[229] but in times of trouble.

"After the sixty-two 'sevens' the Anointed One will be cut off and will have nothing. The people of the ruler who will come will destroy the city and the sanctuary. The end will come like a flood: War will continue

---

226 The word for subdue is actually an ancient Babylonian word, meaning also 'abase', 'put down' or 'humble'
227 Some commentators interpret this to mean the natural order
228 Generally interpreted as "a year, two years and half a year".
229 A moat

until the end, and desolations have been decreed. He [the Antichrist] will confirm a covenant with many for one 'seven'. In the middle of the 'seven' he will put an end to sacrifice and offering. And on a wing of the temple he will set up an abomination that causes desolation, until the end that is decreed is poured out on him."

Now, remember that Daniel's book was written around 530 BC. It clearly predicts that "the people of the ruler who will come will destroy the city [Jerusalem] and the sanctuary [the Temple]".

Even if you want to remain a cynic and go with a late date for the authorship of Daniel of 165 BC – against the evidence I might add – you are still left with a prediction that Rome will destroy the Jewish temple, which indeed they did in 70 AD.

In many respects that's one of the reasons why the constant push by anti-supernaturalists to date the Gospels later than the fall of Jerusalem (to avoid giving the appearance that Jesus' prophecy about the temple came true) is a waste of time. Even if you go with Spong and date all the gospels at 100 AD, you are still left with Daniel making the same successful prediction either 600 years or 235 years in advance (take your pick). And if the only reason to date the gospels late was because you don't believe in fulfilled prophecy, then that reason starts to look kind of weak in the face of Daniel's success.

Even so, the destruction of the temple was not the main point of Daniel's angelic warning. Gabriel talked of seventy 'sevens', but then broke it down to explicitly talk about the first sixty nine 'sevens'. The word 'sevens' means a group of seven years. Now when Daniel was writing his book, there had been no decree to rebuild Jerusalem. That decree was not issued until 457 BC, long after Daniel's death. Sixty-nine times seven gives us a total of 483 years. Adding 483 to -457 on a calculator gives you 26AD. Now, allowing for our artificial BC/AD crossover (there is no year Zero), the adjustment gives us the date of 27 AD. According to the Book of Daniel, the "Anointed One" (Messiah) will appear in Israel in 27 AD.

When did Jesus Christ get baptized and begin his ministry in Palestine? 27 AD.

This is another prophecy that survives irrespective of the date you choose for Daniel, because its target date, 27 AD was still well in the future regardless of when Daniel was written. We know the Essenes had Daniel in the second century BC because we have physical copies of portions of Daniel found in the caves at Qumran[230] and carbon-dated.[231]

---

230 http://home.earthlink.net/~ironmen/qumran.htm
231 Spong, who continues to assert the late date for Daniel, devotes an entire chapter in

Returning to Gabriel's warning, you'll recall he mentioned "seventy 'sevens' " first up, but we've only dealt with the first 69. Let's return to the prophecy. We are told that after his appearance in Israel, the Messiah will be "cut off" and have nothing. The crucifixion of Christ in 30 AD certainly cut the Messiah short.

A series of events to follow the crucifixion were then foretold by Gabriel. They include the destruction of the temple in 70 AD by the empire to come (Rome), and then wars and desolations until "the end". Last century was the bloodiest in world history, and in terms of potential "desolations" the site of the Jewish temple currently has an Islamic mosque plonked on top of it.

Gabriel then jumps from generalities to tell Daniel about the Antichrist, who "will confirm a covenant [treaty, agreement] with many for one 'seven'. In the middle of the 'seven' [ie, three and a half years] he will put an end to sacrifice and offering. And on a wing of the temple he will set up an abomination that causes desolation[232]…"

This 'seven' has not yet begun. No "Antichrist" has yet emerged, and despite the recent re-establishment of the ancient Jewish Sanhedrin Council for the first time in 1,600 years, the Jewish sacrificial system has not yet been re-established.[233]

Understandably, debate about how all these prophecies fit into our current timeframes rages unabated. There are those who argue the destruction of the Temple in 70 AD by the Roman empire (our empire) is the "abomination that causes desolation" and that in fact the tribulation for the entire planet began at that moment and continues today – Christ could in principle return at any moment.[234]

JFTNR to Daniel's 'Son of Man' imagery and its reappearance in the gospels. He does not once, however, tell his readers about the specific prophecies Daniel managed to successfully predict, including that the Son of Man would appear in Israel in 27 AD, before being 'cut off'. I would have thought this 'inconvenient truth' was *directly* relevant to his claim that Christ was *not* the Messiah, and did not see himself as such. Surely anyone making such an assertion must first explain away the pinpoint accurate prophecies?

232 This last sentence can also be translated: "And one who causes desolation will come upon the pinnacle of the abominable temple [Dome of the Rock?], until the end that is decreed is poured out on the desolated city"

233 http://www.haaretz.com/hasen/spages/831646.html

234 *Jesus and the Gospels*, Craig Blomberg, Broadman & Holman, 1997, pp 322-328. It is a battle that modern students know little about, but the Jewish-Roman war resulted in the deaths of one million Jews at the time and the destruction of their entire priesthood, leaving the Jews unable to resume making sacrifices to God because the lineage records of the Levite priests were destroyed by the Romans. To the Jews of the time, this was Armageddon!

The temple was destroyed virtually 40 years to the day after Christ predicted it. Even in this analysis, however, Blomberg concedes: "The language of Revelation and the frequent pattern in Scripture of multiple fulfillments of prophecy suggest that there may be a particular intensifying of 'tribulation' at the very end of the church age. But Jesus, in this context (the Olivet discourse) is probably not limiting his use of the term just to that final period of human history."

Theories, however, remain just that. Speculation, conjecture. The only hard facts on the table are that Daniel, regardless of when he was written, accurately predicted both the destruction of the temple and the appearance of the Messiah – as well as the execution of the Messiah. But despite the execution, his earlier visions clearly show the Son of Man returns at the end of time – the so-called second coming.

These, then, are the cornerstone Messianic prophecies that the four gospels allude to through Christ. With all of these things pointing at Jesus, however, the question to be determined was whether in fact he was the promised Messiah.

CHAPTER 14

RESURRECTION: FACT OR FIGMENT?

"That within a few weeks after the crucifixion Jesus' disciples came to believe this, is one of the indisputable facts of history"
Reginald Fuller, scholar

O F ALL THE STORIES IN the Bible, the question of whether one man transcended death is arguably the most hotly-debated issue of all time. Court cases have been fought over it, civilizations have been built on it, wars have taken place because of it. Because it all comes down to one thing: most of us agree that a supernatural something created our universe and created life. The evidence in *The Divinity Code* shows even the world's most outspoken atheists, when backed into a corner, come up with creation stories that mimic the necessity for God to have flicked the switch.

In a world of competing religious views and beliefs, however, it has been easier to allow "each to their own" rather than confront the central issue: are all or any of the religions true for *all* humanity, and if so which?

Given that all major religions pretty much share the "Golden Rule" – do unto others etc – the test for which one is most likely to reflect the will of the Creator will be higher than merely comparing moral teachings.

In the case of Christianity, there are some unique components that appear nowhere else in any major religion. One of these is the existence of historically-testable fulfilled prophecy. Whilst many religions contain prophetic elements, none are as precise as those that appear in the Bible. And a search for genuine Hindu prophecies will be a short one. The Hindu Bhagavad-Gita lists a prophecy concerning Kalki, born of an eminent family line in a small obscure village, who will be the saviour of the world at the end of this particular cycle of time. Before you get excited, though,

Hindu websites record that this epic was written over a period of centuries, from 900 BC through to around 500 AD. The earliest surviving copies apparently date to around 1400 AD.[235] In that mix, there is plenty of scope for Hinduism to have borrowed from Christianity.[236]

Remember, my purpose here is not to convert you to Christianity. I figure you're intelligent enough to make up your own mind about things. Rather, my task is to test prevailing theories on the existence of God and lay out what I believe is hard evidence of a divinity code in the universe and in life, expressed in a number of ways. One of those ways is the Resurrection, and again I hark back to Richard Dawkins' sage comment: either it happened or it didn't, and that is a scientifically-testable fact relevant to all of us.

As previously mentioned, only Jesus Christ as a historical religious figure has claimed to actually *be* God, rather than simply be God's mouthpiece. Only Christ claimed he could and would beat death, as proof of his divinity.

So did he?

To answer the question, we have only the Pauline epistles, gospel testimony, plus some assorted Roman and Jewish writings, as physical exhibits of evidence.

Christianity, or the truth of it at least, stands or falls on the historical truth of the Resurrection. The apostle Paul reached exactly the same conclusion:

"If Christ has not been raised, our preaching is useless and so is your faith...your faith is futile."[237]

Keeping these thoughts in mind, let's explore the different Resurrection accounts. The earliest known testimony that a resurrection occurred, contrary to your expectations perhaps, comes from the apostle Paul himself.

During the same letter, 1 Corinthians, Paul repeated what is now recognized as the oldest component of the entire New Testament – a creed encapsulating the absolute foundation of Christianity:[238]

"For what I received I passed on to you as of the first importance: *that Christ died for our sins according to the Scriptures, that he was buried, that he was raised on the third day according to the Scriptures, and that he appeared to Peter, and then to the Twelve. After that he appeared to more than 500 of the brothers at the same time, most of whom are still living, though some have fallen asleep. Then he appeared to James, then to all the apostles*, and last of all he appeared to me..."

235 http://www.haryana-online.com/History/mahabharat.htm
236 And of course we have already seen that, with the "Eesa Maseeha" stories
237 1 Cor. 15:14-17
238 1 Cor. 15:3-6

This passage is widely recognized by scholars on both sides of the debate as dating back to the meeting Paul had with Peter and James in Jerusalem, shortly after his road to Damascus conversion.

"In that list two individuals are mentioned by name as having seen the risen Christ, and two only: 'he appeared to Peter' and 'he appeared to James'," writes the University of Manchester's leading Professor of Biblical Criticism at the time, F. F. Bruce.[239]

"It is no mere coincidence that these should be the only two apostles whom Paul claims to have seen during his first visit to Jerusalem after his conversion."

In a moment I will call a star witness to the stand, a hostile witness whose testimony is all the more credible as a result. This witness will consign the theories of Karen Armstrong, Lloyd Geering, John Shelby Spong and others well and truly into the dustbin of history. But first, a brief continuation of the contextual build-up to this dramatic event.

The phrase in 1 Cor. 15:3, "For what I received I passed on to you", is the hint that this is more than mere opinion, this is the gospel Paul received from Peter and James at their historic meeting, probably just four years after the crucifixion.

"The verbs 'receive' and 'deliver [passed on]' in this kind of context are practically technical terms for the passing on of tradition from one individual or generation to the next," explains F. F. Bruce.[240]

Paul uses the codewords again in the now world-famous Holy Communion creed:[241]

"For I received from the Lord what I also passed on to you: The Lord Jesus, on the night he was betrayed, took bread, and when he had given thanks, he broke it and said..."

If you've been to church in your life you'll know the liturgy. But this one received and passed on comes with a highly relevant ending, missing from many church liturgies today:

"For as often as you eat this bread and drink the cup, you proclaim the Lord's death until he comes."

"The last clause, 'until he comes'," writes Professor Bruce,[242] "is in all probability an integral part of what Paul 'received'. It may hark back to Jesus' saying in the upper room that the next time he ate the Passover or drank the fruit of the vine would be in the consummated kingdom of

239 *Paul: Apostle of the Heart Set Free*, F. F. Bruce, Eerdmans, 2000, p. 85
240 Ibid, p. 264
241 1 Cor. 11:23-26
242 Paul, Bruce, p. 265

God; but in any case it reflects the eschatological [end times] significance of the meal in the early church."

As Bruce writes, these are *core* traditions.

"These traditions were summed up as 'the tradition of Christ', which comprised a summary of the Christian message, expressed as a confession of faith, with special emphasis on the death and resurrection of Christ."[243]

OK, I mentioned a star witness. Before I wheel him in, let's re-cap what some of these acclaimed authors are saying about the Resurrection of Christ being mythic in nature.

"Miracles do not appear to be part of the earliest memory the church had of Jesus," writes Spong. "As noted earlier, there are no miracles recorded in Paul, who had died before the first gospel was written."[244]

"It came to be realized," writes Geering, "that the gospels were neither written by apostles nor eyewitnesses of what they recounted. It is now widely acknowledged that the gospels were written in the period 70-100 CE being derived partly from collections of stories circulating in oral tradition, and partly from the creative inspiration of the evangelist in question[245]...as the stories progressed, the risen Christ came to be described in more and more physical terms. It is on the basis of these late resurrection stories that conservative Christians today defend what they call 'the bodily resurrection'[246]...successive generations came to perceive and worship him as the Christ.[247]"

John Spong describes it as "...clearly the power of the mythology that developed around Jesus between the time of his death and the writing of the gospels [60 to 70 years later].[248]

"There was no stylized Last Supper," asserts Spong, "in which bread was identified with his broken body and wine with his poured-out shed blood designed to symbolize his final prediction of death."[249]

Who better to call to the witness stand, then, than John Shelby Spong himself.

The central theme of Spong's, and Geering's, work is that the later gospel writers, who they claim were *not* disciples of Christ and probably never knew him, had gilded the lily – added miracles and mythology about the man-god Jesus Christ that wasn't there at the beginning.

---

243 Ibid, p. 264
244 *JFTNR*, Spong, p. 68
245 *CWG*, Geering, p. 74
246 Ibid, p. 79
247 Ibid, p. 82
248 *JFTNR*, Spong, p. 26
249 Ibid, p. 128

As I've already established, the gospels were not written late and can safely be regarded as authentic. You're about to see why from the mouth of Spong himself.

John Spong's Achilles Heel is the testimony of the apostle Paul. After spending his entire book trying to shred the credibility of gospel-writers, he turns his attention to defending the historical existence of Christ. I quoted Spong on that topic earlier, but I saved the best for here, where Spong is using the fact that Paul met the apostles Peter and James, as proof that Christ must have existed. Check out his reasoning – I've highlighted the killer blow in italics:[250]

"What we learn from this firsthand source [Paul] in Galatians is that within three years of his conversion, Paul had conferred with Peter and seen James, the brother of Jesus. This would have been no fewer than four and no more than nine years after the crucifixion.

"Peter and James, the Lord's brother, were people who knew the Jesus of history. A wider consultation took place with others [disciples] eighteen to twenty-three years later, certainly within the range of an average memory.

"I think we can be clear that full-blown myths are not created in so short a time."

Gotcha!

Cast your mind back a few pages to those earliest creeds that Paul "received" and "passed on":

"That Christ died for our sins according to the Scriptures, that he was buried, that he was raised on the third day according to the Scriptures, and that he appeared to Peter, and then to the Twelve. After that he appeared to more than 500 of the brothers at the same time, most of whom are still living, though some have fallen asleep. Then he appeared to James, then to all the apostles..."

By Spong's own admission, this central nugget of Christianity was passed to Paul probably only four years after Christ was resurrected, and no later than nine years after the event. And as Spong assures us all, "I think we can be clear that full-blown myths are not created in so short a time."

The Resurrection was no myth invented by the gospel writers seven decades after the event! This creed bypassed the gospel writers altogether. It went directly from two men who knew Jesus Christ personally – Peter, and Jesus' brother James – directly to Paul, as early as four years after it happened.[251]

The significance of James testifying to Paul about the risen Christ cannot be emphasized enough, as F. F. Bruce explains:

---

250 *JFTNR*, Spong, p. 211
251 This also blows Spong's claims about the Last Supper out of the water as well, because as we've seen, Paul also recounted the communion liturgy in what scholars believe is another of the products of that early conversation with Peter and James

"James, with other members of the family of Jesus, does not appear to have been a follower of his before his death; indeed, the family as a whole appears to have viewed Jesus' public activity with aloofness, not to say hostility.

"Yet after Jesus' resurrection his mother and brothers are found in association with the apostles and other disciples. The brothers became figures of note in the church at large, and James in particular occupied an increasingly influential position in the church of Jerusalem.

"If we look for some explanation of their sudden change in attitude towards Jesus, we can find it in the statement that in resurrection he appeared to James."

It is one thing to appear to a stranger. It is entirely different for a dead man to walk up and greet his own skeptical brother. And I can guarantee it would take more than a dream or a vision to convince me one of my dead relatives was back in power and glory.

Just to set the seal on this, we should note for the record that in the same Corinthians letter containing the creed, the same chapter in fact, Paul talks about the resurrection body:[252]

"But someone may ask, 'How are the dead raised? With what kind of body will they come?' How foolish! What you sow does not come to life unless it dies. When you sow, you do not plant the body that will be, just a seed, perhaps of wheat or of something else. But God gives it a body as he has determined, and to each kind of seed he gives its own body...So it will be with the resurrection of the dead. The body that is sown is perishable, it is raised imperishable."

Considering he had just quoted the creed about Christ appearing to the masses, it is a fair bet Paul knew the resurrected Christ was far more than a mere ghost (still supernatural) or *quelle horreur*, a mere vision. Our resurrection bodies are real bodies. They may be changed bodies, which would explain why the disciples had difficulty recognizing Christ at first, but they are real, physical bodies. The seed that went into the ground wasn't exchanged for a plant, it became the plant. The caterpillar becomes the butterfly, but its life force remains one, not two. This was Paul's message. And if Christ was resurrected, he walked and talked.

Before moving on to the gospel accounts, it is worth recording what else Paul can tell us about his own understanding of Christ's death, resurrection and second coming.

"You foolish Galatians! Who has bewitched you? Before your very eyes Jesus Christ was clearly portrayed as crucified."[253]

---

252   1 Cor. 15:35-42
253   Gal. 3:1

"May I never boast except in the Cross of our Lord Jesus Christ, through which the world has been crucified to me, and I to the world."[254]

"...This will happen when the Lord Jesus is revealed from heaven in blazing fire with his powerful angels...on the day he comes to be glorified in his holy people and to be marveled at among all those who have believed."[255]

"...And then the lawless one will be revealed, whom the Lord Jesus will overthrow with the breath of his mouth and destroy by the splendour of his coming. The coming of the lawless one will be in accordance with the work of Satan displayed in all kinds of counterfeit miracles, signs and wonders, and in every sort of evil that deceives those who are perishing. They perish because they refused to love the truth and so be saved."[256]

"Just as Christ was raised from the dead through the glory of the Father, we too may live a new life...Now if we died with Christ, we believe that we will also live with him. For we know that since Christ was raised from the dead, he cannot die again; death no longer has mastery over him."[257]

"We wait eagerly for our adoption as sons, the redemption of our bodies. For in this hope we were saved."[258]

"Christ Jesus, who died – more than that, who was raised to life, is at the right hand of God."[259]

"Theirs are the patriarchs, and from them is traced the human ancestry of Christ, who is God over all..."[260]

The above quotes are taken from a series of Paul's letters, written between 49 AD and 57 AD. Paul must have known the story of the virgin birth, contrary to Spong's assertions, otherwise he would not have felt the need to specify Christ's "human ancestry" whilst in the next breath calling him "God over all".

Now remember, the dating of these letters is universally accepted by scholars. They are not controversial in that sense. Remember also John Spong's assurance to us that Paul's writings are too early to have been affected by myth. The same Paul who met the apostles in Jerusalem to learn more about the ministry of Christ and spent 15 days with them, clearly had the factual matrix of those original details in his mind when he talked about the cross, crucifixion, resurrection, ascension and second coming of Jesus. How could he not? Paul never witnessed the crucifixion,

254 Gal. 6:14
255 2 Thess. 1:7-10
256 2 Thess. 2:8-10
257 Rom. 6:4-9
258 Rom. 8:23
259 Rom. 8:34
260 Rom 9:5

he never saw the cross. Yet he testified of these things, and presumably from his background knowledge.

The next set of documents to examine are the gospels themselves.

For many critics, the gospel stories concerning the Resurrection are not only fictional because "miracles can't happen", they are also claimed to be "thoroughly contradictory". Speaking as a journalist, I disagree. Those of us in the news business recognize eyewitness testimony when we see it, because we deal with it every day. Every deadline we are judging the credibility of witnesses, reports and variations in stories.

To illustrate my point, I can think of nothing better than returning to the first book I ever wrote – an investigation into the mysterious death of a man named Paul White, whose car slammed into an overbridge pylon, apparently in front of witnesses:[261]

> …Two witnesses, both of whom had failed to see the actual moment of impact, despite the fact that both were accelerating on a motorway on-ramp almost right behind Paul White's vehicle. On a wet road, in the dark, what kind of evasive action would the two drivers have had to take, especially as White's car had hit the wall and literally stopped dead, right in front of them?
>
> Paul Owen-Lowe, a TV3 news producer, visited the crash site a few days later. He found long skid marks down the motorway and ending at the abutment that White's car hit. Neither of the witnesses reported seeing White applying the brakes. Instead, [witness] Dennis Manson believes White was accelerating heavily at the time. Both witnesses claimed to have lost sight of White's Nissan Pulsar at exactly the same moment, even though they were several car lengths apart.
>
> In fact the police were having trouble with other witness accounts of what happened as well. A motorbike rider, Michael Owen, was third on the scene, but says the only other person there was the Armourguard driver, who was beside the wreck, and a gold Trans-Am just pulling up on the left. Manson sent him back to a nearby service station to call an ambulance, and when he returned Owen says he parked behind a white car which had pulled up 10 metres behind the crash.
>
> Dennis Manson stated to police that the bouncer's white Honda had been parked 20 metres in front of the crash, while the bouncer himself says he pulled up and only had to walk across one and a

261 *The Paradise Conspiracy*, Ian Wishart, Howling At The Moon, 1995, p. 44

half lanes of the road to reach the wreck. Manson, a combat medic in the Vietnam War, says he felt for White's pulse but couldn't find one and assumed he was dead. He later told *3 National News* he may have "looked in the wrong place" for the pulse, in the heat of the moment.

Confusion appears to have reigned also within the emergency services that attended. Police Traffic Senior Sergeant William Steedman remembers going "around to the passenger's door which had sprung open at the time of the accident. It was open far enough for me to put my body in."

But Traffic Officer Kieran McGonigle remembers it differently.

"The Senior [Steedman] was trying to get in the passenger's side but the door was jammed, so he asked one of the *fire* guys [my emphasis] for a crowbar. He used it to open the door. He started looking through some of the documents on the back seat to get a name for the driver."

Confused? Then let firefighter Roy Breeze add his statement to the mix.

"After checking for petrol leaks and things around the car I went around to the passenger side. I found the door easy to open, so I don't think it was secured closed.

"I have worked on the rescue tender for 7 years and in that time have attended a lot of accidents, and so that's why I can clearly remember that the door was easy to open and wasn't jammed locked, closed, like they normally are."

None of this serves to indicate anything untoward took place, but what it does illustrate – as is well known to anyone who investigates accidents or crimes – is that, even with the best of intentions, witnesses – professional or otherwise – often give totally different versions of events...

And these statements were taken within only a day or two of the crash, not years later! Now bear in mind, the significant variations in the *official police witness statements* from trained professionals – police, paramedics, security guards – didn't change the centrality of the event in question – the car crashed, the driver was killed. Everyone agreed on the basic facts. Despite it happening in front of a number of people, however, no two stories matched. People see things from different angles, or viewpoints are obscured, or in the stress of the moment with adrenalin pumping minor details get altered.

The gospels, then, reflect everything I would expect to see in an eyewitness report of any major event. If they were perfectly harmonious, I'd be suspicious.

Mark's Gospel, the earliest of the gospels, records a core story of an empty tomb:

THE GOSPEL OF MARK

1When the Sabbath was over, Mary Magdalene, Mary the mother of James, and Salome bought spices so that they might go to anoint Jesus' body. 2Very early on the first day of the week, just after sunrise, they were on their way to the tomb 3and they asked each other, "Who will roll the stone away from the entrance of the tomb?"

4But when they looked up, they saw that the stone, which was very large, had been rolled away. 5As they entered the tomb, they saw a young man dressed in a white robe sitting on the right side, and they were alarmed.

6"Don't be alarmed," he said. "You are looking for Jesus the Nazarene, who was crucified. He has risen! He is not here. See the place where they laid him. 7But go, tell his disciples and Peter, 'He is going ahead of you into Galilee. There you will see him, just as he told you.' "

8Trembling and bewildered, the women went out and fled from the tomb. They said nothing to anyone, because they were afraid.

The key themes in Mark are simple: By the time anyone got there, it was just after sunrise. The tomb was empty. Its stone was rolled away. The discovery was made by women. The women are identified as Mary Magdalene, Mary the mother of James, and Salome, carrying spices for the body. There is a person inside the tomb, possibly angelic. These six points are the core facts. There are also, of course, ancillary details. We are told it is a young man dressed in white inside the tomb, possibly angelic although this is neither confirmed nor denied by Mark. The second is the man telling them Jesus had risen, as an explanation for the empty tomb, and urging them to tell Peter and the disciples to go to Galilee. The third is that at this point the women said nothing to anyone, because they were afraid.[262]

Some later manuscripts have an extra ending on Mark – which may or may not have been copied from earlier versions than the ones we are left with today. I've left it out of this discussion. Moving ahead to Matthew:

---

262 Clearly they told someone, otherwise no one would have known. It may be that the Roman guards mentioned in Matthew were nearby, and the women were afraid of *them*

THE GOSPEL OF MATTHEW

1After the Sabbath, at dawn on the first day of the week, Mary Magdalene and the other Mary went to look at the tomb.

2There was a violent earthquake, for an angel of the Lord came down from heaven and, going to the tomb, rolled back the stone and sat on it. 3His appearance was like lightning, and his clothes were white as snow. 4The guards were so afraid of him that they shook and became like dead men.

5The angel said to the women, "Do not be afraid, for I know that you are looking for Jesus, who was crucified. 6He is not here; he has risen, just as he said. Come and see the place where he lay. 7Then go quickly and tell his disciples: 'He has risen from the dead and is going ahead of you into Galilee. There you will see him.' Now I have told you."

8So the women hurried away from the tomb, afraid yet filled with joy, and ran to tell his disciples. 9Suddenly Jesus met them. "Greetings," he said. They came to him, clasped his feet and worshiped him. 10Then Jesus said to them, "Do not be afraid. Go and tell my brothers to go to Galilee; there they will see me."

The key factual points in Matthew are these: It is dawn. The tomb is empty. Its stone was rolled away. The discovery was made by women. The women are identified as Mary Magdalene, and the 'other' Mary. They flee the empty tomb "afraid, but filled with joy". They come across the risen Jesus at some point after leaving. They are able to clasp his hands and talk to him. He tells them the disciples must meet him in Galilee. These nine points are the core facts. Again, Matthew also, of course, records ancillary details. The first of these is that Matthew says there was an earthquake. He definitely confirms an angelic presence – also dressed in white. He says there were guards posted, who perhaps fainted at the sight of what was taking place (it was after all, a graveyard!) The angel tells the women Jesus had risen, as an explanation for the empty tomb, and is again recorded as urging them to get the disciples to go to Galilee to meet Jesus.[263]

---

263 We see in Matthew that the empty tomb has clearly become an issue of argument between Christians and Jews – not the fact that it was empty but the explanation for it. Just prior to the resurrection passages, at 27:62-66, Matthew had recorded: "The next day...the chief priests and the Pharisees went to Pilate. 'Sir,' they said, 'we remember that while he was still alive that deceiver said, 'After three days I will rise again'. So give the order for the tomb to be made secure until the third day. Otherwise, his disciples may come and steal the body and tell the people that he has been raised from the dead. This last deception will be worse than the first.' 'Take a guard,' Pilate answered. 'Go, make the tomb as secure as you know how.' So they went and made the tomb secure by putting a seal on the stone and posting the guard." The point of this passage becomes clear later in the resurrection narrative, which records at

THE GOSPEL OF LUKE

1On the first day of the week, very early in the morning, the women took the spices they had prepared and went to the tomb. 2They found the stone rolled away from the tomb, 3but when they entered, they did not find the body of the Lord Jesus. 4While they were wondering about this, suddenly two men in clothes that gleamed like lightning stood beside them. 5In their fright the women bowed down with their faces to the ground, but the men said to them, "Why do you look for the living among the dead? 6He is not here; he has risen! Remember how he told you, while he was still with you in Galilee: 7'The Son of Man must be delivered into the hands of sinful men, be crucified and on the third day be raised again.' " 8Then they remembered his words.

9When they came back from the tomb, they told all these things to the Eleven and to all the others. 10It was Mary Magdalene, Joanna, Mary the mother of James, and the others with them who told this to the apostles. 11But they did not believe the women, because their words seemed to them like nonsense. 12Peter, however, got up and ran to the tomb. Bending over, he saw the strips of linen lying by themselves, and he went away, wondering to himself what had happened.

THEMES: Luke's Gospel, again, identifies certain core truths of the resurrection accounts: It is very early in the morning. Women discover the stone rolled away. The tomb is empty. The women are Mary Magdalene, Joanna, and Mary the mother of James. They are told by an angelic presence that Christ is risen. They left the tomb to tell Peter and the disciples, who didn't believe them and went to see for himself. Ancillary information includes the claim that there were two men/angels rather than one.

THE GOSPEL OF JOHN

1Early on the first day of the week, while it was still dark, Mary

---

Matt 28:11-15: "While the women were on their way, some of the guards went into the city and reported to the chief priests everything that had happened. When the chief priests had met with the elders and devised a plan, they gave the soldiers a large sum of money, telling them, "You are to say, 'His disciples came during the night and stole him away while we were asleep.' If this report gets to the governor, we will satisfy him and keep you out of trouble." So the soldiers took the money and did as they were instructed. And this story has been widely circulated among the Jews to this very day."
This account is seen by many as further proof of an empty tomb. Whilst clearly a Matthean apologetic, Matthew was not defending the *emptiness* of the tomb, but *why* it was empty, i.e. he offered a supernatural reason "Jesus is risen from the dead", against the Jewish argument, "someone stole the corpse". This illustrates that rival Jewish groups were indeed accusing Christians of stealing Christ's body, otherwise there would be no need to have this account in the gospels at all

Magdalene went to the tomb and saw that the stone had been removed from the entrance. 2So she came running to Simon Peter and the other disciple, the one Jesus loved, and said, "They have taken the Lord out of the tomb, and we don't know where they have put him!"

3So Peter and the other disciple started for the tomb. 4Both were running, but the other disciple outran Peter and reached the tomb first. 5He bent over and looked in at the strips of linen lying there but did not go in. 6Then Simon Peter, who was behind him, arrived and went into the tomb. He saw the strips of linen lying there, 7as well as the burial cloth that had been around Jesus' head. The cloth was folded up by itself, separate from the linen. 8Finally the other disciple, who had reached the tomb first, also went inside. He saw and believed. 9(They still did not understand from Scripture that Jesus had to rise from the dead.)

10Then the disciples went back to their homes, 11but Mary stood outside the tomb crying. As she wept, she bent over to look into the tomb 12and saw two angels in white, seated where Jesus' body had been, one at the head and the other at the foot.

13They asked her, "Woman, why are you crying?"

"They have taken my Lord away," she said, "and I don't know where they have put him." 14At this, she turned around and saw Jesus standing there, but she did not realize that it was Jesus.

15"Woman," he said, "why are you crying? Who is it you are looking for?"

Thinking he was the gardener, she said, "Sir, if you have carried him away, tell me where you have put him, and I will get him."

16Jesus said to her, "Mary."

She turned toward him and cried out in Aramaic, "Rabboni!" (which means Teacher).

17Jesus said, "Do not hold on to me, for I have not yet returned to the Father. Go instead to my brothers and tell them, 'I am returning to my Father and your Father, to my God and your God.' "

18Mary Magdalene went to the disciples with the news: "I have seen the Lord!" And she told them that he had said these things to her.

19On the evening of that first day of the week, when the disciples were together, with the doors locked for fear of the Jews, Jesus came and stood among them and said, "Peace be with you!" 20After he said this, he showed them his hands and side. The disciples were overjoyed when they saw the Lord.

21Again Jesus said, "Peace be with you! As the Father has sent me, I am sending you." 22And with that he breathed on them and said, "Receive the Holy Spirit. 23If you forgive anyone his sins, they are forgiven; if you do not forgive them, they are not forgiven."

OK, you're probably getting the basic picture now. John's main themes: the tomb is empty, discovered by a woman, runs to tell Peter, who drags John (the coy yet 'modest' disciple) along. The men find it just as Mary says, and walk off perplexed. Mary goes back, or hangs around, and sees two angels inside the tomb, turns around to find Jesus behind her. Then she races off again to tell the men she has seen the risen Lord.

In this account the only words recorded are Christ asking her not to touch him as he has yet to return to his Father. This does not mean that these were the only things Christ could have said, however. When I do an interview, or write a book for that matter, I leave a lot of comments on the cutting-room floor, so to speak. If I was to repeat everything I obtained verbatim, it would be a very long book and very unfocused. Instead, all journalists and writers "redact" or edit out the bits that are irrelevant to their point.

To understand the resurrection accounts as journalism, you first have to understand the markets each writer was going for. The biggest mistake made by Spong, Geering and others, in my view, has been to impose a simple chronological template on the gospels, from oldest to most recent, and work a basic "myth evolution theory" over the top of them. Yes, the gospels were published sequentially, but far more important than that are the unique audiences each book was aimed at. The style difference between a *Children's Bible* and the *King James Version* is going to be far more significant than the time delay between them.

Mark was a Jew writing for Romans. Whilst not a direct disciple of Christ, there is evidence to suggest that Christ's Last Supper may have taken place in a room owned by Mark's mother. Mark, we know, accompanied Paul and also went with Peter to Rome. His gospel is said to have recorded what Peter preached to Roman audiences. Little wonder Mark doesn't mention a virgin birth – the whole point of the birth story is that it filled an obscure Jewish prophecy that was probably irrelevant to Roman ears. In Jerusalem, the virgin birth meant something. In Rome, it didn't.[264]

---

264 Just developing this little diversion, as it illustrates Mark's careful avoidance of the issue for his Roman readers, scholar Millard Erickson argues that Mark actually does make a veiled reference to the virgin birth at 6:3. In Matt 13:55, the equivalent passage reads "Is this not the carpenter's son?", while in Luke 4:22 it reads "Is not this Joseph's son?". Yet in Mark, where the author had chosen not to divert into a birth narrative, he writes, "Is not this the

Matthew was a Jew writing for a Jewish audience. His gospel evokes more vivid Hebrew imagery and ancient prophecy as part of his attempt to clearly put Christ in the Jewish Messiah context for his Jewish readers.

Luke, from what we can tell, was Greek, certainly a Gentile, and was writing for a primarily Greek/Syrian audience as well as some of the Jewish communities along the eastern Mediterranean coast. He is careful to straddle two worlds without alienating either. In the resurrection accounts, he carefully does not talk of Jewish "angels", but rather "two men" whose clothes gleamed like "lightning". To a Greek or Roman audience, this evokes the imagery of Mercury/Hermes, the messenger god whose specific role was to carry news from "the gods" down to mortals. Of course, Luke knew it wasn't Hermes, but it would have been an effective dog-whistle to his readers about divine events taking place and heavenly messengers heralding the news. Luke and Mark were simply playing to their foreign markets by referring to the angel/s on this occasion as men. Matthew, on the other hand, was well and truly playing to the home crowd. Remember, the Jewish pantheon of divine appearances was full of angelic expectations. So 'Jewish reporter' Matthew's angel is there with bells on, announced by an earthquake, perched imperiously atop the rolled tombstone. Does any of this change the core of Matthew's story? Not in the slightest: the tomb was empty, it was women who found it, and Christ was seen.

John's resurrection account, like his entire gospel, was far more spiritual than the synoptic versions. Knowing that the previous gospels had concentrated on the historic acts and parables of Christ, John preferred to emphasise the transcendent God.

As a reporter, then, John had no interest in Jesus' comments on Galilee – the other gospels had already covered that – but Christ's suggestion that some kind of spiritual purity was needed (hence the request to Mary Magdalene not to touch) was interesting to him in view of the whole thrust of his gospel, which was not the minutiae, so much as the big picture of what the Resurrection meant. He lingers, for example, on his own and Peter's reaction at seeing the linen burial cloth, and says of himself: "Finally, the other disciple, who had reached the tomb first, also went inside. He saw and believed. (They still did not understand from Scripture that Jesus had to rise from the dead)."

carpenter; the son of Mary and brother of James and Joses and Judas and Simon, and are not his sisters here with us?" Says Erickson: "It is as if Mark is taking pains to avoid referring to Jesus as the son of Joseph" because it would, of course, have confused his readers who didn't have access to the birth story and who had been told through Mark that Jesus was the son of God. In the same fashion, when John's Gospel describes Jesus as "God's only begotten son", scholars suggest the phrase has to be referring to the virgin birth. See Erickson's *Christian Theology*, Baker Books, 1984, Vol 2, pp. 750-751

RESURRECTION: FACT OR FIGMENT?

His last comment is exactly right. It is one thing for Jesus to have uttered cryptic comments about rebuilding his temple in three days, it is a totally different thing for the disciples to have pored back over the sacred scrolls looking for verses that might explain what had happened. That would happen, but it had not happened by that first Easter Sunday, because they had no personal expectation that Christ would rise.

Retired judge and barrister Herbert Casteel argues the core truths in the resurrection accounts sometimes get obscured by the debate around the supposed ancillary differences.

"The internal evidence of the resurrection accounts: Each of the four Gospels gives an account of that first Easter Sunday when Jesus arose from the tomb. When we first read these accounts it appears they are in hopeless contradiction. Matthew says it was Mary Magdalene and the other Mary who went out to the tomb. Mark says it was Mary Magdalene, Mary the mother of James, and Salome. Luke says it was Mary Magdalene, Joanna, Mary the mother of James, and the others with them, and John mentions only Mary Magdalene. Furthermore, they all mention different people to whom Jesus appeared on that day.

"Does this mean that these are false reports, made-up by dishonest men to deceive us? On the contrary, this is good evidence that these are truthful accounts, because people who conspire to testify to a falsehood rehearse carefully to avoid contradictions. False testimony appears on the surface to be in harmony, but discrepancies appear when you dig deeper. True accounts may appear on the surface to be contradictory, but are found to be in harmony when you dig deeper," says Casteel.[265]

To me, there are only four important points in the resurrection stories. All four gospels agree the tomb was empty. All four agree that women discovered this first. All four agree that Christ had risen. And three of the four gospels testify that Christ appeared to his followers in the flesh.[266]

Just like Paul White's road crash, those are the kernels of truth that infuse the gospel accounts, regardless of apparent discrepancies.[267] Differences in news stories arise depending on whom you talk to as a source. None of us see the world like a video camera. Instead, we process and remember the information most relevant to our own perspective. Salome? Joanna? Perhaps they were both there, and Mark's source for his

---

265 *Beyond a Reasonable Doubt*, Herbert C Casteel, College Press: 1992, 2nd rev.; p. 211ff
266 This assertion also appears in the added ending to Mark (16:9-20)
267 In fact, there are many well-constructed analyses of these at the following sites:
http://www.christian-thinktank.com/ordorise.html
http://www.tektonics.org/lp/physrez.html
http://www.tektonics.org/tomb/carrier11.html

account was Salome who couldn't remember Joanna's name, but knew the older Marys. Perhaps Matthew found Joanna, who likewise remembered the Marys but couldn't recall the name of the other girl. There are an infinite number of variables. So what do you do as a writer? You drop the reference to a witness you can't name and who therefore offers no backup to your story.

One angel? Two angels? Two men? Who cares? The same logic applies, depending on the viewing angles of their witnesses, whether a tree or bush partially blocked their line of sight – any range of ordinary things. We know all four gospels agree that at least one angel/messenger was there. The problem was that many of these accounts were assembled two or three decades after the events in question. In contrast, let me take you again to the police witness statements in the Paul White Citibank case, taken just *days* after the events in question and narrated and redacted by me for my book as I tried to reconstruct White's final hours:

White told him each of the installments would be worth $15,000. It was during this time that White caught the attention of an off-duty bouncer. The bouncer and White left sometime between 3:00am and 4:00am, heading for the Customhouse Bar. While they were there, Paul White made a comment about how the lights above the bar were looking strange. Moving on, they arrived at the Galatos Bar a short time later. White dropped some cash on the floor.

"It was embarrassing," the bouncer told police later. "Someone asked me 'where was that from?'. I assumed he was talking about the money and I said 'I wouldn't have a clue'. I didn't like the idea of getting into a conversation about it with anybody. I suppose the situation was nerve wracking."

After putting the loot back in a plastic bag, White and his new friend left the bar. They headed back to Grapes, arriving around 4:15am. Theoretically. Once again confusion arises among police witnesses about the exact whereabouts of Mr Paul Gordon Edward White. One staff member interviewed by police says he left Grapes at 4:15am and White was still inside at the time having drinks with other staff. Other staff report White and the bouncer *arriving back* around 4:30am.

Whatever the exact time, all witnesses agree that the bouncer was out in the carpark trying to convince Paul White not to drive himself home. A waitress leaving the club to go home was watching the discussion.

"I remember seeing two guys walk up and stand behind them, a few paces away, for a minute or so," she told police. "I turned away for about three minutes and when I looked back they had gone. I had no idea where they went."

It was just a passing observation, but it echoed Sharon Young's earlier comment about two men standing close to White at the Centra Hotel several hours earlier.

One police witness says he saw Paul drag a wad of money from one of his pockets and wave it around at one point in the carpark, this would be the last documented sighting of a significant amount of cash on White. Eventually however, sometime just before 5:00am, only White and the bouncer were left. Within half an hour Paul White would be deep in a coma and dying. His money would be missing. The last thing he saw was probably a concrete wall.[268]

William Lane Craig, with doctorates from the Universities of Birmingham and Munich, and a professor at Biola University, is widely acknowledged as one of America's leading theologians. He points out that the four gospel accounts of the resurrection are stunningly simple and unadorned with myth, when compared with the pseudo-gospels that emerged a hundred and forty years later.

"Comparison of Mark's account with those in later apocryphal gospels like the Gospel of Peter underlines the simplicity of the Markan story. The Gospel of Peter inserts, between Jesus' being sealed in the tomb and the visit of Mary Magdalene early Sunday morning, an account of the resurrection itself.[269]

"According to this account, the tomb is surrounded not only by Roman guards but also by the Jewish Pharisees and elders, as well as a multitude from the surrounding countryside. Suddenly in the night there rings out a loud voice in heaven, and two men descend from heaven to the tomb, The stone over the door rolls back by itself and they go into the tomb.

"Then three men come out of the tomb, two of them holding up the third man. The heads of the two men reach up into the clouds, but the head of the third man reaches up beyond the clouds. Then a cross comes out of the tomb, and a voice from heaven asks, 'Have you preached to them that sleep?' And the cross answers, 'Yes'.

"This is how legends look," says Craig. "By contrast, Mark's account of

268   *The Paradise Conspiracy*, Ian Wishart, Howling At The Moon, 1995, p. 34
269   *In Defense Of Miracles*, Habermas & Geivett eds, IVP, 1997, p. 254

the discovery of the empty tomb is simple and seems to be pretty much a straightforward report of what happened."

Craig, and others, point out that the gospel reports ran counter-cultural in a whole range of ways, like the fact that women were the first witnesses. Women in ancient Israel, like women in many hardline Islamic countries today, had no credibility. Their evidence could not be used in court. There was no value to the gospel-writers, and in fact a lot of negative baggage, in having women as the prime eyewitnesses of the resurrection. If you were writing a fictional account that you wanted ancient Jews to believe, the male disciples would have been the first to see the risen Christ. So the fact that women are given this prominence, in a series of gospels that proclaim truth, makes it highly probable that Christ did indeed rise, and the women told the world.

There is something else to consider. All but one of the disciples are recorded as having died a martyr's death in defense of the truth of the resurrection.[270] According to contemporary Roman writings, Christians were offered the chance to deny Christ and live, and those who refused to deny Christ were then executed by the Romans.[271] It is one thing to die for something you believe in, or merely "believe" to be true. The Islamic terrorists who flew jets into the World Trade Centre died for something they believed (hoped) was true. It is a totally different thing to lay down your life for something you *know for a fact* is a lie. It just does not happen. If the resurrection was a fake, the disciples themselves had to know, because they are the ones who went around testifying that they had physically seen the risen Christ. The disciples had all borne direct witness to the resurrected Messiah. The reason they went to their deaths as lion-fodder, stoning or crucifixion victims, rather than recant their belief in Christ, is because they didn't just 'believe', they *knew* Christ was God. For them, there could only be one answer to the earthly executioner's challenge: "Deny Christ or die!"

Why would you throw away *eternal* life by denying the risen Christ you yourself had seen, when you knew that within a few bites of the big cat's jaws you'd be joining Christ yourself?

If the resurrection didn't happen, the disciples were liars. Not just mistaken – Liars. The disciples, unlike anyone alive today, had the luxury

---

270 http://www.ccel.org/bible/phillips/CN500APOSTLES%20FATE.htm
271 http://www.mc.maricopa.edu/~tomshoemaker/handouts/pliny.html.
Roman administrator Pliny the Younger spells out how he would give Christians three chances to recant: "Meanwhile, in the case of those who were denounced to me as Christians, I have observed the following procedure: I interrogated these as to whether they were Christians; those who confessed I interrogated a second and a third time, threatening them with punishment; those who persisted I ordered executed."

of coughing up to their lie, and saving themselves from death by beast. It is not as if they were onto a great get-rich-quick scheme; Christianity, a gospel of service to others, was bringing the disciples and their families grief and persecution, when they could so easily have opted for a less stressful life by denying their beliefs. Would a disciple watch his wife and children be put to the sword for something he himself knew was a lie, when he could save them all with a word?

For this reason, a majority of scholars, and even popular commentators like John Spong, are convinced that whatever happened on that first Easter, it was enough to make absolute believers out of all those involved.

"I can, with absolute honesty and deep conviction, say that I believe the resurrection of Jesus was real," writes Spong. "To support that assertion I can point to data that reveal in very objective ways that something of great and significant power happened following the crucifixion of Jesus, something that had dramatic and life-changing consequences.

"In an earlier context we noted what seems to be the absolutely historical fact that Jesus faced apostolic abandonment when he was arrested…What we need to look at now is the equally real fact of history that after the crucifixion some experience of great magnitude brought Jesus' disciples back, empowered them and gave them the courage to take up the cause of this Jesus in the face of persecution and martyrdom.

"They never wavered. The strength of their conviction was such that no threat or fear could now separate them from the God they believed they had met in Jesus."[272]

I'm running with Spong here precisely because he's a hostile witness in this book. He recognizes, despite his overall attack on Christianity, that the evidence in favour of the resurrection being real to the disciples is overwhelming. It cannot be explained as myth, or a fabrication. Whatever it is, it must be fundamental to the understanding the disciples had of Christ and their own role in the new branch of Judaism that Christianity was.

After all, the worship of Christ as God was blasphemy to people who, all their lives, had been orthodox Jews. With daily recitations of the Shema, "Hear, O Israel, the Lord your God is one", it was drummed into the Jews that God could not be two, or three. When Jesus Christ called himself, "I AM", he was giving himself God's name. When the disciples called Christ, "My Lord and my God", they were going where no Jew had gone before. Yet go they did, even into the lions' den.

You've seen the lead-up to the resurrection appearances, and the beliefs

---

272 *JFTNR*, Spong, p. 118

of the early Christians that what they had seen was real. Now, let's test the counter-theories.

THE MASS-HALLUCINATION THEORY

The liberal wing, led by people like Spong, Geering or Armstrong, argue that the high Christology – that is, the belief that Christ was divine – was a late addition to the original Christian stories, as "myths" about him grew and Christians were looking for a "my God is bigger than your god" pitch. Some critics even try to argue this "divine Christ" was invented by the Catholic Church in 325 AD, which as we saw earlier is utterly incorrect based on early Roman writings.

In arguing that the Resurrection as Christianity understands it wasn't real, Geering, Spong and Infidels' Richard Carrier try to appeal to mass hallucination theory – that a bunch of people all experienced simultaneous hallucinations of the allegedly risen Christ.

This review by AnsweringInfidels' David Wood of Richard Carrier's recent book on the topic, sets out the dilemma nicely:[273]

Carrier attributes the origin of life to natural causes, and the resurrection of Jesus to an incredible ensemble of mass-hallucinations....

Since the debate [with Michael Licona], Richard has again argued that Jesus never existed. Thus, we have a problem. Richard believes that Jesus probably never existed. He also says that the theory he thinks is "most probably correct" is that Jesus' disciples experienced visions of him after he died....

Jesus never existed. Nevertheless, he had close companions who did exist. (If you're wondering how a person who didn't exist could have followers, you may be forgetting that nonexistent people can be very, very crafty.) These followers became extremely distraught when Jesus (who didn't exist) was tortured and crucified by Roman soldiers (who did exist). Jesus (who didn't exist) may or may not have been placed in a tomb (which may or may not have existed).

In light of the death of their nonexistent leader, the minds of these followers were so overcome by emotion that they soon experienced grief hallucinations, in which they saw visions of the risen Jesus (whom no one had ever seen to begin with). Strangely, these disciples came to believe that Jesus was resurrected without his body (probably because nonexistent people don't have bodies). This caused them to become bold evangelists of the risen Lord they had never seen.

James (who did exist), the brother of Jesus, also experienced grief hallucinations when he heard that his brother (who didn't exist) had been nailed to a cross (many of which did exist). James joined the other followers, and the group became so bold that it attracted the attention of a man named Saul (who did exist). While Saul wanted to destroy Christianity because it went against everything he believed in, he was overwhelmingly attracted to its humble message of social reform. Thus, in the midst of a murderous rampage against Christianity, Saul also hallucinated and experienced a vision of Jesus (who never existed). The Apostle Paul (who previously existed as Saul) later met with Jesus' followers to make sure that his teachings were in line with those of Jesus. He was pleased to learn that his teachings indeed matched up with the words of the non-existent Jesus, and he continued to spread Christianity throughout the Roman world....

Now *that* makes sense, doesn't it! The problem with all of this, of course, is that science has shown there are no such things as mass hallucinations. A hallucination is something your mind sees that isn't there. For a group of people to share the same "hallucination" would imply that all of their minds have simultaneously given up the reality ghost and all gone with the same hallucination, rather than different ones. This doesn't happen, of course. When people all see the same thing, we call them "eyewitnesses" in modern society.

A group of people could certainly experience a mass optical illusion, which is where a trick of the light or shadow creates an apparent image that our brains all collectively interpret the same way. An example of this is seeing the shape of a dog in the clouds. But mass hallucinations? There are no documented cases in history.

In *Christianity Without God*, Lloyd Geering – like Spong – finds miracles impossible for his own mind to handle, so begins his study by looking for explanations other than supernatural to explain the risen Christ. Unlike Richard Carrier, Geering concedes Christ existed, but like him he believes the resurrection appearances began as a series of "visions".

"The unconscious depths of the human psyche can prove to be extraordinarily creative. The psyche, drawing upon both remembered experience and the basic symbols already embedded there, creates a vision which resolves the issue."[274]

274 *Christianity Without God*, Geering, p. 77

In his footnote to anchor this fluffy piece of psychobabble, Geering says "Jungian analysts document many contemporary accounts of how the unconscious mind can creatively resolve inner tensions by means of visions."

Perhaps, but what Geering *didn't* say is that psychologists have found *no* evidence that your vision can meet my vision and do lunch, becoming the same vision for both of us at precisely the same moment. The reason for this is very simple: each of us has inner tensions that differ. You might be suffering repressed sexual tensions as Freud used to waffle on about, and I might be suffering a phobia. The vision created by our subconscious minds will be unique to each of us.

Geering continues:[275]

"Such is the nature of the enquiring human mind that it was not sufficient for the ongoing Christian community just to say that the glorified Jesus had been seen in visions…As soon as Christians were convinced that some had received visions of the exaltation of Jesus, and since they knew for certain that he had been crucified and gone to the abode of the dead, then it followed that he must have risen from the dead. So the earliest Christian records declare that Jesus had been raised from the dead.

"At first, this was chiefly a synonym for exaltation [a spiritual-only resurrection], for resurrection certainly did not mean the return to life in this world. And yet, during the last third of the first century, several stories began to emerge which seemed to imply just that.

"In John 21 we are even told of Jesus breakfasting with the disciples after their catch of fish."

Let's stop Geering, Emeritus Professor, right there on a factual issue. The resurrected Christ eating fish and bread story *first* surfaces in the Gospel of Luke,[276] written in the late 50s, not John:

"While they were still talking about this, Jesus himself stood among them and said to them, 'Peace be with you'.

"They were startled and frightened, thinking they saw a ghost. He said to them, 'Why are you troubled, and why do doubts rise in your minds? Look at my hands and my feet. It is I myself! Touch me and see; a ghost does not have flesh and bones, as you see I have'.

"When he had said this, he showed them his hands and feet. And while they still did not believe it because of joy and amazement, he asked them, 'Do you have anything here to eat?' They gave him a piece of broiled fish, and he took it and ate it in their presence."

---

275   Ibid, p. 78
276   Luke 24:28-30, and 24:36-43. This "mass hallucination" walked around shaking hands, eating food and generally socializing in front of large numbers of people

How many times have you and your friends been sitting down to dinner and a vision of a dead friend has walked into the room, shaken your hand, pulled up a chair, reached for a slice of bread, grabbed a fish, and started yarning with all of you? Oh, it hasn't happened?

Perhaps now you can see the weakness in the arguments of Lloyd Geering, because this is where the skeptics hit the wall.

Geering's, Spong's and Carrier's theories about "visions" are not new. In fact, Geering proudly cites an 1843 rationalist, David Strauss, who first raised it. In more recent centuries however, the theory has been thoroughly trashed. But why bother with the recent? If it's good enough for Geering to cite one of the original proponents of this rubbishy theory, I can cite one of the original debunkers of it:

"The only other explanation [besides fraud], worthy of attention," writes Alfred Edersheim,[277] "is the so called 'Vision-hypothesis:' that the Apostles really believed in the Resurrection, but the mere visions of Christ had wrought in them this belief. The hypothesis has been variously modified. According to some, these visions were the outcome of an excited imagination, of a morbid state of the nervous system. To this there is, of course, the preliminary objection, that such visions presuppose a previous expectancy of the event, which, as we know, is the opposite of the fact."

Indeed, and Lloyd Geering himself admits as much:[278]

"It is generally agreed, with gospel record support, that when Jesus was crucified the disciples deserted him and fled. They returned to Galilee greatly dispirited."

Hardly the state of mind in which one *expects* to see a resurrection. After all, they saw him die.

Edersheim continues:

"Again, such a 'Vision-hypothesis' in no way agrees with the many details and circumstances narrated in connection with the Risen One, who is described as having appeared not only to one or another in the retirement of the chamber, but to many, and in a manner and circumstances which render the idea of a mere vision impossible. Besides, the visions of an excited imagination would not have endured and led to such results; most probably they would soon have given place to corresponding depression.

"The 'Vision-hypothesis' is not much improved, if we regard the supposed vision as the result of reflection, that the disciples, convinced that the Messiah could not remain dead (and this again is contrary to fact) had wrought themselves first into a persuasion that He must rise,

---

277 Alfred Edersheim, *The Life and Times of Jesus the Messiah*, 1883
278 *Christianity Without God*, Geering, p. 77

and then into visions of the Risen One. This argument might, of course, be variously elaborated, and the account in the Gospels represents as the form which it afterwards took in the belief of the Church.

"But (a) the whole 'Vision-hypothesis' is shadowy and unreal, and the sacred writers themselves show that they knew the distinction between visions and real appearances; (b) it is impossible to reconcile it with such occurrences as that in St. Luke 24:38-43 and St. John 21:13, and, if possible, even more so, to set aside all these details as the outcome of later tradition, for which there was no other basis than the desire of vindicating a vision; (c) it is incompatible with the careful inquiry of St. Paul, who, as on so many other occasions, is here a most important witness. (d) The theory involves the most arbitrary handling of the Gospel-narratives, such as that the Apostles had at once returned to Galilee, where the sight of the familiar scenes had kindled in them this enthusiasm; that all the notices about the 'third day' are to be rejected, &c. (e). What was so *fundamental* a belief as that of the Resurrection could not have had its origin in a delusive vision. This, as Keim has shown, would be incompatible with the calm clearness of conviction and strong purpose of action which were its outcome. Besides, are we to believe that the enthusiasm had first seized the women, then the Apostle, and so on? But how, in that case, about the 500 of whom St. Paul speaks? They could scarcely all have been seized with the same mania. (f) A mere vision is unthinkable under such circumstances as the walk to Emmaus, the conversation with Thomas, with Peter, &c. Besides, it is incompatible with the giving of such definite promises by the Risen Christ as that of the Holy Spirit, and of such detailed directions as that of Evangelising the world. (g) Lastly, as Keim points out, it is incompatible with the fact that these manifestations ceased with the Ascension. We have eight or at most nine such manifestations in the course of six weeks, and then they suddenly and permanently cease! This would not accord with the theory of visions on the part of excited enthusiasts."

As you can see, Edersheim's response to the vision theory is cutting and decisive. More shocking to me is how an expert writing in 1880 can skewer the scholarship of Lloyd Geering more than 120 years in the future – which is the danger of relying (as Richard Dawkins also does) on such old theories in the first place, even though they have been debunked time and again.

Actually, this highlights another weakness in the books written by liberal theologians – they rarely address counter arguments, as I have tried to do here. The danger in that is that your own thinking becomes stale; it is almost as if you are afraid of the truth. If the truth cannot withstand the crucible of informed debate and investigation, then it was never the truth in the first place.

Spong is another who refuses to engage, preferring to live his life in a safe intellectual bubble, preaching largely to his converted and relying on his books to draw people in.

"Sometimes when I have to respond to the constant harassment of those who live within the narrow bounds of yesterday's Christianity, I feel as if I am being gummed to death by a herd of clacking geese."[279]

Perhaps he meant "flock" or "gaggle", rather than "herd". His point is clear, but it rests entirely on there not being a miraculous creation event, and solely a naturalistic scientific explanation for all that exists. Given that top scientists are coming down in favour of a probable supernatural beginning, the Spong/Geering/Dawkins argument has no rational basis; it depends on there being no God. If God exists, their entire theory collapses.

Geering meanwhile makes sweeping appeals in his books to unseen, unsourced experts:

"There is now widespread agreement…"[280]

"It is now widely acknowledged…"[281]

Of the scholars he does cite on page 77, all were born in the 1800s. It is like being trapped in a timewarp, or reading a book written by a living fossil.

But still, the inane theories keep coming:

"Is it really true that there is no such thing as mass hallucination?" writes a desperate atheist academic, Michael Martin in his 1991 book, *The Case Against Christianity*. "In fact, psychologists have studied a closely related phenomenon known as collective delusion or mass hysteria. In this phenomenon…"

You probably missed Martin's subtle segue there, to try and dig skepticism out of the wreckage of their theories. First of all, he challenges the established scientific fact that there is no such thing as mass hallucination. He challenges it, because for his and Geering's arguments to hold up, there has to be such a phenomenon. But instead of challenging it directly by giving examples of genuine mass hallucinations (he couldn't, because there are none), he slides into comparing it to "a closely related phenomenon… collective delusion".

Commentators[282] have picked up on this to trounce Martin:

"Hallucinations are sensory experiences (e.g., "I see the Abominable

---

279 *JFTNR*, Spong, p. 8
280 *Christianity Without God*, Geering, p. 76
281 Ibid, p. 74
282 http://www.theism.net/authors/zjordan/default_files/hallu.htm

Snowman sitting on my sofa drinking coffee, I hear his growl, and I feel his claws ripping my flesh"), whereas delusions are beliefs (e.g., "The Abominable Snowman is out to get me.")

People can certainly share delusional beliefs, and some of the authors I'm addressing in *The Divinity Code* are evidence of that. But sharing hallucinations (without the assistance of drugs and suggestive prompting) is unheard of.

Lastly, if the disciples did all hallucinate about seeing the risen Christ, then presumably his body should have been safely back in the tomb, never having moved at all. Except, of course, it wasn't. So not only does this theory require the unprecedented and unscientific coincidence of mass hallucinations of the same thing, but the equally inexplicable coincidence that, of all the bodies that could possibly go missing in the graveyard that day, it had to be Christ's.

THE SWOON THEORY

This is the doctrine that Christ did not actually die on the cross, but merely passed out, and was revived either with help or on his own in the tomb. I should make clear at this point that no accredited New Testament scholar believes this theory. Even the rationalist skeptic David Strauss, beloved of Geering, scoffed in the mid 1800s when the theory was being debated then.

"It is impossible that a being who had stolen half dead out of the sepulchre, who crept about weak and ill and wanting medical treatment, who required bandaging, strengthening and indulgence, and who still at last yielded to his sufferings, could have given the disciples the impression that he was a conqueror over death and the grave, the Prince of life: an impression that lay at the bottom of their future ministry.

"Such a resuscitation could only have *weakened* the impression which he had made upon them in life and death, at the most could only have given it an elegiac voice, but could by no possibility have changed their sorrow into enthusiasm, have elevated their reverence into worship."[283]

Think about it for a nano-second: the first century Jews were Homo sapiens sapiens, just like you and I. They had the same IQ levels we do. I'm sure in that bloodthirsty society they'd seen plenty of half-dead victims of Roman violence or Jewish stonings. In fact, they probably saw more half-dead people in a week than you have in your life time. I'm equally sure they could work out the difference between a resurrected Saviour coming

---

283 *A New Life of Jesus*, David Strauss, 1879, 1.412

in glory, and the first-century equivalent of a road-traffic accident.

Then there's the inconvenient reality of a Roman crucifixion. They were not designed to be survivable, and the Romans were pretty good at them. Life was cheap, and the lives of Jewish vagabonds even cheaper. The thrashing Christ received first with hook-encrusted whips intended to rip open his back and limbs would have almost killed him, let alone the nailing to the cross part.

One of the key modern proponents of this two centuries old idea is New Zealand author Michael Baigent, who first mooted it in *The Holy Blood & The Holy Grail* and developed the theme further in last year's *The Jesus Papers*: To get around the obvious problem of a blood-encrusted, gasping, crawling and naked Christ (the burial cloth having remained in the tomb) croaking to his disbelieving followers "I have risen indeed!", Baigent's solution is that Christ avoids the resurrection appearances altogether, and takes off into the sunset with Mary Magdalene before anyone gets wind of his hoax:

"In this book, I have proposed that Jesus, with some help from his closest friends and the collusion of the Roman prefect, Pontius Pilate, survived the crucifixion. It was undoubtedly a very close run maneuver. When Joseph of Arimathea went to ask for Jesus' body, Pilate seems to have thought that the plan had not been a success and Jesus had in fact died, as indicated, according to Mark's Gospel, by his use of the Greek work *ptoma* (meaning 'corpse') for Jesus' body.

"Jesus had not died, but it appears that he was in urgent need of medical treatment. He was taken down from the cross and placed in an empty tomb. Then, once night had fallen, according to John's Gospel, Joseph of Arimathea and Nicodemus came with medicinal potions. Once Jesus was considered out of danger, I have suggested they took him out of the tomb and away to safety, to a place where he could recuperate."[284]

Personally, I don't think a couple of Band-Aids and a dose of Rescue Remedy were going to do the trick, no matter how desperately Baigent wants to believe this long-debunked theory.[285]

"And what happened next?" he asks. "We cannot know, but he did not,

---

284   *The Jesus Papers*, Michael Baigent, HarperElement, 2006, p. 262
285   Baigent appeals to the recorded survival of a crucifixion victim by Josephus. The man's legs had not been broken so he had not suffocated and was able to be revived. Jesus, however, had received a double punishment. John's Gospel 19:1-6 records that Pilate tried to assuage the crowd's bloodlust by having Christ severely flogged first. He then re-presented him to the crowd, and only sent him on to crucifixion after the crowd indicated they still wanted Barabbas released, not Christ. Of course, the gospels also record that in lieu of not breaking his legs, the Romans ran Jesus through with a spear to the heart. The Josephus victim had not suffered that fate. The chances of Christ's survival were nil

despite the mythology about him which has been created – vanish from the face of the earth. He went *somewhere*."

Indeed. According to the vast majority of trained scholars, the disciples were absolutely convinced they not only saw Christ but dined with him, on numerous occasions, for about six weeks until his ascension. Baigent's theory – even if you ignore its huge failings and accept it at face value – doesn't explain what got the disciples inspired again and brave enough to face being torn apart by lions.

So, there's an empty tomb because Christ has skipped off somewhere with Mary Magdalene? If all that had greeted the disciples was an empty tomb and nothing further, the history books would have consigned Christianity to a three-year minor Jerusalem sect, which ended in discord when followers accused fellow Jews of stealing the body of their minor prophet. Because that would have been the automatic reaction of the disciples themselves: "The tomb's empty, somebody's nicked our Jesus!"

No, it is the empty tomb *plus* the resurrection appearances that accounts for the religion's dominance of world history. Alone among world religions, it is the Resurrection of a real historical figure, Jesus Christ, that not only suggests the supernatural realm is real but that Christ has control of it.

If that is the case, however, the questions we are about to ask need some answers.

CHAPTER 15

THE PROBLEM OF EVIL

"God cannot do what is actually impossible. It is actually impossible to destroy evil without destroying free choice. But free choice is necessary to a moral universe. Therefore, God cannot destroy evil without destroying this good moral universe"

Norman Geisler, New Testament scholar

IT IS ALL VERY WELL building a case for the existence of God, even one that is compelling, based on the latest scientific data, but if God really does exist, how do we explain one of the biggest arguments against it I know: the problem of Evil?

Richard Dawkins, like me, recognizes that the existence of evil does not – in itself – disprove the existence of God.

"It is an argument only against the existence of a good God," says Dawkins. "Goodness is no part of the *definition* of the God Hypothesis, merely a desirable add-on."

If it were left to both Dawkins and I, we'd probably leave the question there: the presence of evil in the world does not in itself negate the scientific evidence in favour of creation, nor the evidence that Earth has been fine-tuned to sustain intelligent human life.

However, despite the fact I have assembled objective evidence for the divinity code and tried to avoid getting bogged down in touchy-feely moral issues (except in the section on comparative religion where, by definition, we needed to examine competing moral claims), this book would be incomplete without addressing the question at hand.

For many, the issue of apparent divine inaction in the face of evil is a hard pill to swallow. John Spong, for example, tries to justify his lack of belief in miracles by appealing to the problem of evil.

"Once miraculous supernatural power is ascribed to God, then believers need an explanation for why God acts on some occasions and not others. If God has the power to answer the prayers of parents that their son or daughter might be spared death in a time of war, does the death of a prayed-for soldier mean that the parental prayers were ineffective, or perhaps that the victim deserved God's killing?

"If God has the ability to feed the hungry with manna from heaven or to expand the food supply so that hunger disappears, but instead allows deadly starvation to strike a land in a time of drought or blight, is God moral?

"If God had the power to defeat the enemies of the Jews and to destroy them at the time of the exodus, then why did not God intervene to stop the Holocaust?

"If one attributes to God supernatural power, then one has to explain why God uses it so sparingly – why there is so much pain, sickness and tragedy in human life."

The problem for John Shelby Spong here is linking two unrelated things. The *ability* of God to perform miracles, which I think is a given, does not of itself hinge on whether he is a good God or a "capricious" one. If I can draw an analogy, my ability to type exists independent of whether I use my typing abilities for good or evil, or whether I choose to keep my typing to myself. Likewise, God's failure to interact on every occasion that Spong desires it does not of itself disprove the existence of God. It might go some way to figuring out his character, or the disingenuousness of Spong's demands, but you can't use it to prove that God cannot perform miracles.

His questions on the problem of evil are valid, however, and they deserve a response.

Let's take a couple of things as a given. Firstly, we all die. Secondly, all death causes pain (for those few who die a peaceful death with no relatives to grieve, death presumably is not a problem). These facts are inescapable on earth as we currently know it.

At the logical extreme of those who decry evil is a plea for immortality for all. Of course, a person of faith would argue that there is indeed a deal on the table offering immortality for all, it's just that a lot of people refuse to accept it. Take John Spong as a classic case in point. Here's a man who makes a strident argument that he doesn't "want" a "capricious" God intervening in the universe, and expressly would *not* want to worship such a being. Yet, when push comes to shove, he wants precisely that kind of being to intervene to prevent evil. And to prevent evil among humanity such a God would have to intervene billions of times a day across the planet. Every day.

To protect his creatures from grief, such a God would have to invoke *natural*, rather than just spiritual, immortality. Only if no-one died could we spare humans the tragedy of loss – in essence we would forever remain as caterpillars and never progress to the butterfly stage. But this immortality on earth would come at a price. If you think the planet is crowded now, try adding another six billion or so people to the mix (and that's not including the extra number of children each person could have over their immortal lifetimes). Then factor in what kind of society you would end up with if no one ever died. What kind of pecking order would emerge, and how would that have affected the development of human knowledge? In a society that traditionally venerates its elders, we'd sure have a lot of them, but they'd be people who grew up as goat herders thousands of years ago. Would the young ever break through and claim their own place in the sun, or would we have a world forever caught in a primitive timewarp, led by cavemen?

Without the human quest to understand and even cheat death, would our society have advanced, or stagnated? Without risk, would we ever have discovered anything significant?

Clearly, to intervene against death, a miracle-working God would automatically heal all illnesses and injuries. Eat what you like, get as obese as you like, you can never die. Stab someone who annoys you, and know that tomorrow they'll wake up alive and kicking.

I wonder, if we had true immortality in our natural lives, how horrific our society would become.

The vision, if you think about it for longer than a minute, becomes quite appalling to contemplate. Set free from responsibility for our actions, humanity would probably do what it has always done – become even more evil and sadistic than ever. We would be mini-gods, whose sole purpose in life would be fulfilling our every whim because – hey, you'll never have to pay for it

Then there's the issue of quality of life and meaning of life. If we were nothing more than glorified pets with a giant sugar-daddy, with absolutely no control over our personal destinies, would we be slaves or free?

Yes, God *can* step in and save every single one of us from trauma. The fact that he intervenes in some lives by way of miracles is testimony to his ability to do this. But Spong, I think, misses the point of both pain and miracles.

In the miracles story at Matt. 9:1-6, Christ is confronted with a paralysed man. His first response is to say, "Take heart, son, your sins are forgiven." It was this statement that had the Pharisees frothing at the mouth. Only God has the power to forgive sins, they muttered. Who is this Jesus fellow walking in here and making a blasphemous statement like that?

"Why do you entertain evil thoughts in your hearts?" Christ challenged them after a few moments. "Which is easier: to say, 'Your sins are forgiven', or to say, 'Get up and walk'?"

For Jesus, the two statements were actually inextricably linked. But let's face it, anyone could utter the forgiveness line. So his next comment goes to the heart of why we have miracles at all:

"But *so that you may know that the Son of Man has authority on earth to forgive sins*," he said to the crowd as he turned to the paralysed man, "Get up, take your mat and go home."

And the man did. Whilst the man benefited from the miracle, its primary purpose was to testify to the power and authority of Christ.

Capricious? It depends on your perspective on the purpose of God. If you are someone like Spong or Christopher Hitchens who believes God, if he exists, should limit his interference in your life to merely being a sugar-daddy, then I can understand why you would demand miracles as of right. If on the other hand you see God's purpose as drawing more people to a saving faith and eternal life, then you can appreciate the occasional miracle for what it is – a gift that deserves thanks and which reflects God's power.

Christ's direct response to Spong, were he standing here, would probably be exactly what he said to his Hebrew critics 2000 years ago:

"A wicked and adulterous generation looks for a miraculous sign, but none will be given it."

If miracles only take place here and there, we can still find a way to rationalize them away and intellectual dignity is available for all – I can choose to believe, you can choose not to believe, and the world goes on. If miracles were to take place every day in every harmful situation, people would realize pretty quickly (like, within about 24 hours) that God definitely existed, thereby removing the need for faith. Yet Christ says that moment will not arrive until the second coming.

Which leads us to another possible reason for God's non-intervention on a mass basis. There are more Christians alive today, than have existed ever in history. If Christianity is true, that means more people will have the chance to see heaven now than at any previous time. Whilst we live in a dangerous, harm-filled world, most of us nonetheless experience at least some joy in our lives. Taking risks gives us pleasure. Evil and dangerous as the world may be, the existence of that evil has in many cases been a catalyst for people to make an active faith choice.

Does that mean God is using evil as a whip? I don't think so. Left to our own devices, with no God in the picture at all, evil would be a natural end result. If we are not answerable to a higher power, then the law of the jungle, "might is right", becomes the only truth on planet Earth – the same line being pitched by the student behind the Finland school massacre.

Like Vox Day, writing in his new book *The Irrational Atheist*, I believe God is ultimately a libertarian. He's laid down a set of rules – whether we choose to follow them or not is over to us – and we have to live with the consequences of our own choices on that. He's not forcing anyone to believe. And the evil we face in this world is largely of our own making.

"Man has survived millennia of religious faith," Day writes, "but if the prophets of over-population and global warming are correct, he may not survive a mere four centuries of science."

Taking atheists like Richard Dawkins and Sam Harris to task for their rabid attacks on the dangers of religion, Day well and truly takes the mickey:

"The five major religions of the world, in order of their appearance on the scene, are Hinduism, traditional Chinese folk religion, Buddhism, Christianity and Islam. These five religions have approximately 4.85 billion adherents, representing an estimated 71.3 percent of the world's population in 2007, and they have been around for a collective 11,600 years. During the vast majority of those 116 centuries, the world has not been in any danger of extinction from weapons of any kind, nor has the human race been in serious danger of dying out from pollution, global warming, overpopulation or anything else.

"Despite 116 centuries filled with hundreds, if not thousands, of diverse religions, all competing for mindshare, resources and dominance, the species has not merely survived, it has thrived.

"There is no aspect of Hindu teaching which has produced a means of potentially extinguishing Mankind. The occasional 11th century rampages by the Sohei of Mount Hiei notwithstanding, Buddhism provides no method of destroying the planet, while Christians have been waiting patiently for the world to end for nearly two thousand years now without doing much to immanentize the eschaton except for occasionally footing the bill for Jews making *aliyah*. Islam, for all of the danger it supposedly presents, has not produced a significant military technology since Damascene steel was developed in the 12th century and even that is of nebulous connection to the religion itself.

"Modern science has only been around for the last 350 years, if we date the scientific method back to the man known as the Father of Science, Galileo Galilei. One could push that date back considerably, if one wished, to Aristotle and Archimedes, or forward to Newton and the Age of Enlightenment, but regardless, the dire threat to mankind described by Harris only dates back to the middle of the 20th century. In the last sixty years, science has produced a veritable witches' brew of potential dangers to the human race, ranging from atom-shattering explosive devices to lethal genetic modifications, designer diseases, large quantities of radioactive waste and even, supposedly, the accidental production of mini black holes and strangelets through particle collider experiments.

"So, in only three percent of the time that religion has been on the scene, science has managed to produce multiple threats to continued human existence. Moreover, the quantity and lethal quality of those threats appears to be accelerating, as the bulk of them have appeared in the most recent sixth of the scientific era," points out Day.

Far from being the rescuers of mankind "from religious dogma", Dawkins and his cronies represent people with the capacity – for the first time in history – to send humanity back to the caves.

The ability to commit mass murder using airliners is probably a case in point of the "advantages" science has brought to evil, and the 9/11 attacks themselves provide a case study in the problem of evil in our time.

Christian author Philip Yancey landed back in New York after an overseas tour, just a few weeks after the attacks. He wrote this for the magazine *Christianity Today*:

> …I showed up at airports at least two hours in advance, as requested, and in virtually every case got through security in time to hop on an earlier flight. A driver named Eddie met me at LaGuardia in New York. Mayor Giuliani had ordered checkpoints at every tunnel, and vehicle searches were causing huge traffic backups, he told me. Eddie knew a back route through Queens and drove us through neighborhoods unaccustomed to limousines driving by. I told him my destination, the Salvation Army center near Ground Zero, and he said he knew it well. Eddie, a young Puerto Rican with a clean-shaved head, was impeccably dressed in a starched white shirt and tie, wearing gold bracelets and a diamond-studded ring. He had a perfect Brooklyn accent.
>
> "Where were you on September 11?" I asked Eddie, making conversation. "Were you working?" He paused at least ten seconds before answering, no doubt weighing whether he wanted to tell the story again, to a stranger.
>
> "Actually, Mr. Yancey, I was parked just across from the World Trade Center."
>
> "No! Tell me about it."
>
> "I had picked up a ride at the airport, Mr. Firestone, and dropped

him at the Millennium Hotel. I remember his name because I asked him if he owned the tire company, but he laughed and said no. He had a meeting scheduled at the WTC, and I planned to stay with the car and wait for him. I was sitting in this car, reading the paper, when I heard a roar like the sound jet engines make when the planes warm up. I live near LaGuardia, so I hear that roar every morning. Then the ground shook, the car shook, and I heard the explosion. I jumped outside of the car and saw people running everywhere.

"I was standing by my car when the second plane hit a few minutes later. My God, I've never seen a fireball like that. I knew I should get in the car and leave, but something glued me there. It's like when you see an accident, and you know you should drive past without looking, but you can't.

"You wouldn't believe the noise. Car horns were going off all over the place. Police, ambulance, and fire truck sirens were coming closer. I quickly called my wife in Brooklyn and told her, 'Honey, something big has happened down here. Turn on the news. I'm right in front of the twin towers, but I'm OK.'

"And then the people started streaming out. Thousands of people. Some screaming, some holding handkerchiefs over their faces, some covered with blood. I stood by the car as they ran past. I looked in the air and, oh my God, I saw little specks—people jumping. A man in a white shirt. A woman with her skirt flying up. A couple holding hands. A man trying to use his sports coat as a parachute. People would look up, try to figure where they'd land, and dodge the bodies as they hit the sidewalk. I'll never forget that sight as long as I live.

"There was paper and debris and stuff flying everywhere, like a blizzard. I saw a boy, maybe 14, on the sidewalk doubled up, coughing, and when I went over to him he pointed to his pocket. He couldn't speak. I reached in and pulled out an asthma pump, and he sprayed it and got his breath back.

"I was there 45 minutes, I guess—I couldn't tell how long, but that's what they say now, when the first tower collapsed. A woman had fallen down on the sidewalk, an elderly woman. Everybody was running past her, not stepping on her or anything, but running right past her. I waited for a break in the people and went to her. 'Are you all right, ma'am?' I asked. 'I have some water in my car. Can I get you some?' She said she'd made it down something like 58 floors, and I told her she was safe now.

"I could tell she was upset, so I asked if I could say a prayer for her. I'm Catholic, you know. It just seemed the thing to do. She looked relieved, and while I was kneeling there on the sidewalk holding her hand, I heard a noise louder than I thought possible. The entire giant building just collapsed, all 110 stories. And I swear to God, Mr. Yancey, while I'm kneeling there holding that woman's hand, something falls from the sky – a piece of a computer or something – and hits that woman and she slumps over dead. Imagine – escaping from 58 stories and then getting killed like that.

"I look behind me and see a cloud dark as night rushing right towards me. I let go her hand and take off running. It's like a cops-and-robbers cartoon. The faster I run, the closer the cloud gets. I realize I got no chance. I duck into a little space between two buildings to wait it out. When the cloud hits, it's darker than I knew dark could be. At night, even a cloudy night, at least you got space around you, air to breathe. This cloud was, like, solid. You couldn't see anything. You couldn't breathe. You were surrounded by dark you could feel."

Eventually, Eddie told me, he found his way back to his car. Police had already sealed off the area, but he wanted to get his limo out. It was covered with dust like volcanic ash, and he took off his white shirt and wiped the windshield until he could see out. He opened the doors and yelled, "Anybody want a ride outta here?" Eight people, strangers, piled in. He headed for the nearest bridge off Manhattan, crossing over just before the mayor ordered all bridges and tunnels closed.

When he finally got home, four hours after the attack, he found his wife hysterical, his two children huddled in a corner watching Mommy sob. After his phone call, she had stood at her window in Brooklyn and watched the World Trade Center disintegrate, certain that her husband had been killed in the explosion and fire. Phone service was down, and she had not heard from him in four hours.

Eddie was so shaken that the next day he accepted a job to drive someone to Detroit. Airplanes were grounded, people were desperate to get home, and he wanted to get as far away from New York as he could. He drove straight through, took a two-hour nap in the car, and drove 14 hours back to Brooklyn.

"Everything's different now, Mr. Yancey," Eddie said. "I go to my brother's house every night. We sit around, watch TV, play with the kids, play games. Stuff I never used to do. Family stuff. And I haven't missed Mass yet. I'll never be the same."[286]

It is trite for the rest of us to try and rationalize an event and experiences like that, but step back from it a moment and consider this. The death toll in the 9/11 attacks was just under 3,000 people. In terms of normal US death patterns, that accounts for less than half the usual daily total of 7,000 deaths from all causes per day. As an extraordinary event, averaged out across the year, it's equivalent to 7,008 people dying per day on average, instead of 7,000. As I said at the start of this chapter, we all have to die, sometime.[287]

But 9/11 got the world's attention. It focused minds, it sent people back to their churches around the world. It has had a major impact on world history. It was also carried out by humans. God was not flying the plane.

In Yancey's report above, the limo-driver Eddie sees an elderly woman and instinctively offers to pray for her. That act of Christian grace, in what turned out to be the final seconds of her life, gave her comfort at that moment and, who knows, may even have been a saving grace. Given the length of time it could take for a computer to plummet from as high as 400 metres above ground, the woman's fate may have already been determined even before Eddie opened his mouth to pray. With the tower about to collapse, one could also argue that death via plummeting computer – being instant – is a mercy compared to choking to death in ash as the building tumbles around you.

These are mere speculations, and I raise them only to show that there are more ways than one of looking at an event whilst trying to discern the purpose of an unseen God.

Here's another way of looking at 9/11, seen by one American:

"Why am I annoyed? Because every day there are horrible accidents that kill far more people, and the public doesn't seem to take notice. They think those disasters are a normal and routine part of life. If one person is mangled in a car accident, it is treated as no big deal – unless the victim happens to be someone you know and love. The family of the person who dies doesn't make millions because of the death. The families of 9/11 victims were paid a guaranteed minimum of US$250,000 and up to US$4.7 million, with the average death benefit being $1,185,000. Why?"[288]

---

286 http://www.christianitytoday.com/ct/2001/octoberweb-only/10-22-21.0.html
287 To put this firmly in perspective, the total number of deaths in the world each year is 57 million, or nearly 157,000 a day. The 9/11 attack accounted for 25 minutes worth of the world's death toll that day. Even the Indonesian Tsunami – with 300,000 victims – accounted for less than two days' worth of the world death toll that year
288 http://www.tcnj.edu/~hofmann/disasters/Disasters.htm

"If one of my family members gets killed in a car crash, I get nothing. If they were killed in 9/11 I'd be rich. As Rush Limbaugh so aptly pointed out regarding families of solders killed in Iraq, "…the first check you get is a $6,000, direct death benefit, half of which is taxable. Next, you get $1,750 for burial costs. If you are the surviving spouse, you get $833 a month until you remarry. And there's a payment of $211 per month for each child under 18." Evidently tragic death in the service of one's country is not worth nearly as much as tragic death at the office. And perhaps the more people that die with you, the more valuable your death becomes. Dying alone seems to have little value or importance anymore.

"Of course, as unjust as it seems, the real issue here is not how much money someone makes when his or her loved one is tragically killed. The real issue is that our nation has rallied around a huge symbolic disaster while virtually ignoring the fact that many more people are killed every day in mini disasters around the world that, by and large, are treated as normal.

"In the twelve-month periods before and after 9/11 there were 3,287 people killed every day in vehicle accidents around the world. (WHO/World Bank report). Also during these same periods 1,370 people were killed every day by conventional weapons. (*Amnesty* magazine, Issue 22, November-December 2003). Nine/Eleven was a one-day disaster that killed 2,967 people, while elsewhere around the world on that day 4,657 more people died in tragic deaths that went unnoticed. These statistics don't include the many people who were burned to death (4,000 a year on average just in the US according to the FDA), or the 3 million who died from AIDS in 2002, or were killed in other types of accidents at home and elsewhere.

"In the overall picture, 9/11 was no big deal in terms of numbers of deaths. It only accounted for 0.06% of the violent deaths that year, and probably less than half of all tragic deaths that day. But because it happed all at once in a span of a few hours, and represented an intentional attack on the United States, it was a big deal. Let's just keep in mind that it's not just the number of deaths that made it significant, but the act itself and the reasons behind it. If high numbers of deaths were a big deal, cars and weapons would have been outlawed years ago. A 9/11 disaster every day wouldn't match the other deaths in terms of the numbers of people violently killed."

In other words, our own sense of outrage and tragedy can exist independent of the big picture.

Neither the Christian Bible, nor the Jewish one, nor the Qu'ran, nor the Hindu Vedas or Buddhist texts make any promises of divine intervention to save people from their worldly fates. In fact, Christ uses a collapsing tower to make the same point about separating the natural from the supernatural:

"Those eighteen who died when the tower in Siloam fell on them – do you think they were more guilty than all the others living in Jerusalem? I tell you, no! But unless you repent, you too will all perish."[289]

Then there was the case of a group of Galileans who appear to have been slaughtered by Roman soldiers and suffered the indignity of having their own blood mixed in temple sacrifices. Was this a judgment of God against the victims, some of the disciples wondered.

"Do you think that these Galileans were worse sinners than all the other Galileans because they suffered this way?" asked Jesus in reply. "I tell you, no! But unless you repent, you too will all perish."[290]

The message, then, appears to be that bad things happen for no theological reason at all. Part of living in the natural, fallen world. Part of living in a world where humans are negligent or maleficent towards each other. Knowing this, and adopting the later Boy Scout motto – Be Prepared – Christ was at pains to say, if you haven't made peace with God (repented and believed) and disaster then strikes, then it is too late.

I should distinguish, too, that there are two kinds of evil up for debate: moral evil, which is human-caused; and natural evil which, as the name suggests, emanates from nature.

Natural evil includes such things as floods, earthquakes, volcanic eruptions, tornadoes and the like. There is, however, some crossover. Land developers who build cities on flood plains (New Orleans springs to mind), in 'tornado alley' or on earthquake faultlines bear some culpability for the inevitable end result of their actions. Indeed, many disasters that seem natural have actually been caused by human tinkering with the environment.

One community near me has had more devastating flooding in recent years than previously, with all the commentators gravely tut-tutting about "one in 100-year floods" occurring every couple of years, and TV newsreaders warning "Experts are blaming global warming..."

What the experts actually discovered, when they looked a little deeper, is that local county cost-cutting meant rivers were not being dredged of silt (from farm and development run-off) as often as they should have been, meaning river levels rose higher than necessary when heavy rain systems swept through.

I remember one of the first news stories I ever reported on as a newbie

---

289   Luke 13:4-5
290   Luke 13:1-3

radio journalist in 1982 was a honeymooning couple whose car was tragically crushed by a two-tonne boulder that rolled down a gorge on top of them. It was a senseless tragedy and, it seemed, an impossible freak accident. After all, the car was doing 100 km/h; a fraction of a second either side and the boulder would have missed them. Yet despite its freakishness, it wasn't the only accident of its kind I covered, however. There was an almost identical repeat during the 1990s. You could make the same "fraction of a second either side" argument for 90% of road crashes, when you think about it. Rocks fall down gorges. Occasionally, they hit something.

Earthquakes, as we discovered in an earlier chapter, are essential for life to exist on this planet, as are most of the other natural forces we occasionally come into conflict with.

Yes, as an all powerful being, God could have built us a no-risk universe; you might call it a playpen. But for the same reasons I outlined earlier, a no-risk universe or planet would only encourage more and more dodgy behaviour, given the human quest to find the edge of the envelope and push further.

Which brings us back to moral evil – that which we do to each other. I defy any sentient life form to deny it has become worse as a result of the social changes we've made as a result of our own "enlightenment". Take the child raped by a pedophile. Once upon a time, Mr Neck was introduced to Mr Rope was introduced to Mr Tree, and Mr Pedophile never re-offended. It was a pretty strong incentive to mates of Mr Pedophile that they too might suffer the same fate if they didn't watch out.

When the Virginia Tech shootings took place, an email very quickly did the rounds asking where was God at a whole smorgasbord of school shootings:

Dear God:

Why didn't you save the school children at ?...

Moses Lake, Washington 2/2/96
Bethel, Alaska 2/19/97
Pearl, Mississippi 10/1/97
West Paducah, Kentucky 12/1/97
Stamp, Arkansas 12/15/97
Jonesboro, Arkansas 3/24/98
Edinboro, Pennsylvania 4/24/98
Fayetteville, Tennessee 5/19/98

Springfield, Oregon 5/21/98
Richmond, Virginia 6/15/98
Littleton, Colorado 4/20/99
Taber, Alberta, Canada 5/28/99
Conyers, Georgia 5/20/99
Deming, New Mexico 11/19/99
Fort Gibson, Oklahoma 12/6/99
Santee, California 3/ 5/01
El Cajon, California 3/22/01 and
Blacksburg, VA 4/16/07 ?

Sincerely,
Concerned Student

Reply:

Dear Concerned Student:
Sorry, I am not allowed in schools.

Sincerely,
God

How did this get started? Let's see, I think it started when Madalyn Murray O'Hair complained. She didn't want any prayer in our schools. *And we said, OK.*

Then someone said, you better not: Read the Bible in school; the Bible that says "thou shalt not kill, Thou shalt not steal, And love your neighbors as yourself," *And we said, OK.*

Dr. Benjamin Spock said we shouldn't smack our children when they misbehaved, because their little personalities would be warped and we might damage their self-esteem.

And we said, "An expert should know what he's talking about". So we won't smack them anymore.

Then someone said, "Teachers and principals better not discipline our children when they misbehave."

And the school administrators said, "No faculty member in this school better touch a student when they misbehave, because we don't want any bad publicity, and we surely don't want to be sued.

And we accepted their reasoning...

Then someone said, let's let our daughters have abortions if they want, And they won't even have to tell their parents.

And we said, that's a grand idea.

Then some wise school board member said, Since boys will be boys And they're going to do it anyway, let's give our sons all the condoms they want, So they can have all the fun they desire, And we won't have to tell their parents they got them at school.

And we said, that's another great idea...

Then some of our top elected officials said, It doesn't matter what we do in private as long as we do our jobs.

And we said, It doesn't matter what anybody, including the President, Does in private as long as we have jobs and the economy is good...

And someone else took that appreciation a step further and published pictures of nude children, And then stepped further still by Making them available on the Internet.

And we said, everyone's entitled to free speech...

And the entertainment industry said, let's make TV shows and movies that promote Profanity, violence and illicit sex...And let's record music that encourages Rape, drugs, murder, suicide, and satanic themes...

And we said, it's just entertainment, And it has no adverse effect, And nobody takes it seriously anyway, So go right ahead.

Now we're asking ourselves Why our children have no conscience, Why they don't know right from wrong, And why it doesn't bother them to Kill strangers, classmates or even themselves.

Undoubtedly, If we thought about it long and hard enough, We could figure it out.

I'm sure it has a great deal to do with...

"WE REAP WHAT WE SOW"

Why is it our children cannot read a Bible in school, but can in Prison?

Madalyn Murray O'Hair, mentioned in that epistle, is a fascinating example of the tragic life of an atheist fundamentalist. Born 1919 into a Presbyterian family, O'Hair married at 22. While serving with the US military in Italy in codes, she began an affair with a married Catholic officer, William J Murray and became pregnant. He refused to divorce his wife, but Madalyn did divorce her own husband and gave birth to a son whom she named William. Another child, Jon Garth Murray, followed to a different father. She began calling herself Madalyn Murray. In the 1950s she became a member of a Communist organization, the Socialist Workers Party, and tried to take her children and defect to the Soviet Union in 1960. In what must have been a slap in the face, the Russians refused to accept the American defector, and sent her back to the US.

On arrival back, she enrolled 15 year old son William in a Baltimore school, which she promptly sued for allegedly forcing her son to take part in Bible readings, which she regarded as "unconstitutional". Her lawsuit further claimed her son had been threatened with violence for failing to take part. If you want to know who took Christianity out of American schools, Madalyn Murray is the one to blame. Eventually reaching the US Supreme Court on appeal, they voted 8-1 in favour of her case in 1963, prompting *Life* magazine to name her "the most hated woman in America".

On the strength of her notoriety and success, she founded "American Atheists" and went on to become a leading light of the atheist movement, marrying a guy named O'Hair along the way (but not for long).

In 1980 she suffered the first major blow to her public image, when son William converted to Christianity, revealing that the lawsuit his mother had taken to the Supreme Court had contained fabricated evidence.

Madalyn Murray O'Hair publicly divorced her child:

"One could call this a postnatal abortion on the part of a mother, I guess; I repudiate him entirely and completely for now and all times...He is beyond human forgiveness."

She never made up with her son, William, who later revealed his life as a teenage atheist had been hell. He fathered a child during his teens in the sixties (Robin) who was adopted by Madalyn.

In 1995 Madalyn Murray O'Hair disappeared, along with her other son Jon Garth and granddaughter Robin. Also missing was US$600,000 in gold bullion belonging to American Atheists.

A *Vanity Fair* report, based on documents provided by and interviews with American Atheists employees, initially concluded Madalyn Murray O'Hair and her children had fled to New Zealand with the money.

"On August 28, 1995, American Atheist employee David Travis arrived for work bright and early at the global headquarters and discovered the front door padlocked shut. A posted note read, "The Murray-O'Hair family has been called out of town on an emergency basis. We do not know how long we will be gone at the time of the writing of this memo." This truly puzzled Travis, who started opening the mail. He discovered a statement from a bank in New Zealand he'd never heard of, detailing an account in O'Hair's name which contained close to a million dollars."[291]

In 2001, however, another former employee David Roland Waters – under heavy pressure from police – finally confessed to murdering the O'Hair family. He disclosed the location of their bodies, which police discovered had been sawn into small pieces and buried in 55-gallon drums. O'Hair had to be identified via a mutilated prosthetic hip.

Waters had stolen the bullion from the O'Hairs, but through a strange twist of fate the money was stolen from him by a criminal gang who'd managed to copy a skeleton key for bank safety deposit boxes.

As he was led from court in handcuffs, spectators booed and hissed, and one atheist – in his fury – even used a supernatural name to describe Waters.

"Why don't they execute you?" screamed Samuel Miller, who'd been a member of American Atheists for three decades. "You murdered a wonderful woman and tortured her, stinking *ghoul!*"[292]

From the time of his incarceration for suspected murder, until his own death in jail from lung cancer, atheist David Waters served 666 days.[293]

A subsequent audit of American Atheists however found more purloined monies, and the *Texas Atheist* newsletter posthumously accused Madalyn Murray O'Hair of stealing $8 million, noting that she wasn't so wonderful after all.

Her surviving son, William (now a Christian preacher), is also on record about his mother's perpetual dishonesty, saying at one stage she even printed fake stock certificates to aid in the takeover of an atheist publishing company. He also alleges his mother was corruptly stealing cash, possibly "tens of millions" – an allegation later backed up by the executor of her estate who says he found phone logs to Swiss banks, although the banks are refusing to cough up account details.

As for the gruesome circumstances of her death, although O'Hair, her son and granddaughter spent a month as kidnapping victims before they were finally killed, presumably the indignities she suffered while dying worried her not:

"Earlier in her life, O'Hair wrote an essay for American Atheist about her hopes that nothing "special" would ever happen to her body. She didn't want any "dirty Christ-ers" getting their hands on her corpse. She advised that her "carcass should be flung into the water, where the fish could feed on it." A dead body, she wrote, was nothing more than a fallen leaf from a

---

291   http://www.rotten.com/library/bio/misc/madalyn-murray-ohair/
292   http://tspweb02.tsp.utexas.edu/webarchive/04-02-01/2001040207_s03_Waters.html
293   http://en.wikipedia.org/wiki/Madalyn_Murray_O'Hair

tree, a dog killed on the highway, or a fish caught in a net."[294]

Does the fact that the woman, singlehandedly responsible for getting prayer taken out of schools, ended up chopped into pieces at the hands of another atheist killer, signal divine retribution? Whilst many would be tempted to say "Yes", based on the same arguments I made above I would have to say "No".

There is a qualifier to this, however, within Christian theology. There are more spiritual forces at work than just God's. According to Christianity, human rebellion wasn't the only thing God had to contend with. The leading angelic figure, Lucifer, whose name means "morning star", is said to have let pride go to his head and taken a fall from grace as a result, taking a fair few supporters with him. They, according to the Bible, infest planet Earth. It is almost as if God said, "A plague on both your houses," and condemned humans and fallen angels to co-exist.

Angels?, you ask. Let's look at the logic for a moment. We accept that the universe appears created. We accept the fine tuning of life on Earth. Therefore we accept the logical possibility that God created life. Is it possible that God created supernatural creatures as well, like angels?[295] It is logically possible, yes. Can you catch one and put it in an aviary? Probably not. Do people claim to have encountered them? Yes, millions, from virtually all cultures.

Angels have big and ancient pedigree. Christianity, Islam, Judaism, Hinduism, Wicca and the thousands of primitive tribal religions around the world all agree on the existence of a spirit realm inhabited by, well, spirits. Angels, demons, entities, call them what you will. In fact, in Hinduism, tribal animism and Wicca, it is these intermediate-level supernatural entities that become the objects of worship.

"Most Wiccans and Pagans see "god" as more of a job title than a proper name," writes Wiccan Patti Wigington.[296] "They don't worship the Christian God, but that doesn't mean they don't accept the existence of deity. Various Wiccan and Pagan traditions honor different gods. Some see all deities as one, and may refer to The God or The Goddess. Others may

---

294   http://www.rotten.com/library/bio/misc/madalyn-murray-ohair/
295   We also accept that unseen sub-atomic particles must exist, including particles created in the Big Bang and which, to all intents and purposes, are "immortal" Is it possible that some other lifeforms composed of 14 billion year old particles exist and that we simply cannot see them or measure them? Yeah, it's possible. This is a far cry from invoking such a supernatural beastie as The Flying Spaghetti Monster: by definition "spaghetti" is material (made of matter), and supernatural involves immaterial beings. "Flying" is the description of a physical act that takes place in three dimensional space where solid matter (wings) beat against gaseous matter (air) to propel a creature using natural forces. Therefore, whilst vaguely amusing, the FSM argument is a trivial absurdity.
296   http://paganwiccan.about.com/od/faq/f/Believe_God.htm

worship specific gods or goddesses – Cernunnos, Brighid, Isis, Apollo, etc. – from their own tradition. Because there are so many different forms of Pagan belief, there are nearly as many gods and goddesses to believe in.

"Many Pagans and Wiccans are willing to accept the presence of the Divine in all things. Because Wicca and Paganism place a good deal of emphasis on the idea that experiencing the divine is something for everyone, not just select members of the clergy, it's possible for a Wiccan or Pagan to find something sacred within the mundane. For example, the whisper of wind through the trees or the roar of the ocean can both be considered divine. Not only that, most Wiccans feel that the divine lives within each of us.

"It's rare to find a Pagan or Wiccan who sees the gods as judgmental or punishing. Instead, most view the gods as beings that are meant to be walked beside, hand in hand, and honored."

Thus, within the broad "church" that is Wicca and neopaganism, we can see that an original creator God lurks dimly in the background of their belief system, but they would far rather play with the fairies at the bottom of the garden, rather than "walk beside, hand in hand" and honouring the Gardener himself.

Again, like Spong, their rationale for not wanting to approach the supreme deity is a desire not to be judged or punished – which is a similar rationale to the one ascribed to Satan.

In the gospels, Christ suggests Lucifer, or Satan, or Shaitan, or Kali, or whatever name you care to call him in various religions, actually holds earth as a kind of "enemy territory". He talks about, once judgment begins, "The Prince of this world will be driven out".[297] Even though Christ, as God incarnate, walked the streets of Jerusalem he still appeared to acknowledge Satan's power here:

"I will not speak with you much longer, for the Prince of this world is coming. He has no hold on me, but the world must learn that I love the Father and that I do exactly what my Father has commanded me."

The implication from this is that while Christ *could* act unilaterally directly against Satan, apparently he has to play it by the book, dot the i's and cross the t's. This would only make sense if God – as an ultimately pure moral figure – cannot possibly do anything "illegal", even if we want him to.

The Gospels of Matthew, Mark and Luke all record that after his baptism, Christ was tempted by Satan, who promised anything in the world if Christ would abandon his mission. The implication is that Satan had the power to grant anything in the world. This, again, accords with the respect Christ seems to show for Satan's earthly 'authority', if not for the creature itself. After all, Jesus again had the power to act unilaterally against the Devil on this occasion, as it was reportedly right there in front of him. But he did not. Instead of a direct power struggle, Jesus achieved his goal through sacrifice.

A further clue to the bizarre balance between good and evil is found in the Epistle of Jude 1:8-9.

"In the very same way, these dreamers pollute their own bodies, reject authority and slander celestial beings. But even the archangel Michael, when he was disputing with the devil about the body of Moses, did not dare to bring a slanderous accusation against him, but said, 'The Lord rebuke you!'."

Why would the archangel Michael be unable to directly challenge his former colleague, unless for reasons not specified in the Bible? The Book of Job (pronounced "Jobe") provides further clues.

In Job, Satan is portrayed as questioning God about the protection God has put in place around Job's life.

"Have you not put a hedge around him and his household and everything he has? You have blessed the work of his hands, so that his flocks and herds are spread throughout the land."

In theological terms, Satan's point in this passage was that Job was living a charmed life, protected by God, so little wonder the man was always worshipping and giving thanks. Take the protection away, said Satan, and then see what happens.

"Very well, then," God is recorded as saying, "everything he has is in your hands, but on the man himself do not lay a finger."

This exchange is crucial to understanding the affliction of evil. God did not attack Job; he simply removed the divine protection from around him because Satan apparently has a legal right to test people. The "Prince of this world" was then free to throw everything he had at Job to make him "curse you [God] to your face".

I won't re-litigate the entire book, but suffice to say Job lost everything: his children killed while getting drunk and having a party, his property destroyed, his health ruined.

After a while, Job did begin to curse, but the Bible records one of his friends making the counter argument against his complaints.

"How long will you say such things? Your words are a blustering wind. Does God pervert justice?[298] Does the Almighty pervert what is right?

---

[298] Interesting point this, because it flows back to the way Christ and the archangel Michael treated Satan. Can an all-good God bend the rules in order to achieve a "right" goal,

"When your children sinned against him, he gave them over to the penalty of their sin."

In other words, with God's "hedge" of protection removed from the family, Satan had authority to create hell on earth, particularly if there was a trace of sin, but even without. Christ, after all, was sinless but that didn't stop Satan having a crack at him in the desert, according to the gospel writers.

Which brings me back to Madalyn Murray O'Hair. A woman who defied the very idea of God is highly unlikely to have had a divine hedge around her life either. And it showed.

The apostle Peter described Evil this way: "Your enemy the devil prowls around like a roaring lion, looking for someone to devour. Resist him, standing firm in the faith, because you know that your brothers throughout the world are undergoing the same kind of sufferings."[299]

Did O'Hair get "devoured"? Well, if getting butchered counts, the answer would have to be "yes".

Did God actively wield the chainsaw? No.

O'Hair had made it repeatedly clear she never wanted God's help. She was on her own, doing it her way.

Christian prayer is ostensibly made in the hope that God will patch the hedge on your behalf. If you were to study crime records, born-again Christians would show up far less often as either perpetrators or victims of crime, despite the fact that crime rates across the West have skyrocketed the more society has loosened up over the past 50 years. This is not to say there are not tragedies befalling Christians – of course there are. I am reminded of the terribly sad story of an evangelist preaching in Auckland one night about the reality of Evil – and when he returned home that evening he found his son had – like a man possessed – brutally murdered both his brother and their mother, the evangelist's wife.

The rational explanation? These things happen. The spiritual explanation? Does masking the symptoms of people who hear voices in their heads, using chemical drug cocktails, actually address the root cause of why they're hearing voices in the first place?

Either way, we Christians bleed and grieve like everybody else, but we live with the hope and expectation of being re-united with our loved ones after our earthly run has ended. People who refuse to believe do not expect, or have, that hope.

such as defeating Evil? Or would bending the rules be succumbing to the very Evil God stands against? A God of justice has to be just, even to ultimate sinners like the devil
299 1 Peter 5:8-9

The medieval writer Dante Alighieri put his vision of Hell into words, and above the entrance to Hell he suggested a sign was displayed: "Abandon hope all ye who enter here".

The very fact that we perceive "hope", the very fact that we appreciate "good", suggests in itself that God exists. If there is Evil, and we can discern that, why does it exist and why are we drawn to the good?

The central theme of the Christian religion is the cross, but it goes far deeper than merely hanging a guy on a cross and saying "believe in him". Why was Christ on the cross in the first place? Why did he have to die such a gruesome death? If one reads the gospel accounts, it was precisely to combat what we are talking about here: Evil.

If God were to become a man, experience life as a man, and die as a man absorbing all the pain it was possible for a man to absorb, crucifixion would probably be the way to do it. To walk in our shoes, Christ needed to take everything humans could throw at him. To be able to truly comfort the victim of a pedophile, or a rape, or a brutal murder, he needs to be able to say, "I know your pain" and mean it.

According to Christian doctrine, in order to accomplish his task Christ had to die on the cross as a man, not as God. This meant the absolute withdrawal of any spiritual power at all; Jesus could no longer sense God. It was at this moment, says Matthew's Gospel, that Jesus cried out in agony on the cross:

"Eloi, Eloi, lama sabachthani?" – which means, "My God, my God, why have you forsaken me?"

A few moments later, he was dead.

Except, of course, God had not forsaken him. Death, in the Christian writings, is but a doorway through which all of us must pass. For some, like Christ and the victims of crime, natural disasters and disease, the passage through is a painful one, culminating in a point where your nerve cells shut down, the pain stops and you die. It is the totality of the journey, however, rather than merely Part 1, that needs to be examined in the context of how we relate to the presence of Evil.

John Spong, Hitchens and others make sweeping references to the inaction of God in the face of evil, ignoring the fact that the handbook for this particular God hypothesis clearly indicates he won't be stepping in on a wholesale basis until the end of time, at which point everything will be sorted out and every wrong repaid. For God to break his word would raise the issue I touched on earlier about perverting the course of justice.

But what Spong and Hitchens also overlook is what lies on the otherside of the doorway. The caterpillar cannot conceive how life must be for a butterfly – it is a totally foreign idea and beyond the caterpillar's ability to experience. In just the same way, the restrictions, perils and turmoil of our natural universe may well be directly relevant to our future lives as spiritual butterflies, and this may be something that we simply cannot understand until it happens.

If, as the science now strongly indicates, a creator God exists; and if, as Christianity alleges, that God is a theistic one who does in fact care about humanity (which would explain the fine-tuning of the universe for life to exist on Earth in particular), then one can also take it as a given that eternal life will make up for any pain or persecution we suffer on earth no matter how terrible. Whatever the ultimate pain or suffering you went through just before death, it is forgotten and replaced by a feeling of bliss.[300] That is the central message of the Gospels: the victory of Good over Evil and the final expulsion of evil from the universe, once time has run its course.

Let's return to John Spong's original challenges:

1. "Once miraculous supernatural power is ascribed to God, then believers need an explanation for why God acts on some occasions and not others. If God has the power to answer the prayers of parents that their son or daughter might be spared death in a time of war, does the death of a prayed-for soldier mean that the parental prayers were ineffective, or perhaps that the victim deserved God's killing?
2. "If God has the ability to feed the hungry with manna from heaven or to expand the food supply so that hunger disappears, but instead allows deadly starvation to strike a land in a time of drought or blight, is God moral?
3. "If God had the power to defeat the enemies of the Jews and to destroy them at the time of the exodus, then why did not God intervene to stop the Holocaust?
4. "If one attributes to God supernatural power, then one has to explain why God uses it so sparingly – why there is so much pain, sickness and tragedy in human life."

Taking into account everything so far, the answer to 1) is this: God has never intervened to create immortality in the natural world. Therefore, a prayer for intervention ultimately is a choice between death now or death later. That's all – a postponement of the inevitable. As we've seen from the biblical passages, there's not a suggestion that a soldier deserved to die (although a theological argument can be made that the "Prince of this

---

300 In the hundreds of Near Death Experiences now documented, this transcendence from suffering to beauty is an overarching theme

world" has the power to throw whatever he likes at us, including death).

Jesus Christ chose not to save himself from the Cross despite his power, then rose again to show that death is beaten for all who believe. If the prayers of all parents were answered, none of their offspring would ever die regardless of occupation. Clearly, that's not an option. But maybe there's an issue of meaning involved. Maybe the death simply has to happen in order for a series of other events to unfold.

If you take the view that God not only created the universe but sees through time and can see how the story ends, then arguably the future is set in stone. One of the key philosophical conundrums with the idea of time travel is the damage that could be done if we went back into the past and altered an event – theoretically, we could change the present in major, unanticipated ways. Michael J Fox's *Back To The Future* movies played on this theme, where a family photo Fox's character carried began to erase because of changes he had caused.

Under this scenario, we are fortunate to get any miraculous input into the world at all, because conceivably it could potentially require God to "re-wire" the path to the future to compensate so as not to change the end result. On the flipside of this argument is the possibility that because God knows the future he knows at what points he can intervene, and if you happen to be a case that sits outside those parameters you won't be getting miraculous assistance. This doesn't remove the need for prayer and religious faith, because we mortals can't see the future and will never know whether or not we are one of the fortunate ones. In the Christian community millions of people report minor miracles in their lives every day, so I don't find it difficult to argue that God has allowed for many interventions in the lives of his believers, just not always the big ones.[301] The real test, I suspect, would be to ask the parents of the prayed-for soldier how many times they had prayed over the years and how many of their prayers had been answered.

---

301 Literally as I was proofing this book ready for printing, our local paper carried the story of a 48 year old delivery driver whose van was hit by a train at a level crossing I use every day. The freight train ploughed into the vehicle, throwing it into a ditch and pinning the driver underneath the wreck. Being a rural area it took emergency services time to reach the crash scene, where they found the man almost drowning in hot engine oil that had been pouring down his throat. "Emergency workers initially doubted whether the man would even survive the rescue helicopter flight to hospital," reported the paper. His condition critical, he lapsed into a coma and remained that way for a fortnight, while his mother and wife prayed constantly for a recovery the doctors said would probably not happen.. You know what I am going to say, so I'll let his mother say it instead: "He is a miracle! I thank God as I feel luckier than ever that my prayers were answered and those of all our friends..." Although he cannot speak yet, he's well on the way to a full recovery, and will be home for Christmas. Undoubtedly Dawkins would ask, 'Why him and not others?" or "If God really cared, why did he let the train hit him in the first place?" We've already dealt with the divine sugar-daddy myth. Bad things happen. It is how we respond to those things that shows our character

The answer to 2) and 3) is this: Spong confuses the actions of God in directing the destiny of the pre-Christian Israelites, with the actions of God generally. If Spong wants to raise the "chosen people" argument, which is effectively what he's doing, then it needs to be raised in its complete context. In the Old Testament, God was guiding the Jews to provide the human genetic component of the eventual Messiah for the entire planet. It was for this reason, if you read your Old Testament carefully, that there was repeated "smiting" of pagan tribes. God wanted nothing to infect the spiritual purity he was trying to create for the line of Mary, mother of Christ.

If pagan tribes worshipping demonic gods and carrying out child sacrifice and other nasties were in danger of influencing wayward Jews (as the evidence clearly shows they were), then God gave the instruction to obliterate them from the face of the planet. As the being accredited as the giver and taker of life, one can argue that God has every right to decide that the time is up for a debauched group of humans. If he chooses to use the Jews as his weapon of choice to achieve that, so be it. If a factory CEO discovers the factory has produced defective or even unsafe units, those units are recalled from the shops and destroyed. Likewise, as head of the human-making factory, a Creator deity has a right to destroy defective product.

Significantly, for those hooked on the issue of Old Testament violence, whenever the Jews went off and did their own "smiting" without God's blessing, they lost. Which seems to tell us something about what happens when God mows down his "hedge".

God supplied manna from heaven to feed the people whose genetic line would give rise to the Messiah. He defended those people from attacks both physical and spiritual, for the same reason.

After Christ, that need was no longer there. The Jewish leaders rejected the Messiahship of Christ, and within a generation their temple had been torn asunder and the Jews scattered to the four corners of the known earth. The "hedge" had been removed and Satan, using the Job analogy, threw everything he had at God's "chosen people" for the next 1900 years. The Holocaust, of course, fell into this latter period.

But there is one final piece in this contextual jigsaw that we haven't touched on – the Jewish mission in the biblical epic did not end with the events of 70AD and the destruction of the temple.

One of the overarching themes of Old Testament prophecy was the eventual return of a Messiah in power at the end of time. Many of the prophets had predicted the Jews would be scattered, as indeed they later were. But some of the prophets also predicted that after a time of reckoning,

THE PROBLEM OF EVIL

the Jews would be re-united, shortly before the end of time.

In the book of Isaiah, the prophet is writing about 100 years *before* the first exile of the Jews, to Babylon. But here's what he says of the end of times:

"In that day, the Root of Jesse will stand as a banner for the peoples; the nations will rally to him, and his place of rest will be glorious. In that day, the Lord will reach out his hand *a second time* to reclaim the remnant that is left of his people from Assyria, from Lower Egypt, from Cush, from Elam, from Babylonia,[302] from Hamath and from the islands of the sea."

Jesus Christ, according to the genealogies, was descended from Jesse (King David's father). But the key phrase here is "a second time". Isaiah speaks of a time in his future, in the "day" (not a specific day but a period of time immediately leading up to the end, when God will for a second time gather the Jews back to the Holy Land. The first time happened about 200 years after Isaiah wrote, when the Jews were permitted to return to Jerusalem from Babylon. But this prophecy talks of a second time. For this prophecy to be fulfilled, the Jews had to be scattered again, as they were by the Romans.

The prophet Jeremiah, writing just before the Babylonian exile, homes in even closer to the events of 1948. To understand his prophecy that follows, however, you need some further background context: When the Jews were crushed by the Romans in 70AD, Israel was still split into two kingdoms, Judah in the south and Israel in the north. Both were subject to Rome, but both were independent from each other. The country we know as Israel had not been united since the days of Solomon.

Here's what Jeremiah says will happen towards the end:

"In those days the house of Judah will join the house of Israel, and together they will come from a northern land to the land I gave your forefathers as an inheritance."

This prophecy was finally fulfilled in our time, 1948. Jews from across Europe – the northern land – flooded into the newly created state of Israel – brought together for the first time in 1900 years. Significantly, modern Israel is the first time since Solomon that Judah and Israel have been reunited, and it took 2,500 years for Jeremiah's prophecy to come true.

Had the Holocaust *not* happened, it is doubtful that the prophecy could have been fulfilled. Did God create the Holocaust? No, but he knew it was

---

302 It is significant that when the state of Israel was created in 1948, the response of the surrounding Arab countries (Syria, Egypt, Iraq (Babylon) etc) was to expel all the Jews living in those countries. Nearly one million Jews were deported virtually overnight, leaving behind homes, businesses and bank accounts. In contrast, the number of Palestinian Arabs displaced was significantly lower. Instead of transferring the seized Jewish homes and property to displaced Palestinians, the Arab countries refused to let the Palestinians in either

coming and was therefore able to predict in advance that the Jews would undergo tremendous persecution before the end, before they were recalled to Israel.

"He will raise a banner for the nations," says Isaiah, "and gather the exiles of Israel; he will assemble the scattered people of Judah from the four quarters of the earth."

Thus, in my final answer to Spong on points 2 and 3 (and for that matter 4 as well), I would argue the Holocaust was an event of history that had to happen. God *could* stop a lot of things, but I keep coming back to the question of "why?". The sort of intervention Spong demands would turn us into nothing more than pets. Why should God feed the victims of African famine, when the better answer is that the rest of us on planet Earth should step up to the plate. God's inaction, to me, requires humanity to take on that mantle. If we truly wanted to end world poverty, we could. Why are we appealing to what Richard Dawkins would call the "great Sky Fairy" to do what we are too lazy to?

It's the same with crime, and similar types of evil. How much of it is caused by human greed and desires? Is that God's problem or ours? Should he continually wave his magic wand, or do we have a responsibility to clean up our act?

In terms of disease, we are undergoing a sexually-transmitted disease epidemic across the world, and AIDS may wipe out up to a third of the population of Africa. We know how STDs are transmitted. We know that virgins who marry and stay together monogamously will never catch an STD. You argue that this is "too hard" in today's modern society, and "unrealistic". Is that our fault, or our designer's? We're the ones who wanted the freedom, and with freedom comes risk.

Part of living in a natural world, likewise, is that it comes with natural bugs. These things make possible much of the beauty of life that we enjoy. But they can also cause problems. Water is great to drink, but horrible to drown in. Cars are fantastic to drive, but a pain to be run over by. Life has risks. The kind of perfect world that Spong and Hitchens throw down the gauntlet over is promised, but only for those who accept the conditions of faith. Given that neither Spong nor Hitchens want such a God, they are unlikely to ever see such a perfect world.

Christian philosopher Greg Boyd expressed a similar view in his book, *Letters From A Skeptic*:[303]

"It may be that a good deal of what we call 'evil' is simply due to the

---

303 *Letters From A Skeptic*, Dr Gregory Boyd & Edward Boyd, Victor, 1994

fact that anything which God could create would be limited in certain respects. The very fact that what God creates is less than Himself introduces limitations and imperfections into the picture. Any created thing, for example, possesses a limited set of characteristics which rules out the possibility of it possessing other characteristics incompatible with these. But this can lead to some unfortunate consequences.

"The rock which holds you up must also be hard enough for you to stub your toe on it. The air which you breathe must also be thin enough to allow you to fall through it when not supported by a hard surface... and so on. The dependability of the world which makes it possible for rational, morally responsible creatures to live, works against us in certain circumstances. Indeed, every positive feature of any created entity is a potentially negative feature in certain circumstances."

Like me, Boyd believes that most evil in the world can be put down to human failings (war, hunger, bad town planning etc), or the limitations of living in a created natural world. But there are some things – like deformed babies – that he agrees don't appear to fit.[304] He argues that the balance of the remaining evil can be sheeted home to the spiritual realm:[305]

"The Christian understanding, based on Scripture, is that these entities are, like us, personal and free and, like us, some of them have used their freedom for evil. These evil spiritual forces – 'demons' if you will – are now in a state of war against God and everything that is good, and the earth is (perhaps among other places as well) their battlefield.

"In the Christian view, then, the earth has been literally besieged by a power outside itself. There is a power of pure evil which now affects everything and everybody on the earth. The Creator is not the only influence any longer. This is why the earth can be so incredibly beautiful on the one hand, and so incredibly nightmarish on the other.

"We live, individually and collectively, amidst a contradiction of good and evil...My claim then is that the earth is a battlefield. We are, like Normandy in World War II, caught in the crossfire of a cosmic battle.

---

304 Assuming, of course, that the deformity has not been caused by a drug, medicine, bad diet or human caused environmental factor.

305 The "Skeptic" in the book title was Boyd's father, who raised some tough questions of his own to Boyd's claims. How could a graduate of Yale and Princeton, lamented his dad, "really believe in angels and demons and the like". Boyd shot back along the lines of, 'well, we exist, so what's so hard to believe about the possibility of unseen thinking beings existing as well?' After all, added Boyd, we're quite happy to accept the existence of a wide range of scientific particles no one has ever seen nor will ever see, and all we can see are the effects they cause, their fingerprints. What makes belief in spiritual entities that also leave fingerprints any different? Science says a quark 'might' cause a particular phenomenon, while I argue that parents worshipping a demonic "goddess of destruction" who then go out and ritually slaughter their own kids 'might' have invoked a demon, based on the same laws of cause and effect

And on battlefields as you know, all sorts of terrible things happen. In such a situation, everything becomes a potential weapon and every person a potential victim. And thus the entire cosmos, the Bible says, is in a state of chaos (Rom. 8)."

Gregory Boyd, incidentally, is a proponent of an idea called Finite Godism, which I talked about earlier. This is the belief that God is not "all powerful", that his ability to influence world events is "finite". Finite Godism is the same argument raised by Jewish Rabbi, Harold Kushner, in his book, *When Bad Things Happen To Good People*.

"Where was God while [the Holocaust] was going on? Why did he not intervene to stop it? Why didn't he strike Hitler dead in 1939 and spare millions of lives and untold suffering, or why didn't he send an earthquake to demolish the gas chambers. Where was God?"

Kushner, working through the issues, later concludes that God's powers are limited.

"There are some things God does not control…"

Boyd's analysis runs deeper. He argues that while God certainly is omnipotent, that he has voluntarily – as part of giving humanity and spiritual entities free will – relinquished his ability to control everything in nature and in humanity. Otherwise, says Boyd, we would not truly be free. Only the truly free can truly love, he argues, and God desires true love rather than forced love from humans (hence the decision to "choose" Christ, rather than be compelled to worship).

Boyd, Norman Geisler, C S Lewis and many other Christian writers are all of the view that – rather than disproving God, the existence of Evil points to the existence of God. And spiritual evil, usually manifested through humans, points strongly to the existence of some kind of spiritual power struggle.

Which is exactly what I found when I went looking for evidence in the natural, rather than supernatural, realm.

CHAPTER 16

DARKNESS AT THE EDGE OF TOWN

"Contemporary forms of deception, especially deception on a worldwide scale never possible before, might spur our meditation on the meaning of the legend of Antichrist as the image of essential human evil"
Bernard McGinn, *Antichrist*

IT IS ONE THING TO pontificate about "Good vs Evil" as an esoteric argument. But if such a battle was really taking place, wouldn't we expect to see spillover in the natural world? Clearly, as I explored in the last chapter, there's a strong allegation that spiritual evil is a motivating force in much of the apparent human evil we see on this planet. But the evidence is circumstantial to non-believers. Surely, we would see something direct?

Indeed, we can.

If the "Church" is to be God's outpost on planet Earth, and God really exists as a spiritual force for "good", then direct attacks on the Church itself from hostile forces could be evidence. Why do we find pedophiles and corruption in churches, for example?

The biggest spiritual attack on the Christian church has not come, ironically, from major rival religions like Islam or Buddhism. The biggest attack has come from those listed as ancient enemies in the Bible – pagans and Wicca.

Originally, along with druidism, part of ancient Celtic practices in Europe, Wicca largely died out with the coming of Christianity. The supernatural power of Christianity, as described in the Book of Acts and still seen in churches and prayer meetings today, eclipsed anything any other religion, including Wicca, could rustle up.

An example of this is spelt out in Acts 13:9, where Paul confronted a man described as a Jewish "sorcerer" who'd been trying to interfere with the apostle's mission:

"Paul, filled with the Holy Spirit, looked straight at Elymas and said, 'You are a child of the devil and an enemy of everything that is right! You are full of all kinds of deceit and trickery. Will you never stop perverting the right ways of the Lord? Now the hand of the Lord is against you. You are going to be blind and for a time you will be unable to see the light of the sun'.

"Immediately, mist and darkness came over him, and he groped about, seeking someone to lead him by the hand. When the proconsul saw what had happened, he believed, for he was amazed at the teaching about the Lord."

Similar supernatural events in Ephesus saw the townsfolk "who had practiced sorcery" openly confess their error, and they "brought their scrolls together and burned them publicly."[306]

While Wicca, in any of its forms, was never going to match the spectacular signs and wonders that accompanied Christ and his apostles, it survived in isolated pockets as the "alternative" religion for those who secretly wanted to reject Christianity but were forced outwardly to accept it for social reasons.

Wicca and the occult bubbled along in the background for centuries, surviving the occasional blitz from Catholic and Puritan witchsniffers, but the movement had a huge boost last century when a seemingly mild-mannered British civil servant named Gerald Gardner published his book, *Witchcraft Today* in 1954. According to many, Gardner's rituals and stories became the inspiration for the modern resurgence in 'The Craft', although there is debate about whether Gardner told the truth in his book or not.[307]

Coming as it did, however, on the heels of Aleister Crowley's controversial writings on ancient 'magick' and satanic rituals (albeit that Crowley professed not to buy into the Christian version of 'Satan'), Gardner's book became a slow boiler.

But from its timid re-emergence (even in the early 1980s journalists were extremely hard-pressed to find anyone who would publicly confess to practicing witchcraft), Wicca has spread everywhere, aided and abetted by TV shows like 'Charmed' making it appealing to young girls.[308]

From hiding in the shadows only two decades ago, today, a massive and no longer totally secret push is underway by Wicca to infiltrate "mainstream" Christian churches and change liturgical practices, feminize certain bible readings used in rituals and gradually introduce pagan worship symbols

---

306 Acts 19:17-20
307 *Embracing The Witch & The Goddess*, Kathryn Rountree, Routledge, 2004, p. 6
308 There are generally two main strands of Wicca, the general version which can include men and women, and the more feminist strain, who call themselves 'Dianic witches'

into the churches. The most obvious of these, and a sure sign of occultism in a church near you, is the Labyrinth. Do a Google search for the words church and labyrinth. You'll find more than 800,000 references.

Where a church once had a cross, now many have a labyrinth, either in their floors or in their gardens. Why?

"The labyrinth is a large, complex spiral circle which is an ancient symbol for the Divine Mother, the God within, the Goddess, the Holy in all creation. Matriarchal spirituality celebrates the hidden and the unseen…"[309]

You didn't know there was a "Goddess" in Christianity? Don't worry, Christ didn't know it either. On the basis of "if you can't beat them, infiltrate them", Wiccans worldwide have risen to positions of power in many liberal churches. The quote just referenced is from Lauren Artress, an Episcopal Anglican priest at San Francisco's Grace Cathedral and a colleague of New Ager Matthew Fox, also a priest at Grace. Artress has founded a movement called Veriditas, which loosely translates as "the greening power of God".

"When I am in the centre of the Labyrinth," she writes, "I pause to honour and bring into my being first the mineral consciousness, then the vegetable, then animal, human, and angelic…When walking the Labyrinth, you can feel that powerful energies have been set in motion. The Labyrinth functions like a spiral, creating a vortex in its centre."

The idea that labyrinths, or magic wands, familiars or other objects can concentrate spiritual power is pure witchcraft in concept. Christian theology says the only power Christians are authorized to call on is the Holy Spirit, through prayer. The idea of a "Goddess" in cathedrals across the US, New Zealand,[310] Australia, Canada and Britain would appear to be a major breach of the First Commandment.

As you can see then, this is one of the reasons liberal Christianity in the West is rapidly becoming Christian in name only. There is a massive powershift taking place as genuine Christians abandon the mainstream churches to cackling covens, while themselves flocking to the new evangelical mega-churches.

"In the Labyrinth Project newsletters published between 1996 and 2001," writes author Lee Penn, "there is no mention of the Trinity, the Crucifixion, the Resurrection, the Empty Tomb, God the Father, or God as Lord and King. The words – and the concepts – of sin, divine judgment, heaven, hell, repentance, redemption and salvation are likewise absent."

309 *False Dawn*, Lee Penn, Sophia Perennis, New York, 2004, p. 148
310 http://wwll.veriditas.labyrinthsociety.org/locate-a-labyrinth-results?action=locate&country=New+Zealand&state=

Penn adds that the Labyrinth project "has the approval of the highest authorities in the Episcopal Church. In 1999, 2000 and 2001, Phoebe Griswold – the wife of the Presiding Bishop of the Episcopal Church in the USA – led Labyrinth pilgrimages." Griswold also wrote articles about them for a major Anglican journal,[311] proof if any were still needed that Western Anglicanism is crashing and burning back into the Dark Ages faster than you can say "Trinity".

Nor is it just the Episcopal/Anglican church. A briefing paper compiled by a Catholic theologian in Australasia reveals a massive influx of paganism into the Catholic Church as well.

"The driver behind the "Goddess Cult" is feminism, which dissenters have placed higher than the Revelation entrusted to the Church. Sadly the ranks of the "Goddess Cult" are mainly made up of religious orders of nuns for whom feminism is the new orthodoxy, and prime amongst them seem to be key members of the Sisters of Mercy. As nuns are a mainstay in Church structures they wield influence well beyond their numbers," writes Simon Dennerly in a major report.

"It is of the gravest concern that dissenters, and most prominently the Sisters of Mercy, are practicing the Occult. The practice of the Occult is a core part of the Goddess/New Age movement, and it is no different for those dissenters in the Church who ascribe to such beliefs. The Archdiocese of Brisbane is an example of what happens if dissent of this type is allowed to spread. *The Wanderer* articles give examples, such as Nuns at Womenspace offering guidance from pagan Celtic Oracles. Of course with the practice of the Occult the demonic is never far behind."

The Womenspace scandal in Brisbane is an ongoing one, again involving the Sisters of Mercy who appear to be hell-bent on introducing pagan goddess worship to Catholic women under the guise of "sisterhood".

"In the latest newsletter from the Four Winds website," reported AD2000 magazine,[312] "advertising the women's centre in Brisbane, called "Womenspace", where talk of Gaia the earth goddess is commonplace, there was a course advertised for 3-4 December 2005 called "Singing the Chakras: Finding the goddess", to be run by an Anique Radiant Heart who is called a "priestess of the goddess". Goddess worship and environmentalism are linked in an esoteric blend.

"The reading list linked to this site is even more revealing: in it are works by well-known new-agers such as Fritjof Capra, Matthew Fox, Joan Chittister and Paul Collins, and works such as Rosemary Radford Ruether's new age

311   http://web.archive.org/web/20010629211940/http://www.swts.nwu.edu/atr/wn01_issue.htm
312   http://www.ad2000.com.au/articles/2006/feb2006p10_2146.html

eco-feminist work *Gaia and God: an Ecofeminist Theology of Earth Healing.*"

The Feb 06 *AD2000* report drew this response from one reader:

"Wanda Skowronska's article on the danger of New Age paganism (February AD2000) prompted me to visit the Womenspace website. There I learned that the 2006 spirituality program will focus on Wild Women, Gathering Women and Earth Women. The current Newsletter (January-April 2006) also refers to Whistling Woman, Star Woman, Women Celebrating Women, Women who Run with the Wolves and The Wild Mother.

"Healing rituals are scheduled, as are Goddess Rituals and also ancient Celtic Guidance in spirituality. There will be rituals in celebration of the Autumn and Spring Equinoxes, and the Winter and Summer Solstices. A video entitled "Burning Times" will be screened, depicting "the Inquisition and women's holocaust known as the witch hunts". It includes interviews with one Starhawk, described as a prominent writer, teacher and activist. And the three aspects of the Triple Goddess – Virgin, Mother, Crone – will be contemplated, as will the untamed Dark Goddess.

"To anyone with a spare half hour I do recommend a visit to the Womenspace website. It displays the most consummate drivel imaginable."[313]

Starhawk, incidentally, is a self-proclaimed "witch"[314], and you may have also picked up reference to the nuns promoting a kind of 'unholy trinity', the "Triple Goddess – Virgin, Mother, Crone".

The other irony is that the Catholic church's "Womenspace" centre in Brisbane was also leased to pro-abortion groups for meetings, by the nuns who operate the centre.

New Zealand and the US don't escape this phenomenon. A major Wicca conference addressed by Wiccan author Carol Christ[315] (if you can't beat 'em, steal the name) in Auckland, New Zealand in 2005 not only had prominent Catholic nuns in attendance but even staff from the evangelical protestant Bible College of New Zealand.

Another 2005 visit to NZ by US-based Dominican Sister Miriam McGillis ended with a Labyrinth walk in Wellington and a Wiccan ceremony invoking Earth, Water, Air and Fire, the four elements of witchcraft:

"To conclude, Margaret Megwyn led the group in a dance and chant "Earth my body, Water my blood, Air my breath and Fire my spirit" which affirmed, embodied and gave voice to women's connection with the earth and with the cosmos."[316]

---

313   http://www.ad2000.com.au/articles/2006/mar2006p14_2183.html
314   http://www.starhawk.org/starhawk/bio.html
315   http://www.futurechurch.org.nz/carolchrist.htm
316   http://www.catholicculture.org/library/view.cfm?recnum=7620#8

Remember, these are ostensibly "Catholic" nuns. Also heavily involved in paganism is an organization called FutureChurch,[317] fronted in New Zealand by a Bible College lecturer, Steven Taylor and pagan Anglican Rosemary Neave, who also runs a bed and breakfast network for lesbian and Wiccan tourists.[318] The FutureChurch website offers links through to San Francisco's Grace Cathedral and its Labyrinth.

Former US Josephite nun Joan Keller-Marsh runs workshops she calls "From Convent to Coven: A Journey to the Old Religion of the Goddess", and remarked at the opening of one workshop, "I was in one of these once where almost everyone was a nun".

Although she still attends a Catholic Mass, she confesses, "The words of the Consecration make me sick".[319]

I raise all this, not in a Twilight Zone way with the appropriate theme music but to illustrate the split that is taking place within what you perceive as The Church at this very moment. In the media it is generally portrayed as "liberal Christian" vs "conservative Christian". It isn't really. The liberal wing, or "progressives", are largely already committed to a blend of Wicca and New Age rituals and perspectives. They retain the name "Christian" for mainstream credibility and because it would spook the horses if they just came out openly and called it the Church of Wicca. It is these pagan "Christians" who still speak on behalf of "mainstream" churches to the media, and who denounce "fundamentalists" and tell journalists that the Bible stories are "really just mythical".

As I mentioned a moment ago, one of the key change agents is San Francisco priest Matthew Fox, whose agenda catapulted witch Starhawk into New Age stardom and who is based at Labyrinthine Grace Cathedral.

"Fox's teachings have led Anglican prelates to greater sympathy for New Age beliefs," records Lee Penn in *False Dawn*. "George Carey, who was Archbishop of Canterbury from 1991 through 2002, 'said he had initially been 'hostile' to New Age ideas but had come to appreciate their emphasis on creation and the environment. He told a conference on new religious movements at the London School of Economics that the Church had much to learn from New Age spirituality. He first thought New Age was a muddle of beliefs at odds with mainstream Christianity until he read Christian writers such as Matthew Fox on the subject'."[320]

The West is sinking back into pagan darkness at the same time as the

317 http://www.futurechurch.org.nz/about.htm
318 http://www.womentravel.co.nz/html/aboutus.htm
319 *Ungodly Rage*, Donna Steichen, Ignatius, 1991, p. 48
320 http://www.telegraph.co.uk/news/main.jhtml?xml=/news/2001/04/20/ncarey20.xml

rest of the world (outside Islam) is abandoning paganism for Christianity. Issues like the ordination of gay bishop Gene Robinson,[321] which looks set to cause an official split within the Anglican movement, are merely the tip of a much larger iceberg. These are not initiatives put forward by the Christian wing of the Church, but the Wiccan wing, using "Christianity" as a cover.

In New Zealand Catholic schools, Wiccans have managed to wangle their way into the 'Religious Education' unit that sets the curriculum for Christian studies in those schools. Instead of Christian prayers, the Dennerley report discovered prayers based on Native American chants, and links (again) back to Wiccan and Labyrinth sites on websites set up for Catholic schools.

In the recommended reading list for all Catholic high school students are resources that teach things like this:

"A male chauvinist meets Thea, the feminine side of God, who explains that God transcends all human categories. This helps the man accept the feminine side of himself and leads to reconciliation with his wife. Available from Catholic Communications Wellington."

'Thea' is a pagan interpretation of the Goddess, and writer Carol Christ talks not of 'theology' but 'thealogy'. In other words, the name is no accident.

Another heretical text[322] for students suggests Jesus knew he was actually a goddess.

"The earliest Palestinian theological remembrances and interpretations of Jesus' life and death understand him as Sophia's messenger and later as Sophia herself. The earliest Christian theology is sophialogy. It was possible to understand Jesus' ministry and death in terms of God-Sophia because Jesus probably understood himself as the prophet and child of Sophia."

Except, as anyone who has paid attention to this book knows, the statement is an absolute crock. I've taken you through the earliest documents in existence relating to Christ, and not one of them mentions "Sophia". Yet this is approved literature for schoolkids.

Fiorenza's heresy gets worse, however:

"As Child of Sophia he stands in a long line of prophets sent to gather the children of Israel to their gracious Sophia-God. Jesus' execution, like John's, results from his mission and commitment as prophet and emissary of the

---

321 It is no coincidence, for example, that Robinson's ordination was championed by presiding Episcopal Bishop Frank Griswold whose wife, you'll recall, is a Labyrinthian. Grace Cathedral is also a heavy backer of Robinson, as is John Shelby Spong

322 Elizabeth Schussler Fiorenza's "In Memory of Her: A Feminist Theological Reconstruction of Christian Origins", cited at http://www.catholicculture.org/library/view.cfm?recnum=7620#8

Sophia-God... *The Sophia-God of Jesus does not need atonement or sacrifices. Jesus' death is not willed by God* but is the result of his all-inclusive praxis as Sophia's prophet... The suffering and death of Jesus, like that of John and all the other prophets sent to Israel before him, are *not required in order to atone for the sins of the people* in the face of an absolute God, but are the result of violence against the envoys of Sophia who proclaims God's unlimited goodness and the equality and election of all her children in Israel."

All of which prompted Simon Dennerly to exclaim:

"Denying the necessity of the Crucifixion, denying Christ became incarnate for such a purpose, denying Christ is the second person of the Trinity and denying there is a need to atone for our sins to fix our relationship with God to gain salvation: this is completely against the Catholic Faith. This is text book feminist theology and has no place in the formation of our Catholic Educators, but most of all our children."

Regardless, across the Western world, the Christian churches have been infiltrated.

According to New Age movement leader John Randolph Price, "there are more than half a billion New Age advocates on the planet at this time, working among various religious groups."[323]

"No religion is immune from the zeal of the enthusiasts, converts and disciples of the New Age movement," adds Father Malachi Martin, the late Vatican insider and papal envoy whose work exposed a satanic Black Mass group within the upper echelons of the Vatican itself.

"New Age simply borrows all the words, melts them down like so many gold chalices and crosses, and pours them into the mold of their New Age globalism.

"Networked throughout the Roman Catholic Church and all the mainline Protestant churches in the United States, for example, are teams of former Christian believers – bishops, priests and laity – who are subtly and gradually transforming the meaning of Baptism, Confirmation, the Eucharist, Marriage...Sacraments all, they become instead celebrations of "Earth festivals", cultivating man's relationship not with a loving God but with his own earthbound destiny in the global village to come," explains Martin.

Nor is it just Christianity under siege; Israeli journalists have recently reported on the infiltration of New Agers into orthodox Judaism as well.[324] I'm not a betting man by habit, but were I to take a wager I'd say that the 'New Age' will steal enough of the key principles of all the main world religions to cobble together a seemingly credible new world religion of the kind Christ envisioned the Antichrist would assemble, and that followers of New Age beliefs are carrying "the mark of the Beast" – especially in light of comments by one of New Ageism's leading lights.

A man widely regarded by religious studies departments as one of the "founders of the New Age movement" is David Spangler,[325] who helped establish the Findhorn New Age Centre in Scotland – described by Malachi Martin as "to New Agers what the Vatican is to Roman Catholics". Spangler also helped establish the Lindisfarne Association of New Agers, whose alumni have included bestselling *Gnostic Gospels* author Elaine Pagels and Gaia theorist James Lovelock.

Spangler's writings include a claim that "Lucifer" has been given a bum rap.

"Lucifer…is the angel of man's inner light…Lucifer, like Christ, stands at the door of a man's consciousness and knocks…If a man say, 'Come in', Lucifer becomes…the being who carries…the light of wisdom…Lucifer is literally the angel of experience…He is an agent of God's love…and we move into a new age…each of us in some way is brought to that point which I term the Luciferic initiation.

"Lucifer comes to give us the final gift of wholeness. If we accept it, then he is free and we are free. That is the Luciferic initiation. It is one that many people now, and in the days ahead, will be facing, for it is an initiation into the New Age."[326]

Vampire Bat or Fruit Bat? You be the judge. But don't let anyone fool you into thinking the New Age/Pagan movement isn't plugged into darkness.

The even bigger problem with the New Age/Pagan movement, however, is that around half to 75% of self-help seminars and business "gurus" brought in by corporates to train staff are pushing New Age principles under the guise of "team building".

As you saw in an early chapter, New Age mediums have already figured out how to make a lot of money from the great unwashed by purporting to talk to dead people; but big business New Agers have figured out how to make $500 a head out of talking to live people.

"One of the biggest advantages we have as New Agers is, once the occult, metaphysical and New Age terminology is removed, we have concepts and techniques that are very acceptable to the general public," wrote New Ager Dick Sutphen 20 years ago.

"So we can change the names… demonstrate the power… open the door to millions who normally would not be receptive."[327]

325 http://en.wikipedia.org/wiki/David_Spangler
326 *The Keys Of This Blood*, Fr Malachi Martin, pp. 309-310
327 Dick Sutphen, "Infiltrating the New Age into Society," *New Age Activist*, Summer 1986, p.14

As we've already demonstrated, New Age "power" is pretty low-watt, but the entertainment value can be high, and that's what they bank on.[328]

Take Neale Donald Walsch's alleged 'conversations with god'. The god he allegedly talks to is nothing more than a front for New Age mysticism.

"Whatever you do," this 'god' says to Walsch,[329] "do not believe what is said here. Do not believe a single thing I say. Listen to what I say, then believe what your heart tells you is true. For it is in your heart where your wisdom lies, and in your heart where your truth dwells, and in your own heart where God resides in most intimate communion with you."

OK, let's take Walsch's god at face value. First of all he contradicts himself, telling people not to believe a single thing he says – except, presumably, that statement. Then he gives the warm-fluffy that all New Agers want to hear – trust your own heart.

Great, I'm a Papuan cannibal and Neale's god says I should listen to my heart when it says 'eat your enemies'! What about those pedophile priests who keep telling themselves they're doing kids a favour by deflowering them? New Age religions endorse evil under the guise of 'tolerance'.

"Take then, each of you, your own path to Me," says Walsch's god to pedophile and cannibal alike. "Undertake your own journey home. Do not worry or render judgments about how others are taking theirs. You cannot fail to reach Me, and neither can they. Indeed, you will all meet again when you are together at Home, and you will wonder why you quibbled so."

Walsch and Deepak Chopra are new variations on a dangerous old theme – concocting one religion for the planet based on New Age doctrine.

In 1893, a meeting called the World Parliament of Religions was held in Chicago. It was the birth of what we now know as the "interfaith dialogue" movement. It led, in 1906, to an organization calling itself the "Universal Religious Alliance" which was set up with the goal of finding common ground between all the world's religions, and the forging of a new planetary unity. It has been through various incarnations over the decades as it has grown, the movement tagged as the United Religions Initiative in the 1990s and spreading its tentacles via the United Nations "Alliance of Civilisations" doctrine now signed up for New Zealand schools. The World Council of Churches is part of this outreach.

The United Religions Initiative, which includes interfaith councils,

---

328 A classic current con by the New Age is *The Secret*, an alleged expression of "the Universe's wish" to give you your heart's desire. Brought to you by the marketing arm of the New World Order. If you want to see one of *The Secret*'s gurus busted, this clip from TV's *A Current Affair* is a must-see: http://www.youtube.com/watch?v=icklckUsOGM
329 *Home With God*, Neale Donald Walsch, Atria, 2007, p. 25

is tracking to take control of religious education in schools under the Alliance of Civilisations banner:

Specifically, the URI website[330] recorded in October 2007 the existence of a "cooperation circle"[331] with the specific task of lobbying the government:

"The purpose of this cooperation circle is: 'Through education, to promote understanding and cooperation between different religions. In particular, to promote and lobby for religious studies in Schools and Universities'."

If you think "Bible in Schools" is a problem, just wait until the Wiccan/New Agers get their claws into your kids through Government-ordered "religious education".

"Discrimination, hatred and many other forms against peace have their origin in ignorance. Education is a fundamental piece of our work. Our guidelines for action express this in a clear way: URI will serve as a moral voice and a source of action grounded in contemplation in each of the following areas ... Nurturing Cultures of Healing and Peace – actions to develop cultures in which all people can live without fear of violence."

Who could argue with a group that wants "peace"?

Did I mention the real 'kicker', however? The United Religions Initiative is controlled by Bishop William Swing, head poobah at none other than the home of the Labyrinth and Wicca Central, Grace Cathedral.

"Like many other 'one world' groups," writes Malachi Martin, "New Agers look forward to the elimination of existing political systems and national boundaries. They are prepared to welcome the subsequent blending of all nations and peoples into one planetary culture, with a single court of justice, a single police force, a single economic and educational system – all under a single government dominated by a super-bureau of 'enlightened ones'."

New Age doctrine speaks of, and websites are abuzz with, the idea of a coming "Maitreya", or Messiah, who will lead this new global faith. This person won't be God like Jesus Christ, but merely what the New Agers call an "avatar", a human with a divine calling from Mother Universe to lead humanity.

---

330 http://www.uri.org/CC_News/SE_Asia_%26_the_Pacific/SEAPC.html
331 A clue to the terminology here can be found in the works of pagan academic Rosemary Radford Ruether, who talks of the need for groups focused on "feminist spirituality and social praxis...to work toward the new social order". The groups may include Christian, Wiccan, Jewish and shamanistic elements, but Ruether says they should meet in "circles", the optimal number for which (or should that be 'witch'?) is thirteen, "the size of a proper coven". Cited in *Ungodly Rage*, Donna Steichen, p. 33

Make no mistake, however, the New Age Wicca movement is not offering eternal life:

"Classical theism states that the goal of human life is to rise above the changing body and to share in the immortal life of God. Process philosophy [Wicca/New Age] asks us to enjoy finite and changing life that ends in death," writes Carol Christ.[332]

Let's get one thing straight: if the Wicca/New Age movement had a credible cosmology to explain the existence of the Universe – rather than one which flies absolutely in the face of the scientific evidence and everything we now know about the world – I'd be gentler with them. Their creation myth, however, is pantheistic, that 'god' is everything and lives inside the universe, and the universe is eternal therefore. These people do not have a skerrick of credibility. Their entire religion is built on a proven fantasy, similar to the flat earth fad of the 1800s.

It doesn't help, either, that over the course of this book we've laid out evidence strongly indicating the existence of not just any God, but the Christian God in particular.

So I come back to the question I began the chapter with:

"It is one thing to pontificate about "Good vs Evil" as an esoteric argument. But if such a battle was really taking place, wouldn't we expect to see spillover in the natural world?"

Here's my thesis in a nutshell: If there was no truth to the supernatural, then Christianity and Judaism should not attract any special attention in the world. Each belief system would pretty much do its own thing. Can you think of a rational, natural explanation was to why the New Age/Wicca movement should focus its energies *so much* on infiltrating Christianity? Why bother? Yet they are drawn to it like moths to a flame. Not only that, the New Age/Wicca movement is heavily pushing, with the assistance of the United Nations and compliant liberal states like New Zealand or Canada, to set up a new world religion – the real New World Order. Why?

The most incredible irony in this is the fact that New Age/Wicca is walking into a trap – because these people would appear to be fulfilling the final strands of biblical prophecy leading to Armageddon, *even though they don't believe in biblical prophecy!*

The apostle Paul foresaw a time "in the last days", when a group of people "having a form of godliness but denying its power" would "worm their way into homes and gain control" of the "weak-willed".[333] In both the Old Testament and the Book of Revelations, a forecast "Antichrist"

---

332 *She Who Changes*, Carol Christ, Palgrave, 2003, p. 198
333 2 Timothy 3:1-9

is to arise who a large chunk of the world population will think is a great leader, who brings peace and establishes a new godless religion:

"The whole world was astonished and followed the beast...The beast was given a mouth to utter proud words and blasphemies and to exercise his authority for 42 months. He opened his mouth to blaspheme God, and to slander his name and dwelling place and those who live in heaven. He was given power to make war against the saints and to conquer them. And he was given authority over every tribe, people, language and nation. All the inhabitants of the earth shall worship the beast – all whose names have not been written in the book of life belonging to the Lamb that was slain..."[334]

Now, contrast that prediction with this one from the New Age website, Share International:[335]

"He has been expected for generations by all of the major religions. Christians know him as the Christ, and expect his imminent return. Jews await him as the Messiah; Hindus look for the coming of Krishna; Buddhists expect him as Maitreya Buddha; and Muslims anticipate the Imam Mahdi or Messiah.

"Although the names are different, many believe that they all refer to the same individual: the World Teacher, whose personal name is Maitreya (pronounced my-tray-ah).

"Preferring to be known simply as the Teacher, Maitreya has not come as a religious leader, or to found a new religion, but as a teacher and guide for people of every religion and those of no religion.

"At this time of great political, economic and social crisis Maitreya will inspire humanity to see itself as one family, and create a civilization based on sharing, economic and social justice, and global cooperation.

"He will launch a call to action to save the millions of people who starve to death every year in a world of plenty. Among Maitreya's recommendations will be a shift in social priorities so that adequate food, housing, clothing, education, and medical care become universal rights.

"Under Maitreya's inspiration, humanity itself will make the required changes and create a saner and more just world for all."

And *that's* how it will be sold to you. Expressed another way, welcome to *The Matrix*. In the hit movie, the red pill represents hard, edgy, politically-incorrect Truth. The blue pill represents the mind-numbing, cocooning, tolerant, can't-we-all-just-get-along, syrupy, peace-and-love-to-all-humanity drug that keeps humans sedated while the Matrix sucks the life out of them. The hero of the movie, Neo, chooses the red pill of

---

334 Revelation 13:3-8
335 http://www.share-international.org/maitreya/Ma_main.htm

reality rather than continue to live a soft and comforting lie. He wakes up to see for the first time the real nature of the bewitching evil attacking humanity. Watch the movie, you'll get the point.[336]

The Truth hurts. It really does. It is so very tempting to lurch back into the "world peace" mantra where Truth is eased out of the debates so as not to offend anyone, until after a while nobody remembers the Truth. But if the New Agers are wrong about the universe, that doesn't give us any confidence that they are right about spiritual matters.

Many of you will remember the words of John Lennon's dirge, *Imagine*. Writer Andrew Klavan certainly does:

"Of all the silly pop songs ever written, perhaps the silliest is John Lennon's *Imagine*. 'A wop bop a loo ram a lop bam boom' has more philosophical depth as a lyric – and indeed contributes more to the happiness of human society – than Lennon's thudding inanities, which are rendered truly inspiring only by being reduced to a one-word poster on a teenager's wall. Lennon, you'll no doubt remember, asks us to imagine humanity without faith, countries, or possessions. With nothing to kill or die for, he promises, 'the world will live as one.'

"Now you may call me a dreamer, but it seems to me just such a world was imagined long before, in the 1956 film *Invasion of the Body Snatchers*. There, aliens begin to transform the human race into Lennon's world: a soulless army of automatons living as one without any of those bothersome passions that give rise to religions, nations, or private property. 'Love, desire, ambition, faith,' one of the aliens intones, perfectly prefiguring Lennon, 'without them, life is so simple.'

"Of course, what the horror film considers, which the utopian song ignores, is the nature of the human beast. The dark side of our humanity – the killing, the greed, the injustice – is exactly that: the dark side of our humanity – our love, our yearning, our loyalty – everything that makes us what we are. You can have a perfect world, or you can have people to live in it – you can't have both."[337]

The attack on Christianity, and before that the Jews, is an ancient one, but this massive upsurge in spiritual tension around the world makes no sense, unless Christianity is indeed in the middle of an unseen warzone, as the Bible predicts. The re-establishment of the state of Israel in 1948 was utterly against all odds, yet suddenly there it is, and it remains the most controversial piece of real estate in the world – still at the epicenter of the biggest events in world history. The Iraq War, the War on Terror, Iran's

---

336 http://www.arrod.co.uk/essays/matrix.php
337 http://www.claremont.org/publications/crb/id.848/article_detail.asp

nuclear ambitions – these and other major tensions can all be traced back to the existence of Israel.

Why? In a random, natural world, there is no sane and rational explanation for this ongoing foundational attack on both Christianity and a tiny piece of real estate in the desert. Yet if the Bible is true, the jigsaw pieces start to fall into place.

Ah, yes, argues pagan Carol Christ in *She Who Changes*, but all truth is relative. There is no real truth.

But what if she is wrong?

CHAPTER 17
THE DEATH OF RIGHT AND WRONG

"The Left has had to restrict individual freedom of thought and deed in order to destroy the concept of judgment and undermine notions of right and wrong that have been held nearly universally for millennia. This is the result of the wrong people getting control of our culture at a time when we were vulnerable. It's that simple, and that scary"

Tammy Bruce, *The Death of Right and Wrong*

MID 2007, IN A CITY near where I live, a little toddler was rushed to hospital with critical injuries. She died a few days later. As details of the police investigation filtered out, the community was horrified at allegations that the child, a little girl, had not only been beaten over a long period, but that she had been tortured.

It is alleged the 16 year old boyfriend of the child's *34 year old* mother was one of those involved in her demise. Neighbours reported seeing the three year old hanging from a clothes line and spun around until she fell off, while detectives also discovered the child had been locked into a spin-dryer while the machine was going. Other witnesses reported seeing the toddler crying, standing on the roof of the family house while people living there laughed at her terror.

No public onlookers apparently felt they had any right to intervene.

I argued on my blog that the cause of this evil was ultimately spiritual, as society slides further and further away from basic values towards a hotch-potch of tolerating not just the "good" but also the "bad" and the downright "ugly". I was particularly incensed, given the sexual relationship between a 34 year old woman and a 16 year old who was not the father of the toddler, and whose mates also lived at the house, at the family situation the child had died in, and just about hit the roof when I heard a welfare group suggest "It takes a village to raise a child" – an idea that has been well and truly debunked. They argued that the "whanau" concept, "where no one owns the child, not even the parents" and where children are passed around various caregivers as if all are equal, is the answer to the problem.

It isn't. Exposing children to people who have weak or no biological ties to them is similar to exposing lion cubs to adult male lions. Child abuse rates in these situations are higher than in wider society – even after socio factors are filtered. I argue that's because the village concept doesn't actually work.

By undermining the nuclear family, and undermining structures and values that underpin the family, we have sown the seeds for our child abuse epidemic.

This is especially so when you factor in the spiritual decline. If the majority or whole of your society follow the Christian faith, as we used to, then belief in that particular law giver tended to moderate the worst excesses.

Take away spiritual belief, as post modernists have largely done, and you are left with a generation lacking that inner moral compass anchored in the idea of an unseen watcher who ultimately judges.

Sure, you can proscribe "morality" through social engineering in schools but, as liberals tell me so often, "you can't legislate for morality". Not really. It has to be a choice, as Christianity is, something that requires allegiance.

And for the "me" generation, the kneejerk responses are "why should I?", "says who?" and "you can't force me".

Short of adopting the "might is right" stance to bring these people to heel, they're right: who are you (in the absence of God) to tell anyone else how to live? Where do you draw any moral authority from?

Torturing a three year old in the way this one was is incomprehensible, except as a consequence of the increasing spiritual death of society. Change won't happen, I argued, without a return to the Christian faith.

Naturally, my post on the blog created a lot of debate about morality, and whether it was objectively true (i.e., that some things are wrong at all times) or merely relative (i.e., who are you to tell others how they should live?).

"Treating others as you'd want to be treated is much more succinct and comprehensive, really, than lists [like the Ten Commandments]," ventured Ryan, one of those commenting.

That sounds feasible, until you consider that a sado-masochist's definition of how they wanted to be treated might not match his neighbour's.

Whilst Christ himself narrowed down the Commandments to ultimately two, it seems modern liberals have conveniently dropped reference to the cornerstone first commandment:

"Jesus replied: 'Love the Lord your God with all your heart and with all your soul and with all your mind'. *This is the first and greatest commandment.* [my emphasis] And the second is like it: 'Love your neighbour as yourself'. All the Law and the Prophets hang on these two commandments."

Stripped of its reference point, the second commandment is meaningless. A person who puts the teachings of God first will have those in his heart as he interacts with his neighbours. A person who doesn't will not necessarily treat his neighbours so well; for example, he might be a member of a sexual 'swinger's club', so his idea of loving his neighbour might be totally contradictory to the biblical concept.

"What I believe and feel is moral or immoral has no bearing on what is legal or illegal, or what any Government does or says," argued Ryan.

In my view he was ignoring that Governments are comprised of individuals who largely follow their own morality in making laws, thereby divorcing state laws from any anchor outside their own opinions.

Follow our debate as it unfolded:[338]

IAN: Actually Ryan...your argument rests entirely on a pedestal of moral relativism, which is shaky and inconsistent at the best of times. The Christian perspective is God first, government second. Where a state's laws contradict God's laws, the NT says Christians should resist the evil.

RYAN: *Moral relativism is a logical necessity. I can show you why, if you're interested.*

IAN: With respect, Ryan. No, it's not.

Is it ever moral for an adult to have sexual relations with a baby, or is that objectively wrong for all times, all places and all people?

The problem with relativism is that people choose apparent grey examples to argue, thus muddying the waters.

All I have to establish, however, is one objective truth, and the point has been established for all time.

Is rape subjectively wrong or objectively wrong?

Sexual promiscuity of any kind leads to increased health risks. Objectively, at an empirical level, promiscuity is negative for the individual.

Now you can argue till the cows come home that we shouldn't judge, or shouldn't make moral judgments etc. Doesn't change the objective reality that some things, no matter how much we like them, are bad for us.

Drugs are morally wrong because scientifically we know they screw you

338 http://briefingroom.typepad.com/the_briefing_room/2007/07/child-abuse-is-.html
You can follow the debate, in its full context, at this link. What appears in the book is edited for brevity

up. You might not like the moral judgment, but that doesn't change the bottom-line evidence.

The existence of objective truth, in itself points to the existence of an objective truth giver. Otherwise, why does objective truth exist at all?

RYAN: *"Is it ever moral for an adult to have sexual relations with a baby…?"*

It is certainly wrong to me, wrong to you, and may well be wrong to everyone, but that doesn't change the fact that it is logically necessary that morality is subjective, even if all subjects share a given value – as in the case of raping a baby. You may not be able to find a person in the world who likes the taste of crude oil. Does that make tastes objective?

"Is rape subjectively wrong or objectively wrong?"

To whom? It's certainly been right to some people in the past, considered an acceptable spoil of war, as recorded in the Old Testament, if I remember correctly. Slaughtering infants was right to them too.

The statement, say, "Psychoactive drugs have a high chance of triggering latent mental illness" can be true or false. It does not follow that "drugs are bad" unless you are saying "drugs are bad to anyone who values mental health more than pleasure, given the odds". Not everyone does.

I don't disagree that truth exists – that statements are true or false. I disagree that value judgments are true or false.

IAN: Ah Ryan. I'm glad to see you accept the need for logic: "it is logically necessary that morality is subjective, even if all subjects share a given value – as in the case of raping a baby."

The first part of your comment is – if it is to carry any weight in the slightest – an objective truth claim about morality. You say it is "logically necessary" for all other truth claims about morality (except yours) to be "subjective".

All arguments from relativists fail at the first hurdle in this regard. Either they confine themselves to saying nothing: "It's just my opinion", or they step into the breach as you have and dare to objectively assert that subjectivism is the only truth, thereby cancelling out their own argument.

I could leave it there, because obviously your own argument relies on objective moral truth, and the existence of even one objective moral truth actually makes the rest of your argument obsolete.

However, I want to tackle some of the other points you make.

You make a differentiation between a general truth claim and a moral or value truth claim. I think this approach is unnecessary.

If the God of the Bible exists, (a truth claim that must be based in fact, not value) and the Bible accurately records his views (ditto), then it would also be a truth claim of fact (not value) that objective moral truth existed as well.

Do you see the point I am making? Regardless of whether 100% of us refuse to believe in such a God, his existence is not dependent on our belief. Planets and star systems exist that humans have not discovered and may never discover. Their existence is still objectively true.

The ONLY way your claim that relativism is "logically necessary" could be objectively true is if you can PROVE (and no one has) that the God of the Bible does not exist.

I agree with you. If he doesn't and we are all just superior pond scum, then true morality is a human construct and thus subjective, based on the whim of changing opinions and mores.

Which is why an atheist's appeal to some sort of secular moral code is hollow: if I choose to disobey a set of mere human-imposed laws and morals, who are you to tell me I am morally wrong? You might not like it, but so what? Your only recourse to control me is physical force, because you have no superior intellectual argument. Raping a child might be wrong to you but it might feel good to me? Yes?

On the other hand, as I said, if the God of the Bible exists then my actions are wrong regardless of whether you support me or oppose me.

And they are wrong regardless of whether I swear allegiance to such a God or not.

Which is why, Ryan, Christianity must ultimately be a rational faith, because so much actually hinges on the existence or non-existence of God.

As Paul said, we are the most tragic of people if Christianity is not true, and Christ did not rise.

In a previous comment you alluded to "coming through" the other side of Christianity, and appreciating the other faiths as well.

This is where liberal seminaries (and Auckland University is a classic case of the blind leading the blind) utterly miss the boat.

Compare Christianity to Buddhism. The earliest known documents laying out Buddhist belief date from about 600 years after the death of Buddha, IIRC. They also were written at least a hundred years after the death of Christ, so the possibility of Christian influence on the entire Buddhist teachings as we know them cannot be ruled out, especially if the disciple Thomas did indeed venture into India to preach the gospel.

In contrast to Buddhism, the Christian documents can be pegged to within half a generation of Christ's death, being published at a time when large numbers of witnesses to the events in question were still alive and capable of challenging them if they were untrue.

The Hindu manuscripts on the other hand...are written as epic poetry and, unlike the New Testament, are not anything remotely like historical documents. They are more akin to the Roman and Greek polytheistic pantheons.

One can actually make the Hindu/Roman/Greek myths reconcile to the Old Testament in one interesting way: Genesis 6:4. That verse describes a time on earth when god-like creatures came to Earth and mated with human women...similar to the polytheistic legends.

Hinduism, with its belief in millions of minor deities (spirit entities, or what the Bible would call demonic entities) makes no significant truth claim capable of historical verification (unlike Christianity which claims to be based on entirely real events capable of being tested).

Which leaves us with Islam. According to one Islamic scholar in Germany recently, the original Qu'ran was probably written in Aramaic, not Arabic, and when the book is approached from that perspective it is much more Christian in tone and much less Islamic.

However, Arabic is what we are left with, so let's deal with Islam's truth claims. Firstly, we are to believe that an angel of the Lord just about choked Muhammed to death in order to make him write the Qu'ran. We are also to believe that the Qu'ran with its repeated assertions to dominate and slay Christians, Jews and atheists, is written by the same God who published the Jewish Torah and the Christian NT.

Have you read the Qu'ran? It is wildly inconsistent, and utterly unreconcilable in its current form to the person of Jesus Christ revealed in the NT.

You said elsewhere that apologetics are only a comfort to believers. Rubbish. The historical evidence for the truth of Christianity is greater than the historical evidence for any other religion on the planet. And that is an objective, not subjective statement. There are more manuscripts, earlier manuscripts, and more independently verifiable facts than any other religion has.

Now sure, you can "come through" that and hold to this nebulous belief that all faiths are valid in their own way...but they're not really. Not if you really actually sit down and compare them.

The evidence for objective Christian truth far exceeds evidence in favour of fluffy pantheistic vagueness from the East.

It is easy to stand back, look at all the different religions without really knowing much about any of them, and generalise about all roads leading to Rome and "whatever works for you, man".

But those who know the vastly different worldviews of the different religions know they cannot all be equally valid.

If one of them is objectively true, we have a responsibility to ourselves to find that truth, because our lives may depend on it.

RYAN: *My point is that the factual existence of the God of the Bible can no* *more prove the existence of "objective morality" any more than it could prove the existence of "square circles". If he exists and there are particular ways he wants us to act, ways he rewards us for and punishes us for straying, that doesn't make his standard "better" by any moral standard – because such an evaluation would require some other ("higher") moral standard by which to evaluate God's morality. His omniscience, omnipotence, and penchant for reward and punishment merely make it selfishly pleasurable in the long run to obey his law. That doesn't make his morality objectively better than anyone else's, because one must adopt a moral stance before evaluating his moral stance.*

…It's not about power structure, it's about logical priority. Either God can be described as good (conforming to a separate standard) or God decides what is good. It can't be both.

IAN: The third option is simply that God IS good, by definition as part of his nature, and epitomises the ultimate goodness that can ever be aspired to. This is a more subtle definition than simply describing God *as* good (which is a subjective viewpoint for humanity), because it essentially addresses an innate characteristic of God, rather than merely describing his behaviour or choices.

He does not "decree" goodness (except in the administrative sense of communicating to lower life forms)…in the sense that he has a choice to be good or bad…

Thus it is logically possible for God to be the ultimate moral arbiter because he is goodness incarnate – there is no higher authority or better definition of "good".

The possibility of God doing something objectively evil (as opposed to doing something that we may subjectively perceive as 'evil') is as logical as the possibility of square circles – being a contradiction in terms.

RYAN: *Well, here's a question, Ian. If God said that raping children was good, would it therefore be good?*

IAN: Ryan, If you read my comment carefully, it would be impossible for God to make such a decree – certainly in the manner you have phrased it.

This is not because the moral law is "higher" than God but because God in his very nature IS the moral law.

The shades of grey that arise as we try to interpret these things arise because of our human-centric emotions and perspectives. Morality, to us, is often a subjective issue. But just because we might perceive it as "subjective" does not negate the possibility that – looking through a glass darkly as we do – an objective, ultimate moral standard exists in the nature of God himself.

RYAN: *The question really still remains. Forget all this talk of it being*

"God's nature". Did he choose his nature? Then how did he choose what would be good and what would be bad? Did he not choose his nature? Then what is the prior idea of goodness that he embodies?

When you come down to the bottom of any morality and the series of justifications below it, you reach unjustified justifications. It's a logical necessity.

IAN: Au contraire...if morality is actually innate to God himself, not by decree but by essence, then it follows that true goodness is far more important than our second-hand perceptions and definitions here on earth.

The key question then becomes not whether my version of morality is better than yours or vice versa, but whether a path exists that can lead any person directly to the source of ultimate morality.

Putting it another way...supposing Buddhism has 7 points right out of a possible 10, or that animism has 1 point out of a possible 10, and so on... then it is possible to see that some religions and belief systems are closer to the mark than others.

This is where establishing the truth claims of Christianity becomes important, because it is impossible to know which religion is closest to God if one does not actually compare their claims and test them.

Like a maze that has only one correct exit, we can easily be distracted by the view – that all paths in the maze offer views of green hedges – so that we become focused on the similarities between religions (the green hedges) instead of looking at their substance (where they ultimately lead).

And in regard to your second point...the idea of God "choosing" his nature implies that Good can "choose" to be bad, that circles can "choose to be squares or that the number 5 can "choose" to be 821. It is a false construction.

Firstly, the Bible talks of God being timeless. He speaks of himself always in the present tense: "I AM that I AM".

From a scientific perspective, we now have corroboration that Time is a law that only came into existence after the Big Bang, and that it has no application outside the Universe. Thus, a supernatural God existing outside of the fish tank is not timebound, did not need to be created. As such, there was no linear flow whereupon he "chose" how to grow up or develop. He simply IS. The Bible records his nature as unchanging, which again fits the scientific perspective, because anything existing in timelessness would not be subject to change (change being a linear progression over time).

God is good not because he "chooses" to be good, but because that is simply what he is: good incarnate.

There is no "prior" idea of goodness that he embodies, because in timelessness there is no "prior" fullstop.

RYAN: *Ian,*

Why should I be good? More specifically, why should I be good when some of the things you say are good are evil to me?

Let's look at it this way. I use "good" and see the idea "good" used to mean "preferable". I observe that when asked "why" enough, a person runs out of justifications for what they see as good, and up saying, "I just do." At that point, their morality is unjustified, but that's okay, because all morality is unjustified – which doesn't stop it being compelling to the person who holds it.

Now you introduce this "objective good" thing. Let's call it holiness to make a distinction, because I don't see any similarity between what you mean by "good" and what I mean by it. At least, it doesn't mean "preferable", since everyone in the world could find God's plan repulsively sick, but it would still be "good" – according to your model.

So here's my question. What is so good about being holy? What reason is there to be holy?

IAN: Ryan...you ask:

"Why should I be good? More specifically, why should I be good when some of the things you say are good are evil to me?"

My point exactly. Without any external reference point, morality is entirely subjective. Clearly you don't have to be 'good' merely because I say so.

I may of course be right, but my authority is no higher than yours to establish the point.

But if goodness is not a decree of God, but in fact his very essence, then regardless of what you or I define goodness or morality as, an external standard nonetheless exists to measure us against.

But the only way for you or I to know – on the balance of probabilities or higher – is to test the truth of our particular belief systems – not on the basis of "how it feels to me" (because that defines religion entirely subjectively with no external meaning) but instead by measuring it objectively: does it make truth claims? Can those claims be tested? Does the evidence support belief in one religion over another?

Thus, while there a millions of people who like Buddhism because "it works for me", such a statement goes nowhere to proving the objective rationality of Buddhism as a belief system.

I'm not picking on Buddhism by the way...the same logic applies to someone who chooses Christianity purely because "it works for me".

They may have chosen the right path, but they chose it for the wrong objective reason.

If one religion emerges better from empirical testing of its claims than others, then this would make that religion more believable than others.

It is from that credential that the authority for a particular moral code flows.

There are many moral factors common to all major religions. But if one religion is substantially more credible than the others, we should allow the possibility that this particular religion is indeed God-driven, rather than man-driven: we believe the religion because it works, fullstop, rather than believing it because "it works for me".

RYAN: *I still don't know what you're saying by an action when you say that it is "objectively good". Are you saying I should behave that way?*

IAN: Your use of the word "holiness" is probably apt...

Christian theology says God (as goodness/holiness incarnate) cannot be in the presence of evil. Not by choice but by nature.

Humanity cannot be holy in our earthly state. Hence the doctrine of atonement. God says only those who seek him will find him, but this again appears prefaced objectively rather than subjectively. After all, there are many who claim to seek God, but are they prepared to seek God as he really is, or are they preferring to search for God as they want him to be?

Thus, we are offered a smorgasbord of God definitions in human culture.

Modern western spiritualism is very seeker-focused rather than God-focused, and indeed many groups emphasise trying to find the divine within, preferring to ignore the possibility that their entire definition of God may be wrong.

This is why testing the truth claims of different belief systems becomes important, because you can invest your entire life in something that isn't objectively true no matter how "good" it makes you feel.

Perhaps the "good" from being "holy" is that it allows you to then re-unite with your creator.

Now given that in Christian terms none of us are holy so we need Christ as our intercessor, that underlines the need for the salvation of Christ via the doctrine of forgiveness.

And if Christianity truly is the only way to reconcile with God, then only Christianity would then be objectively "good" as a religion.

I know you don't like discussing things beyond comprehension, but sometimes needs must: none of us know what the afterlife (assuming its existence for the sake of this argument) is like. We genuinely cannot comprehend it, any more than a caterpillar can anticipate being a butterfly.

The "good" that you query in regard to "why should I be holy?" may only be fully apparent in how your life is once you reach that state.

Regardless of whether we can fully apprehend it, it certainly does not make it "irrelevant" as you suggest.

Ryan, you ask: "I still don't know what you're saying by an action when you say that it is "objectively good". Are you saying I should behave that way?"

As I say, my views on your behaviour are irrelevant at this level.

I am saying that God is actually the ultimate definition of goodness, and that if this is true then you will personally benefit by engaging with him.

Thus, there is "good" for you in an objective sense depending on the choices you make – as opposed to the "good" you feel (the preferential good you talk of) when you do certain things for pleasure or gain.

This is not to say it is a selfish good (any more or less than your preferential good, or the Darwinian espousal of survival of the fittest).

While it is true that you as an organism derive "good" from reconciliation with the ultimate Good via Christ, it is also true that the process has benefits for the wider society, so that good is shared more widely than the Darwinian good or the preferential one.

RYAN: *Ian,*

Your views on my behaviour are hypothetically relevant. I'm not asking about what you think is right or wrong. I'm asking what, in your objective-morality model of the universe, it means for me that an action is objectively good or objectively bad.

IAN: Ryan: your actions in the objectively moral world that I believe exists are irrelevant to me personally (except obviously insofar as they impact on me or on wider society). But if the Christian God exists then your actions and beliefs have an impact on you in the first instance.

Secondly they can have an impact on others relative to the objective ultimate good.

If Christianity is true, for argument's sake, then anything any of us do that leads people away from reconciliation to God can be said to be evil, because the ultimate Good wants us to return to him for our benefit. In Christian theology, the alternative destination is ruinous.

Conversely, anything we do or say that leads people to a reconciliation with Good and a glorious afterlife rather than a hell-hole, has a positive impact not just on us but on the wider community.

Of course, if Christianity is not true then my entire argument is void, but if it is true then Christianity is the single most important piece of news this universe has ever offered humankind and we are fools if we kick it aside without first giving it genuine objective consideration.

EPILOGUE

A RATIONAL FAITH

"There are none so blind as those who will not see"

14th century proverb

"I DON'T BELIEVE IN GOD BECAUSE nobody has proven his existence. It's not up to me to prove god doesn't exist, it's up to theists to prove that he does. The unfortunate thing is that theists seem to think that the burden of proof is on atheists because we're the minority," wrote one internet atheist.

Actually, I don't have to prove anything to an atheist. If I warn you a train is coming, and you insist on walking through the tunnel because "I don't believe", well, whose problem is that? From what I've written in this book, it seems to me that proving God does *not* exist is actually much harder than simply accepting that he does. To believe there is no God, I actually have to suspend the mathematical side of my brain and then blatantly ignore the laws of probability. Probability was the test that Richard Dawkins threw down in *The God Delusion*, because he recognized that "certainty" is not a realistic state, not even in science. There are many things we accept in science on the basis of probability, and we jail criminals – taking away every freedom they have – often on the basis of probability, not certainty.

I'm not here to force anyone to convert, although I have listed the salvation prayer at the end of this epilogue as a courtesy to those who would otherwise email to ask. Rather, my aim has been merely to argue the case for faith – the sole task of this book has been to document the hard evidence that actually does exist in favour of the God Hypothesis, in response to some of the waffle published by Richard Dawkins, Christopher Hitchens, Sam Harris and John Shelby Spong, among others.

Look, whatever your belief: atheist, Hindu, Buddhist, Muslim, neopagan,

Wiccan, whatever – I salute you as a fellow human being, a brother or sister here on planet Earth. The belief that we should not debate religion is a cop out; none of us should be afraid to discuss our faiths, for out of discussion comes understanding. Even if you depart this book as you came to it, I believe you will at least have gained a deeper understanding of the issues discussed here.

The divinity code seems a certainty to me, and a growing number of leading scientists. You can choose to believe the objective evidence, as many are now doing, or you can choose to reject it – like Spong – not because it isn't there but because it doesn't fit with the way you "want" the world to be.

Me? I long ago recognized that you follow the scientific evidence where it leads, not just where you "want" it to lead. You can try to avoid the implications, you can stamp your feet, you can hiss all you like about how evil it all is; but the reality you face is that every morning you get up to a sun beaming in your window that is positioned "just right" in the universe, and you look up at a moon, which, if it wasn't there, you wouldn't exist either. You turn on a switch at the wall for your morning fix of coffee, knowing that the electromagnetic forces had to be balanced "just right" for you to have a body, let alone a coffee. The water in the jug only exists because you live in the "just right" section of the solar system on a planet that had to be forced into a collision with another planet as big as Mars in order for you to be here. Even if you believe in the theory of evolution via natural selection, which I personally find staggeringly unconvincing, there remains no known process by which your primeval 'ancestor' could have arisen from pond scum, let alone developed the crucial ability to reproduce itself before it died out. One of the leading pioneers in discovering DNA is on record as admitting the whole idea is so impossible that it must be the work of "space aliens". Your leading atheistic scientists at Oxford University in 2007 are reduced to theorizing that every time you personally touch something during the day you create an entire new parallel universe for that event, and every time the parallel you touches something, he or she creates a new set of parallel universes and so on it goes.

Your computer, in its spare time, quietly processes radio telemetry data for Carl Sagan's SETI project seeking anything, even a primitive Morse code, that proves aliens exist. After 28 years of scouring the night sky they haven't even found so much as a recipe for muffins. Meanwhile your radio reports that scientists working on the human genome project say DNA is an intelligent code so powerful that one human cell contains more data than a 30-volume set of the Encyclopedia Britannica; the morning paper's

Science column details the discovery of a tiny molecular engine, similar to a Mazda RX7 in design, found inside a bacterial cell. Your reaction to both these pieces of news is to loudly scoff at the notion of "Intelligent Design", and instead you marvel at the power of "Mother Nature" and evolution to provide such things.

Then, as you finish your coffee, you shake your head with a soft chuckle to yourself – apparently secure in the belief that Dawkins, Hitchens and Spong know what they're talking about – and accuse *me* of believing in a Sky Fairy?

To top it all off, ten years ago scientists discovered the unthinkable – the expansion of the universe is speeding up, not slowing down. Everyone knows that with a normal explosion, bits and pieces are flung far and wide but eventually slow down so much that they fall to earth and stop. That's the laws of physics at work. So imagine the scientific surprise when they found that after billions of years of slowing down after the Big Bang, the outward expansion of galaxies is now speeding up in defiance of what we currently know.

Rather than a long lasting universe, the night sky we see above us at this time in human history will one day be gone, as the galaxies streak out into nothingness, the glow of their suns burnt out; the lights of the universe itself will be switched off.

Perhaps the final word, then, belongs to a report in the science journal *Nature*:[339]

"Our Universe is so unlikely that we must be missing something. In an argument that would have gratified the ancient Greeks, physicists have claimed that the prevailing theoretical view of the Universe is logically flawed. Arranging the cosmos as we think it is arranged, say the team, would have required a miracle."

"An ever-more-rapidly expanding Universe is destined to repeat itself, say Leonard Susskind of Stanford University, California, and his colleagues. But the chances that such re-runs would produce worlds like ours are infinitesimal."

"So either space is not accelerating for the reasons we think it is, or we have yet to discover some principle of physics, the researchers conclude. Like a guardian angel, this principle would pick out those few initial states that lead to a Universe like ours, and then guide cosmic evolution so that it really does unfold this way."

"The incomprehensibility of our situation even drives Susskind's team

---

339 *Nature*, Aug 14, 2002

to ponder whether an "unknown agent intervened in the evolution [of the Universe] for reasons of its own"."

"Either there is no cosmological constant after all – in which case, why is the Universe accelerating? – or we're missing something fundamental."

Or maybe, just maybe, the fundamentalists are on to something, after all...[340]

***

"Nation will rise against nation, and kingdom against kingdom. There will be great earthquakes, famines and pestilences in various places, and fearful events and great signs from heaven. But before all this, they will lay hands on you and persecute you...all men will hate you because of me... by standing firm you will gain life. When you see Jerusalem surrounded by armies, you will know that its desolation is near...There will be signs in the sun, moon and stars. On the earth, nations will be in anguish and perplexity at the roaring and tossing of the sea. Men will faint from terror, apprehensive of what is coming on the world, for the heavenly bodies will be shaken...*Heaven and earth will pass away, but my words will never pass away*" – Luke 21:10-33

---

340 For those of you who wish, of your own free will, to take sides in this cosmic struggle and choose Christ, it is a very simple thing and I've included it here because there are always enquiries. All you have to do is consider where you are in your life, recognise that – like the rest of us – you are not perfect and that you and the rest of the human race suffer under what the Hebrews called "sin" and which, to all intents and purposes, means a lack of holiness. In recognising our mortality, our weakness in the face of various temptations, and our failures, we take the first steps to removing the most fundamental block between ourselves and God: human pride. If you want to recoonect with God, no amount of "good deeds" are going to cut it. We are saved and reconciled only by God's grace through the sacrifice and resurrection of Jesus Christ, not via our own efforts (which is why New Age and Eastern faiths are a dead-end). We are not gods, there is no "goddess within". Only Christ ultimately saves. The choice is yours, but if you genuinely want to begin that journey, it can begin right now with the following prayer:
"*Lord, forgive me for the things that I have done wrong, the people I have hurt. I am asking for a fresh start, as part of your Holy family. God I thank you for allowing your son Jesus Christ to pay the ultimate price for me on the cross, and in his resurrection promising eternal life to all who seek you in his name and who are baptised in the name of the Father, the Son and the Holy Spirit. Jesus, please come into my life and be my Lord and Saviour. I trust in your forgiveness. I now believe. Amen*"
Now, find yourself a church – a real one – and discover the freedom that Christ promises to every person of every race and culture on the planet

119, 120, 128, 129, 130, 132, 133, 135, 154,
160, 162, 163, 180, 182, 183, 199, 222,
223, 227, 231, 232, 249, 252, 281, 283
concedes proof of God need not be
100%, 7
he does believe in God, 67
miscalculations by, 50
'one in a billion' argument collapses,
50
Day, Vox, 231
De Duve, Christian, 41
Dead Sea Scrolls, 26, 117, 119, 126, 190
death
daily and yearly totals, 235
necessity of, 228
Death of God movement, 158
Death Valley, 48
deism, 66, 67, 70, 73, 74
Dennerly, Simon, 258, 262
Dennett, Daniel, 7
Deshpande, Pawan, 78
Dever, William, 25
Devil. *See* Satan
Dhariwal, Navdip, 79
Diodorus of Sicily, 152
disciples, 77, 134, 155, 157, 158, 161, 176, 177,
185, 192, 201, 202, 203, 207, 208, 209,
210, 213, 216, 217, 218, 220, 221, 224,
226, 237, 262
did not expect the Resurrection, 213
significance of their martyrdom, 216
Discover, 54
*Divine Harmony, Christ in the Holy Books
of the East*, 148
Dixon, Jeanne
failed prophecies of, 101
DNA, 39, 40, 42, 43, 50, 53, 66, 282
Doherty, Earl, 136, 137, 141
Dominican sisters
involvement in Wicca, 259

Down Syndrome, 173
Drosnin, Michael, 39
dualism, 72
Duwell, Dr Eric
witnessed a miracle, 171
Earth festivals, 262
Earth, the
daily rotation slowing, 45
designed for scientific discovery, 53
fine tuned for life, 43
giant impact and, 69
held in place by the moon, 48
Earth, Water, Air and Fire, 259
earthquakes, 14, 41, 45, 46, 47, 186, 237,
285
crucial to life, 46
Easter, 142, 213, 217
Eastern religions, 27, 71, 73, 78, 87, 88, 89,
90, 144, 175, 284, *See also* Hinduism,
Buddhism
directly contradict Christianity, 89
Eber, 26
Ebla, 22, 23, 25, 26, 27
clay tablets of, 22, 23, 25, 27
creation story mirrors Genesis, 22
Sodom and Gomorrah mentioned in
records, 27
eco-feminist, 259
Edersheim, Alfred, 221
Egypt, 14, 25, 121, 143, 151
Egyptians, 16
Einstein, Albert, 49, 56, 88, 112
electromagnetism, 55
Embracing The Witch & The Goddess, 256
Emerson, Scott, 166
empty tomb, 207, 208, 209, 216, 225, 226,
257
Encyclopedia of Bible Difficulties, 191
Energy Flow in Biology, 52
enlightenment, 78, 81, 82, 83, 87, 238

Entwisle, Tim, 61

Enuma Elish. *See* creation stories

environmentalism, 258

Ephrathah. *See* Bethlehem

Episcopal church, 257, 258, 261
   involvement in Wicca, 257

Erickson, Millard, 211

Esau, 25

Essays on the Trinity and the Incarnation,
   147

Essenes, 190, 195

Eve, 25
   appearance in Hindu veda, 148
   mentioned in Ebla tablets, 25

Eve's Bite, 6, 39, 50, 62, 81, 103, 191

evil
   religious views of, 72, 74, 79, 81, 86,
      102, 106, 127, 138, 185, 204, 227-232,
      237, 238, 245-248, 252, 253-255, 264,
      268, 270, 272, 276-282

evolution, theory of, 9, 10, 18, 20, 24, 42,
      51, 60, 61, 62, 63, 70, 282, 283, 284
   and the 'God gene', 18
   antibiotic resistance and, 62
   macro-evolution, 62
   top-level scientific disagreement about,
      63
   hobbits and, 15

extraterrestrials
   possible source of Earth life, 40

Ezekiel, 108, 110, 111

Faletaogo, Ethan
   miracle cure of, 167, 168, 171, 175

Faletaogo, Ripene
   witnessed a miracle, 168, 169

False Dawn, 257, 260

false prophets, 151, 187

familiar spirits, 99

feminism, 258

Fernandes, Phil, 65

Festus, 140, 155

Findhorn New Age Centre, 263

finite godism, 70, 72, 74, 254

Finkelstein, Israel, 25

Flew, Antony, 68, 178

floods, 237

Flores Island, 15
   'hobbits' discovered on, 15

Flying Spaghetti Monsterism, 64

Flynn, Tom, 130

fossil record
   incompleteness of the, 10

Fox News, 17

Fox, Matthew, 257, 258, 260

Fox, Michael J, 170, 249

Fox, Robin Lane, 129, 132

free will, 179, 254, 284

Furlong, Jayne, 97

FutureChurch NZ
   involvement in Wicca, 260

Gabriel, archangel
   in the Bible, 194
   in the Qu'ran, 91

Gaia, 258, 259, 263

Gaius Vibius Mazimus, 129

Galilee, 116, 117, 120, 140, 142, 207, 208,
      209, 212, 221, 222

Galileo, Galilei, 38, 231

Gardner, Gerald, 256

gay bishops, 261

Geering, Lloyd, 7, 14, 15, 16, 20, 23, 24, 25,
      26, 106, 161, 190, 200, 201, 211, 218-224
   avoids the evidence from Ebla, 23

Geisler, Norman, 70, 71, 72, 74, 143, 176,
      177, 254

Gelder, Stuart & Roma, 83

ghosts, 99, 110, 143, 203, 219, 220
   public belief in, 17

Gilbert, Walter, 41

Giuliani, Rudi, 232